Practicing to Aim at Truth

Practicing to Aim at Truth
Theological Engagements in Honor of Nancey Murphy

EDITED BY
Ryan Andrew Newson
AND Brad J. Kallenberg

CASCADE Books • Eugene, Oregon

PRACTICING TO AIM AT TRUTH
Theological Engagements in Honor of Nancey Murphy

Copyright © 2015 Wipf and Stock Publishers. All rights reserved. Except for brief quotations in critical publications or reviews, no part of this book may be reproduced in any manner without prior written permission from the publisher. Write: Permissions. Wipf and Stock Publishers, 199 W. 8th Ave., Suite 3, Eugene, OR 97401.

Cascade Books
An Imprint of Wipf and Stock Publishers
199 W. 8th Ave., Suite 3
Eugene, OR 97401

www.wipfandstock.com

ISBN 13: 978-1-62564-994-2

Cataloguing-in-Publication Data

Practicing to aim at truth : theological engagements in honor of Nancey Murphy / edited by Ryan Andrew Newson and Brad Kallenberg.

x + 280 p. ; 23 cm. Includes bibliographical references and index(es).

ISBN 13: 978-1-62564-994-2

1. Murphy, Nancey C. 2. Philosophy and religion. 3. Theological anthropology—Christianity. 4. Metaphysics. 5. Political ethics. 6. Postmodernism. I. Title.

BT28 P63 2015

Manufactured in the U.S.A.   09/30/2015

The Athenians who condemned Socrates to death, the English parliament which condemned Hobbes' *Leviathan* in 1666, and the Nazis who burned philosophical books were correct at least in their apprehension that philosophy can be subversive of established ways of behaving. Understanding the world of morality and changing it are far from incompatible tasks.

—Alasdair MacIntyre, *A Short History of Ethics*

All men philosophize; and as Aristotle says we must do so if only to prove the futility of philosophy. Those who neglect philosophy have metaphysical theories as much as others—only they [have] rude, false, and wordy theories. Some think to avoid the influence of metaphysical errors, by paying no attention to metaphysics; but experience shows that these men beyond all others are held in an iron vice of metaphysical theory, because by theories that they have never called into question.

—C. S. Peirce, *The Collected Papers of Charles Sanders Peirce, Volume 7, Science and Philosophy*

Muddy water is no sign the spring is deep.

—Walter Thomas Conner; quoted in James Wm. McClendon, Jr., *Doctrine: Systematic Theology, Volume 2*

Contents

Contributors | ix

Introduction | 1
—Ryan Andrew Newson

I. Orienting Engagements

1. The Crucial Importance of Nancey Murphy's Deployment of Lakatos's Methodology for Theology and Science | 13
—Robert John Russell

2. Beyond Liberalism and Fundamentalism for the Theological "Others": Notes from a Converted Fundamentalist | 26
—Richard Heyduck

3. Postmodern Insularity? Epistemological Holism and Its Discontents | 44
—Ryan Andrew Newson

II. Theological Anthropology

4. Beyond the Isolated Self: Extended Mind and Spirituality | 67
—Warren S. Brown and Brad D. Strawn

5. Practicing Religious Conversion: What Nancey Murphy Taught Me about Spiritual Development in a Physical World | 83
—Paul N. Markham

6. Then Sings My Soul | 102
—Brad J. Kallenberg

III. Metaphysics

7   Divine Action in a Dynamic World: Towards an Anabaptist Understanding of Active Matter and a God of Love | 125
    —*Christian E. Early*

8   Possibility Spaces: Their Nature and Implications for Cosmology and Theology | 146
    —*George F. R. Ellis*

9   God: Discovering Yet Another Empiricist Dogma? | 171
    —*J. B. Phillips*

IV. Politics and Ethics

10 Radical Kenosis as Radical Politics: Murphy's Political Vision With and Beyond Radical Democracy | 185
    —*Andrew C. Wright*

11 Preaching on Rough Ground: MacIntyre, Yoder, and Murphy's Embodied Philosophy | 206
    —*Greg D. Walgenbach*

12 "So Far As It Depends on You, Live Peaceably with All": On Pluralism, Particularity, and Proselytizing | 227
    —*Mark Thiessen Nation*

13 Sexy Theology: Evolution and the Formation of a Theological Concept of Sexuality Based on Kenosis | 243
    —*James A. Van Slyke*

14 Defacement and Disappearance: The Practice of Mourning with the Church of the Benevolent Self | 261
    —*Craig Hovey*

Subject Index | 277

Author Index | 279

Contributors

Warren S. Brown is the Director of the Lee Edward Travis Research Institute and Professor of Psychology in the Department of Clinical Psychology at Fuller Theological Seminary. He is the coauthor of *Did My Neurons Make Me Do It?* (2007) with Nancey Murphy.

Christian E. Early is Professor of Philosophy and Theology at Eastern Mennonite University in Harrisonburg, Virginia.

George F. R. Ellis is the Emeritus Distinguished Professor of Complex Systems in the Department of Mathematics and Applied Mathematics at the University of Cape Town in South Africa. He is the winner of the Templeton Prize in 2004, and coauthor of *On the Moral Nature of the Universe* (1996) with Nancey Murphy.

Richard Heyduck is Assistant Professor of Religion at Wiley College in Marshall, Texas.

Craig Hovey is Associate Professor of Religion at Ashland University, and Executive Director of the Ashland Center for Nonviolence.

Brad J. Kallenberg is Professor of Theology at the University of Dayton in Ohio.

Paul N. Markham is Director of Community-Based Learning and Research at the University of Washington, Bothell.

Mark Thiessen Nation is Professor of Theology at Eastern Mennonite Seminary in Harrisonburg, Virginia.

Ryan Andrew Newson teaches in the Department of Religion and Philosophy at Campbell University in North Carolina.

J. B. Phillips is Tutor in Philosophy and Theology, Westcott House, Cambridge; Director of Studies in Philosophy, St. Edmund's College, Cambridge; and Affiliated Lecturer, Faculty of Divinity, University of Cambridge.

Robert John Russell is the Ian G. Barbour Professor of Theology and Science at the Graduate Theological Union, and the Director of the Center for Theology and the Natural Sciences.

James A. Van Slyke is Assistant Professor of Psychology at Fresno Pacific University.

Brad D. Strawn is the Evelyn and Frank Freed Professor of the Integration of Psychology and Theology in the Department of Clinical Psychology at Fuller Theological Seminary.

Gregory D. Walgenbach is the Director of Life, Justice, and Peace for the Diocese of Orange in Orange County, California.

Andrew C. Wright is a Doctoral Candidate in Christian Ethics and Philosophical Theology at Fuller Theological Seminary, and teaches as an Adjunct Professor in the Division of Religion and Philosophy at Azusa Pacific University.

Introduction

—Ryan Andrew Newson

I INITIALLY HEARD OF Nancey Murphy in my first year of grad school. It was during a class discussion about the theological concept of "providence" that I innocently asked the professor in what ways our conversation might affect the foundations of Christian faith. Dr. Tupper looked as though he had eaten an unripe lemon, and the next day marched into class with handouts explaining Murphy's Lakatosian, MacIntyrean approach to theological rationality, complete with diagrams and critiques of philosophical foundationalism scribbled in the margins. At the time, I was perplexed; I had no grasp of the problems Murphy was trying to solve (or dissolve)—but these problems would arise for me soon enough, as I delved further into my studies.

From that day on, Murphy's name would continually surface as a creative and perceptive voice who sharpened my thinking as I wrestled with important questions of contemporary philosophical theology. As I sought to understand the contours of theological rationality in a broadly "postmodern" culture that questioned theology's legitimacy; as I struggled with "the" problem of evil and divine action, especially in relation to evolutionary biology and the nature of reality at the quantum level; as I worked to conceptualize a healthy relationship between theology and science in general; as I deepened my sense that the conviction "Jesus is Lord" entails the renunciation of coercive violence by the Christian; and as I reconsidered my inherited notions of human nature and moral formation—time and time again, Murphy's work stood out as a bright light in dark places. Nancey Murphy was clearly someone who had thought hard and well about these matters, while remaining firmly committed to the Anabaptist vision of the Christian life. This made Murphy a kind of rarity: a Radical Reformation philosophical theologian of science.

After having moved to California to study with Nancey, I soon heard stories from other students who shared similar experiences, as well as the common realization of her brilliance. As she gave to each of us a chance to think alongside her, only much later did we start to catch on to all that she was about. To think *with* Nancey, I came to find, was an exercise in submitting even one's most cherished convictions to rigorous scrutiny, not in order to demolish one's faith but to deepen it, to avoid speaking nonsense while passing it off as speaking Christian.

I also learned that to think with Nancey was to move "betwixt and between," as Alasdair MacIntyre puts it,[1] since Nancey herself, as a Christian academic, had not followed the well-worn paths others had taken. Raised in Alliance, Nebraska by a family with a cattle ranch and a strong Catholic faith, Nancey found herself torn between wanting to be a nun and a horse rancher.[2] At Creighton University, Nancey excelled in her studies, having to spend much of her free time laying floor tiles to earn extra money. As a doctoral student in philosophy at the University of California, Berkeley, this devout rancher's daughter studied in a department in which atheism was the norm rather than the exception: "Members of the faculty were divided only over the question of whether religion was still worth arguing *against*."[3] Nancey spent half her time with a charismatic prayer group in her local parish, and the other half studying with some of the best, typically atheistic, philosophers in the world. Nancey was drawn to the "anarchic" method of Paul Feyerabend, but soon became a defender of Feyerabend's (friendly) rival, Imre Lakatos. Eventually, Nancey earned a second doctorate in theology at the Graduate Theological Union—another "betwixt and between" that set her apart from her one-dimensional peers. Nancey's first (and as it turned out, only) major teaching position was at Fuller Theological Seminary in Pasadena, California, making her an odd duck indeed: a Nebraskan, ex-Catholic, Anabaptist, philosophical theologian of science (with two disparate doctorates from prestigious institutions), now teaching in the largest evangelical seminary in the world with deep roots in the Reformed tradition! If this wasn't enough, Nancey came to articulate (with her second husband and theologian Jim McClendon) a postmodern philosophical the-

---

1. Alasdair MacIntyre, *Whose Justice? Which Rationality?* (Notre Dame: University of Notre Dame Press, 1988) 397.

2. Nancey Murphy, "Wind and Spirit: A Theological Autobiography," *Dialog: A Journal of Theology* 46:3 (2007) 301.

3. Ibid., 302.

ology that was *almost* as ill-at-ease with "postmodern" philosophy as it was with "modern" philosophy.[4] Neither liberal nor conservative, Nancey has moved between both worlds, even while goading them to surrender their allegiance to the Enlightenment Project that was impoverishing both. By her own admission, all this "betwixting and betweening" has kept her in something of a perpetual state of "culture shock."[5]

However, many of Nancey's more creative, surprising contributions have come about precisely *because* she worked and moved in and around "the margins." Using the results of communal discernment as "data" for theology,[6] strongly critiquing the notion of a soul (at least as typically understood),[7] elucidating the political and cosmological analogues of Jesus' renunciation of worldly power,[8] and defending the actuality of special divine acts—"miracles"—as a scientifically coherent position[9] are all examples of contributions to contemporary philosophical theology made because of her atypical vantage point. To *really* think with Nancey, then, is to never *quite* fit in. And yet by not fitting in one discovers a community of inquiry capable of giving surprising and *lasting* theological gifts to the church catholic, the academy, and the world at large.

Thus, as important as the theological "content" that I learned from Nancey was the *form* of theologizing that she instilled in me. One of Nancey's abiding convictions is that questions of philosophical theology ought not float above the fray, disconnected from ordinary experience, but that such matters should always "touch ground," as it were, in the life of the scholar and the implications they carry for ordinary Christians.[10] To borrow a line

4. Nancey Murphy and James Wm. McClendon, Jr., "Distinguishing Modern and Postmodern Theologies," *Modern Theology* 5:3 (April 1989) 191–214.

5. Murphy, "Wind and Spirit," 305.

6. Nancey Murphy, *Theology in the Age of Scientific Reasoning* (Ithaca, NY: Cornell University Press, 1990) ch. 5.

7. See Nancey Murphy's introduction and chapter in Warren S. Brown, Nancey Murphy, and Newton Malony, eds. *Whatever Happened to the Soul? Scientific and Theological Portraits of Human Nature* (Minneapolis: Fortress, 1998) 1–29, 127–48; Nancey Murphy, *Bodies and Souls, or Spirited Bodies?* (Cambridge: Cambridge University Press, 2006); and Nancey Murphy and Warren S. Brown, *Did My Neurons Make Me Do It? Philosophical and Neurobiological Perspectives on Moral Responsibility and Free Will* (New York: Oxford University Press, 2007).

8. Nancey Murphy and George F. R. Ellis, *On the Moral Nature of the Universe: Theology, Cosmology, and Ethics* (Minneapolis: Fortress, 1996).

9. Nancey Murphy, "Divine Action in the Natural Order: Buridan's Ass and Schrödinger's Cat," in *Chaos and Complexity: Scientific Perspectives on Divine Action*, edited by Robert John Russell, Nancey Murphy, and Arthur R. Peacocke (Vatican City: Vatican Observatory, 1995) 325–57.

10. This is one reason (among many!) that Murphy says she was originally drawn

from Stanley Cavell, Nancey models an approach to philosophical theology that looks "beneath our feet rather than above our heads."[11] Indeed, Nancey assumes that philosophical theology is always done *from somewhere*; there is no "view from nowhere" from which to go about one's work, and therefore, one's inquiry (and conclusions) ought never be disconnected from the life of faith. Of course, as will be clear to anyone familiar with Nancey's work, this in no way entails a denigration of precise, challenging thinking, nor a "dumbing down" of complex ideas for the sake of accessibility.

Pierre Hadot's description of the ancient philosophical task also epitomizes Nancey's contemporary philosophical style: philosophical theology is not a set of techniques for clear individualistic thinking but the achievement of a community; it is, in fact, a communal *way of life*. As an articulation of this approach to philosophy, Hadot cites this passage from Plutarch:

> Most people imagine that philosophy consists in delivering discourses from the heights of a chair, and in giving classes based on texts. But what these people utterly miss is the uninterrupted philosophy which we see being practiced every day in a way which is perfectly equal to itself. . . . Socrates did not set up grandstands for his audience and did not sit upon a professorial chair; he had no fixed timetable for talking or walking with his friends. Rather, he did philosophy sometimes by joking with them, or by drinking or going to war or to the market with them, and finally by going to prison and drinking poison. He was the first to show that all times and in every place in everything that happens to us, daily life gives us the opportunity to do philosophy.[12]

Nancey Murphy indeed sat on a professional chair; she tended to have a fixed timetable for talking, and she even had "grandstands" (of sorts) set up for her audience, being a lecture-circuit all-star. Still, this passage aptly illustrates Nancey's *approach* to philosophical theology: the task did not end

---

to the work of Jim McClendon; see Nancey Murphy, "Foreword," *The Collected Works of James Wm. McClendon, Jr., Volumes 1 and 2*, edited by Ryan Andrew Newson and Andrew C. Wright (Waco, TX: Baylor University Press, 2014) xii.

11. Cavell is describing the work of Ludwig Wittgenstein: "But what other philosopher has found the antidote to illusion in the particular and repeated humility of remembering and tracking the uses of humble words, looking philosophically as it were beneath our feet rather than above our heads?" Stanley Cavell, "Declining Decline," in *The Cavell Reader*, edited by Stephen Mulhall (Cambridge, MA: Blackwell, 1996) 323.

12. Plutarch, *Whether a Man Should Engage in Politics When He is Old*, 26, 796d. Quoted in Pierre Hadot, *What is Ancient Philosophy*, translated by Michael Chase (Cambridge, MA: Harvard University Press, 2002) 38. I am grateful to Scott Looney for first directing me to this passage.

once one left the classroom. Philosophical theology done well continues as one goes along, as one works for peace, justice, and reconciliation in a broken world, as one eats and drinks and enjoys the company of friends. Indeed, some of the more profound conversations I have had with Nancey have been at her house over dinner, with students both past and present engaged in lively debate. The essays in this book function as examples of the kinds of appropriations, extensions, critiques, and conclusions that one might hear over dinner at Nancey's house, theological engagements that are variously indebted to her work.

Why This Book, Why Now?

This book stands as a testament and a witness—in J. L. Austin's terms, a speech-act—to Nancey Murphy's continued influence on and contribution to contemporary Christian scholarship. Strictly speaking, this book emerged in the wake of Murphy's retirement from Fuller Theological Seminary after twenty-five years of teaching and service. But really, that was just an excuse. As Murphy's colleagues, friends, and students heard the news of her retirement, it became clear that Murphy's work had made an indelible mark on the thinking of many people working in diverse disciplines. Even as these people may have argued with Murphy on certain points (Nancey would be quick to underline MacIntyre's observation that any healthy tradition progresses by means of argument), few left the argument unchanged, or without being sharpened by the encounter. As such, the essays in this book, for all their variance, embody appreciation for Murphy's influence. And as the highest honor one can give a scholar is *engagement*, even critical engagement, this book stands as a tribute to Murphy, a collection of theological essays that continue in the spirit of Murphy's work.

To this end, the title of this book, *Practicing to Aim at Truth*, is drawn from a line in one of Murphy's more obscure essays. In it, Murphy speaks of her indebtedness to MacIntyre's means of judging between large-scale traditions of inquiry (within which all humans think, whether they realize it or not). Without abandoning MacIntyre's insights, Murphy notes that there may be aspects of MacIntyre's understanding of rationality of which a good Anabaptist should be suspicious,[13] particularly regarding the will-to-power as a ubiquitous and distorting phenomenon. On Murphy's view, the best way to retain MacIntyre's "practical" insights while avoiding his "overly optimistic" evaluation of the potentiality inherent in social practices is a synthesis "that grafts MacIntyre's epistemological work onto a Radical

13. This claim also shows up in Murphy, "Wind and Spirit," 308.

Reformation social analysis."[14] In particular, Murphy writes that what is needed to subvert the will-to-power and provide a coherent Christian witness in the contemporary world is the adoption of Radical Reformation practices of the sort typically identified (nonviolence, simple living, revolutionary subordination), and less typically, what Murphy calls "Christian epistemic practices," meaning *"communal practices aimed at the pursuit of truth."*[15]

This is but one way to describe Murphy's contribution to Christian scholarship: as a lifetime of explicating practices that give witness to the kenotic path taken by the crucified and risen Lord, and which provide "a school for learning to live in the world without the use of worldly power."[16] Even more, Christian scholarship is a matter of participating in the sorts of "Christian epistemic practices" that focus the community's vision such that it is better able to see the myriad ways the gospel impinges on all manner of disciplines. The essays collected in this book attest to the existence of a community of scholars, loose yet sharing a family resemblance, who continue to think with Murphy, aiming at a truth whose scope is wider than any one of us, and more dynamic than any "foundation."

Summary of Contents

The scholarly contributions in this book are made by students of Murphy (both old and current, master's level and doctoral) as well as colleagues with whom she has worked, and who have been influenced by her friendship and scholarship. The essays deal with a diverse set of topics; as will be clear as one reads through the contributions, Murphy's influence has reached scholars working in a wide array of fields, with a range of interests, such that while this group constitutes a family of sorts, it is by no means a family that agrees on everything. As such, the essays rub up and even push against each other at certain points, but in so doing show just how fecund her scholarship is, how her research has resonated with diverse philosophies and theologies, and how Murphy enriched the world by making so many friends, catalyzing so many different kinds of conversations. Even so, the contributors are united by something besides Murphy's influence on their work (which in most cases is the direct influence of a teacher): they inhabit a certain kind

---

14. Nancey Murphy, "Missiology in the Postmodern West: A Radical Reformation Perspective," in *To Stake a Claim: Mission and the Western Crisis of Knowledge*, edited by J. Andrew Kirk and Kevin J. Vanhoozer (Maryknoll, NY: Orbis, 1999) 116.

15. Ibid. Emphasis added.

16. Murphy, "Wind and Spirit," 308.

of conversation, a mode of attention, a common *approach* to the questions under consideration, that if nothing else is marked by carefulness of thought and "interdisciplinarity." Certain "regulars" show up as interlocutors, philosophers and theologians who have influenced Murphy's work and continue to shape her students—Imre Lakatos, Alasdair MacIntyre, John Howard Yoder, Ludwig Wittgenstein; also present are interlocutors who are being brought into Murphy's orbit by her students—Romand Coles, Stephen Mulhall, Jeremy Begbie, Ilya Prigogine, Andy Clark. Both the newer directions Murphy is taken, and the uses these more familiar interlocutors are put to, represent only a small sample of the possibilities available to those who would engage Murphy's work in the years to come.

The essays have been organized into four categories drawn from Murphy's areas of research over the years: her initial interest in what she has broadly called "theological methodology," including the relationship between scientific and theological reasoning; theological anthropology; questions of ontology or metaphysics, focused in part on the dialogue between cosmology and Christian theology; and the ever-present question of the ethical, political convictions implied by these theological investigations.[17] There could be a book of essays devoted to Murphy's influence in any one of these categories, but the holistic, interdisciplinary nature of Murphy's work—perhaps best on display in *On the Moral Nature of the Universe*, which the editor at Fortress Press remarked might have been titled, "All about Everything"[18]—lends itself to including each of these categories as a fitting testament to Murphy's influence. And in any case, while disciplinary distinctions remain important, Murphy has always recognized the ways in which each discipline carries unavoidable implications for the others, or is marked by questions that are only answerable by reference to entities or processes available in another.[19]

The first section is made up of essays that orient the reader to Murphy's work, constellating around issues of "methodology," broadly conceived. These essays are helpful for readers who may be unfamiliar with Murphy's work, and it is for this reason that they appear first—not any implied belief in their precedence. Bob Russell's essay opens the volume, which is fitting, given that of the contributors Russell has known Nancey the longest. Russell recounts how Murphy's use of Imre Lakatos's methodology was seminal to the formation of the Center for Theology and the Natural Sciences and his

---

17. Murphy names and summarizes each of these areas in ibid., esp. 304–9.

18. Ibid., 308.

19. Murphy calls the latter "boundary questions." For more on their nature and function in the hierarchy of the sciences, see Murphy and Ellis, *Moral Nature*, 16, 219–20.

own conception of the relationship between science and theology. Russell's essay assumes a semi-autobiographical tone, which is similarly employed by Richard Heyduck. Whereas Russell restricts his scope to Murphy's appropriation and extension of Lakatos, as what most influenced his own work, Heyduck picks up where Russell leaves off, exploring the importance of Murphy's move to Alasdair MacIntyre and the ways this helped awaken him from his fundamentalist slumbers. Combined with the "baptist" theology of Jim McClendon, Heyduck recounts how Murphy helped him move *beyond* the options of liberalism and fundamentalism. In the process, Heyduck wonders whether certain theological "others"—Pentecostals and Mennonites, for example—complicate the formal, binary picture presented in *Beyond Liberalism and Fundamentalism*, which is rightly complexified by her use of Lakatosian and later MacIntyrean resources. Finally, my own essay examines Murphy's postmodern holism in light of certain frequently waged criticisms of this approach, which tend to gather around a shared concern that Murphy may accidentally foster a kind of epistemological insularity. While this criticism turns out to be a nonstarter, I end by arguing that Murphy ought to pay heed to concerns about the possibility of communities not listening well to voices from outside of one's own tradition—concerns Murphy can address with these same philosophical resources, and the resources available to her from her own Anabaptist tradition.

Essays in the second section fall under the umbrella of theological anthropology, the area that Nancey has done her most recent and perhaps most well-known work. Warren Brown and Brad Strawn begin by offering a robust defense of a view of human nature that is at one and the same time wholly embodied and yet which extends well beyond the "limits" of one's skin. Brown and Strawn helpfully examine the implications this account of the human person has on Christian spiritual practices. Paul Markham continues by examining how the physical yet nonreductive vision of human nature he learned from Murphy changed the way he approached ecclesiology in general, and religious conversion in particular. Markham's essay includes attention to complex systems, and the ways theology, philosophy, and science must necessarily interrelate if one is to provide a sufficiently complex conceptualization of human nature and formation in relation to conversion experiences. Finally, Brad Kallenberg writes in an intentionally constructive mode. Kallenberg asks how best to account for the grammar of "inner" and outer in human experience if one follows Murphy's path of nonreductive physicalism. One solution is to model the boundary between inner and outer as a series of "skins"—obviously epidermal, but also ocular, auditory, and olfactory. Kallenberg then extends the model first to language as a skin, and second to technology as a skin. Kallenberg finally uses music to demonstrate the limits of technology as a skin, particularly in the way it distorts human perceptions of time.

The third section gathers essays that relate to Murphy's interest in cosmology, and more generally in our pictures of "the way things are." Christian Early begins by arguing for an addendum to those who would follow Murphy in reconceptualizing divine action: an understanding of the world itself as *dynamic*, and matter as *active*. For Early, this affects not only how one pictures the created order, but also one's view of the nature of God, who to act in such a world must be just as dynamic and adventuresome as the created order itself. In the second essay, George Ellis unpacks the concept of a "possibility space" to provide a supplement to his and Murphy's *On the Moral Nature of the Universe*. Ellis argues that affirming the existence of "stuff" that is non-physical—including entities that are mental, "possible," and even Platonic in nature—is crucial to defeating scientism and recognizing the moral *telos* embedded in the very structure of the universe. Finally, J. B. Phillips works as a philosopher to critique recent shifts in approaching the philosophy of religion, which Phillips argues tend to suffer from a reluctance to deal explicitly with questions at a metaphysical, or metaphilosophical, level. Through a critical engagement with W. V. O. Quine, Phillips argues that work in philosophy of religion must pay attention to the metaphysical assumptions that necessarily frame any such inquiry, whether acknowledged or not, and suggests a renewed approach to the relationship between religion and philosophy that does not give automatic preference to a particular (and in his view, deficient) vision of "god."

The concluding section contains essays that engage the ethical, political weight of Murphy's "practiced," Anabaptist approach to philosophical theology. Andrew Wright begins by arguing that Murphy's philosophical work entails an underdeveloped and (usually) unperceived strand of political radicalism, which he sees as of a piece with the more commonly recognized postmodern shifts she advocates and defends. Wright traces some exciting connections to be made between Murphy's emphasis on kenosis (self-limitation in service to the other) and radical democratic political philosophy. Next, Greg Walgenbach argues that Murphy's unique read of MacIntyre's philosophy provides a window for better understanding her use of John Howard Yoder. Walgenbach traces the way Murphy's MacIntyre provides suitable frames within which Yoder's "lenses" fit, and that the *use* to which Murphy puts this combination is the fostering of grounded, "earthy" spaces of resistance to the principalities and powers. Third, Mark Thiessen Nation uses internalized resources from Murphy to assess three responses Christians have had to the irreducibly pluralistic world that we all share. Nation articulates a response to plurality that eschews both pluralism and parochialism, arguing instead for a "particularism" that recognizes that *everyone* is a member of *some* convictional community, without therefore letting this recognition minimize the normativity of the Christian story. Fourth, James Van Slyke investigates the sense in which Murphy's defense of nonreductionism and top-down causation in the hierarchy of the sciences enables one to affirm both the evolutionary inheritance that is necessarily tied up with human sexuality, as well as an ordering of that inheritance drawn from the higher-order discipline of theology. Van Slyke sees the key to integrating scientific views of evolution and the morality needed to negotiate human and divine relationships in a reclamation *kenosis*. Finally, Craig Hovey honors Murphy's turn toward ethics and Christian practices, which helped pave the way for the current resurgence of political theology as the study of Christian social existence in its own right. Hovey examines the practice of *mourning* in the face of injustice and political banishment as a distinctively political Christian practice that highlights the non-sovereign quality of Christian political existence and remembrance—a quality that the Anabaptists are known for, but who were by no means the first to do so in Christian history.

Conclusion

It is our hope that these essays honor the influence Nancey has had and continues to have on theologians working in a variety of fields. Nancey's intellectual rigor is matched only by her dedication to her students and friends both past and present, including her non-human friends. Nancey has been stunningly prolific over the past several decades, having often quipped that one can write and edit under *any* circumstances if one can write a dissertation with a child in tow. And while Nancey has a knack for writing in ways and on topics that are accessible to a wider audience, she has remained an academic's academic.

Nancey once wrote that she wouldn't mind if the last words of Wittgenstein were engraved on her tombstone: "Tell them I've had a wonderful life."[20] The essays collected here are a small testament to one aspect of that life. In the years to come, the church and the world will be in ever greater need of scholars who embody the virtues of intellectual inquiry that one finds in Nancey, to the glory of God.

---

20. Ibid., 309.

SECTION I

Orienting Engagements

1

The Crucial Importance of Nancey Murphy's Deployment of Lakatos's Methodology for Theology and Science

—Robert John Russell

Biographical Background

1981 was, for me, a life-changing year. I was thirty-five, and after a series of educational and teaching shifts between scientific and theological communities I was moving permanently from academic physics into the unique ecumenical and inter-religious world of theological studies at the Graduate Theological Union, Berkeley (GTU). I had studied physics as an undergraduate at Stanford University (1964–68), along with minors in music and religion. I had received an MDiv and an MA in theology from the Pacific School of Religion in 1972 (a member of the GTU) and an MS and PhD in physics at the University of California (Los Angeles and Santa Cruz, respectively) in 1970 and 1978. I had just completed three years at Carleton College in Northfield, Minnesota, teaching physics, teaching science and religion with Ian Barbour, and serving in campus ministry through ordination in the United Church of Christ, Congregational. My career had come to a pivotal turning point: Would I continue in the world of physics, perhaps occasionally writing about science and religion? Or would I follow the call I felt from God to accept "theology and science" as my lifelong vocation? I chose the latter, and together with my spouse Charlotte and our young daughters Christie and Lisa, returned to the Bay Area.

In Berkeley I created a Center that, hopefully, would invite the religious and scientific communities out of conflict or isolation and into mutually respectful, constructive dialogue and interaction for the benefit of both and for their mutual service to the world. Such an interdisciplinary interaction would require academic excellence on topics drawn from a wide range of theological disciplines (including contemporary systematic and philosophical theology, ethics, spirituality, and biblical studies), rigorous input from historical and contemporary philosophy (especially philosophy of science and philosophy of religion), from the history of science and religion, and from key fields in the natural sciences and mathematics (including physics, cosmology, evolutionary and molecular biology/genetics, and the cognitive neurosciences). It would require theologians who would come to recognize the crucial role science should play in their constructive work. It would require scientists who would be willing to reach beyond the limits of science and explore, or at least be open to, the philosophical and theological implications of their work, as well as the philosophical and theological elements often hidden, but surely present and influential, within their work. It would flourish best in an ecumenical and inter-religious academic context that would include practicing representatives of the world religions. It would mean developing an interdisciplinary methodology to enable and support the dialogue. And it would need to be a place where my own scholarship in theology and science could find a home and evolve without any agenda of it becoming a dominant factor in the process. And so in 1981 the Center for Theology and the Natural Sciences (CTNS) was born with the motto: "a dream worth loving, a reality worth building."

From the outset I used the metaphor of a bridge to represent CTNS. The bridge I chose to symbolize the new interdisciplinary methodology was the Golden Gate Bridge. San Francisco and Marin County are connected by this bridge of dialog and interaction; the bridge does not attempt to "move" one land mass—San Francisco or Marin—onto the other and take it over (the conflict model); nor is the bridge allowed to fall into ruin out of neglect, as if the two land masses have nothing to do with one another (the independence model). Instead, each territory, San Francisco and Marin, are respected and cherished in their own right and yet vibrant commerce can flow between the two—the traffic flows in *both* directions, as I claim should also be the case with theology and science. The bridge metaphor provided the "picture" for what I came to call the "creative mutual interaction" (CMI) between scientific and religious communities. For all this I owe an immense debt of gratitude to Nancey Murphy.

As one of my first doctoral students at the GTU in the early 1980s, fresh from her PhD in philosophy at University of California, Berkeley with

Paul Feyerabend, Nancey introduced me to the work of Imre Lakatos in the philosophy of science and to its potential for theological method.[1] Lakatos's method, generalized to apply to the interaction between theology and science, is deeply embedded in the structure of the bridge metaphor and thus CMI. As Murphy explains, Lakatos viewed scientific theories as structured by a central "hard core" surrounded by a belt of auxiliary hypotheses. He then delineated a set of criteria by which we can decide rationally whether a given scientific research program is "progressive" compared to its competitors. The key criterion is a research program's ability to predict "novel facts" which are later corroborated.[2]

Murphy made a crucial modification of Lakatos' conception of "novel facts" in order that it could be extended beyond natural science and into theology. In this publication Murphy argued that a fact "is novel if it is one not used in the construction of the theory T that it is taken to confirm.... [It is] one whose existence, relevance to T, or interpretability in light of T is first documented after T is proposed."[3] With this modification of the concept of novel facts, Murphy was able to develop a theological method that explicitly used Lakatos's work even though the idea of "prediction" seemed foreign to theology. If we adopt this method we could, in principle, decide between competing theological research programs using criteria which transcend the programs themselves! And in so doing, we could demonstrate *progress* in theology, to use the term which Murphy took from Lakatos' writings. This is a *singular* claim by Murphy, which most practicing theologians have yet to appreciate fully.[4] In my opinion, Murphy's work added a crucial piece to the overall argument for what can be called the scientific status of theology.[5]

In what follows I hope to suggest three ways Murphy's approach can be used to choose between competing theologies: according to their

---

1. As a recent PhD in physics, what I learned from her about Lakatos described and illuminated the ways I had pursued my own scientific research at UCSC in competition with other research groups in my field.

2. Imre Lakatos, "Falsification and the Methodology of Scientific Research Programmes," reprinted in *The Methodology of Scientific Research Programmes: Philosophical Papers*, volume 1, edited by John Worrall and Gregory Currie (Cambridge: Cambridge University Press, 1978) 8-101. Cited in Nancey Murphy, *Theology in the Age of Scientific Reasoning* (Ithaca, NY: Cornell University Press, 1990) 58.

3. Ibid., 68.

4. Murphy's approach was thoroughly implemented by Philip Hefner in *The Human Factor: Evolution, Culture, and Religion* (Minneapolis: Fortress, 1993).

5. Nancey's dissertation on Lakatosian methodology in theology, published as *Theology in the Age of Scientific Reasoning*, won the American Academy of Religion's "Award for Excellence in the Study of Religion" in the Constructive-Reflective Category in 1992.

willingness to engage with science, their ability to continue the engagement as scientific theories change, and their ability to make empirical predictions based on this engagement. Accordingly, I will focus on three specific theological doctrines, and use Murphy's methodology to judge between rival contemporary understandings of these doctrines in light of the theology and science dialogue. In doing so my intention is to demonstrate the astonishing fruitfulness of Murphy's approach in theology and science based on her appropriation of Lakatosian scientific methodology.

All this reflects my continuing indebtedness to Nancey for introducing me to the work of Lakatos in the philosophy of science and for our many conversations over the decades that have followed. Over time Nancey has moved beyond Lakatos to utilize the work of other scholars, especially that of Alasdair MacIntyre.[6] Nevertheless, it is to her crucial impact on *my* career starting in the early 1980s, and for the following decades of shared scholarship and deepening friendship, that I dedicate this essay with the warmest appreciation.

Can a theology of creation that incorporates scientific cosmology be progressive with respect to its competitors that either do not incorporate cosmology or refuse to change as cosmology changes?

Rarely do Christian theologians who write about the doctrine of creation *ex nihilo* engage in a dialogue with science, particularly with scientific cosmology. My hope for some time now has been to show that those theologies which do so represent research programs that are "progressive" compared with those theologies which do not, following Lakatos's understanding of "progress." But this strategy is complicated by the fact that scientific cosmology has changed repeatedly over the past century, and continues to do so today. Could a theology which incorporated the scientific cosmology of the 1950s and 1960s, when "standard Big Bang cosmology" reigned supreme, continue the dialogue even as this cosmology was replaced by more recent "inflationary" and "quantum" cosmologies? If not, my argument in support of the progressive nature of the theology and cosmology dialogue would dry up.

---

6. See Nancey Murphy, *Anglo-American Postmodernity: Scientific Perspectives on Science, Religion, and Ethics* (Boulder, CO: Westview, 1997); and Nancey Murphy, Brad J. Kallenberg, and Mark Thiessen Nation, eds., *Virtues and Practices in the Christian Tradition: Christian Ethics after MacIntyre* (Harrisburg, PA: Trinity, 1997).

In several places,[7] I have discussed the possibility that the absolute beginning of time (t=0) in Big Bang cosmology might be relevant to the doctrine of creation *ex nihilo*. Some scholars saw t=0 as directly relevant to belief in God the creator. A notable example is Pope Pius XII. In his allocution of 1951, Pius wrote that the beginning of the universe in the finite past would lead an unbiased mind to move beyond the material universe and "ascend to a creating Spirit."[8] Another notable example is Ted Peters.[9] Other scholars saw the beginning of time as basically irrelevant to theology, including Arthur Peacocke and John Polkinghorne.[10] Instead of speculating about a distant past event as significant for faith, these scholars stressed the dynamic and irreversible nature of the Big Bang universe compared with the static cosmology of the Bible. This in turn led to an emphasis on the importance of contemporary cosmology for the doctrine of creation, in particular God's relation to nature as its continuous creator. I took a third position similar to that taken by Ian Barbour[11]: cosmology as indirectly relevant to theology. I framed this approach specifically in terms of a Lakatosian research programme in theology and science.[12] Here, following the theological approach reflected in the Wesleyan quadrilateral, faith in God is primarily based on Scripture, tradition, reason and experience; I add to this that science can be understood as a self-limited form of reason and thus a new (but not a fifth) voice within Wesley's four-fold structure. In this way we can bring science—and in particular t=0—into the theological picture: our universe has a temporally finite past, suggesting its existence depends on God its Creator.[13]

7. See my "Finite Creation without a Beginning: The Doctrine of Creation in Relation to Big Bang and Quantum Cosmologies," *Quantum Cosmology and the Laws of Nature: Scientific Perspectives on Divine Action*, edited by Robert John Russell, Nancey Murphy and C. J. Isham (Vatican City: Vatican Observatory, 1993) 293–329. Republished in my *Cosmology from Alpha to Omega: The Creative Mutual Interaction of Theology and Science* (Minneapolis: Fortress, 2008) ch. 3.

8. For a careful discussion of Pius's allocution, see Ernan McMullin, "How Should Cosmology Relate to Theology?" in *The Sciences and Theology in the Twentieth Century*, edited by A. R. Peacocke (Notre Dame: University of Notre Dame Press, 1981) 30–32.

9. Ted Peters, "On Creating the Cosmos," in *Physics, Philosophy and Theology: A Common Quest for Understanding*, edited by Robert John Russell, William R. Stoeger, and George V. Coyne (Vatican City: Vatican Observatory, 1988) 273–96.

10. A. R. Peacocke, *Creation and the World of Science: The Bampton Lectures, 1978* (Oxford, UK: Clarendon, 1979) 77–79. John C. Polkinghorne, *The Faith of a Physicist: Reflections of a Bottom-Up Thinker* (Princeton: Princeton University Press, 1994) 73.

11. Russell, *Cosmology from Alpha*, 83–86.

12. Ibid., 88–89.

13. Clearly this is an indirect argument, since even for an infinitely old universe, its sheer existence leads to creation *ex nihilo*, as Thomas Aquinas argued. As William

But what ought we do when cosmology changes? In the 1980s standard Big Bang cosmology was replaced with inflationary (or hot) Big Bang cosmology. On this account, in the first moments ($10{-}36$ seconds to $10{-}32$ seconds) of the universe's existence, it expanded extraordinarily rapidly in a process called "inflation" before settling down to the usual Big Bang rates. The inflationary model accounts for several technical problems in the standard model, such as the near equivalence of the amount of matter and antimatter in the universe and the fine-tuning of the fundamental physical constants of nature. It does so by suggesting that there are, in fact, countless domains in the actual universe produced by the initial inflationary expansion and that our visible universe is only one of them. The natural constants can vary from domain to domain, and at least in our visible universe, the physical preconditions exist for the biological evolution of life.

The problem is that in inflationary cosmology the empirical status of t=0 is undermined. In some versions it remains; in others, it is impossible to decide whether or not t=0 exists. This makes it much more difficult to import its meaning into a theology of creation.[14] In response I have argued that the concept of t=0 in standard Big Bang cosmology includes two elements: the observation that our visible universe has a finite past (~13.7 billion years), and the conviction that this finite past includes the event t=0. But even in inflationary cosmology our visible universe has a finite past of some 13.7 billion years. The only change is the possible loss of the event t=0; the *visible* universe in inflationary cosmology is still temporally finite and thus still allows us to interpret it theologically in terms of creation *ex nihilo*. In this way I claim that a theology of creation could continue to incorporate cosmology even when we move from standard to inflationary cosmology, and thus be "progressive" compared with its competitors: those theologies of creation that either 1) ignore cosmology altogether or 2) that stick with standard Big Bang cosmology with its t=0 and ignore the rapid changes in cosmology that tend to leave t=0 behind.[15]

Carroll writes, "Thomas Aquinas saw no contradiction in the notion of an eternal created universe. . . . For, even if the universe had no temporal beginning, it still would depend upon God for its very being. The radical dependence on God as cause of being is what creation means." William Carroll, "Thomas Aquinas and Big Bang Cosmology," paper presented at the annual Thomistic Institute sponsored by the Jacques Maritain Center at the University of Notre Dame, July 25, 1997, http://www3.nd.edu/Departments/Maritain/ti/carroll.htm.

14. The problem becomes even more acute when one considers current approaches to quantum cosmology and eternal inflation.

15. A example of the latter is represented in the literature produced by the organization, "Reasons to Believe," founded by Hugh Ross. "Reasons to Believe" insists that science supports t=0 and thus provides evidence for God. See http://www.reasons.org.

Can a theology of the "Cosmic Christ" offer empirical predictions and thus be progressive in comparison with those theologies which talk about the "Cosmic Christ" without engaging science?

In several writings I have also suggested ways in which a Lakatosian method in theology and science can lead us to make empirical predictions about the universe we live in. By combining a Christian theology of redemption through the Christ event on planet earth with Big Bang cosmology, I have argued that we have reasons to predict that wherever life has evolved in the universe to the level of self-consciousness and moral capacity, it will need salvation: that is, extraterrestrial intelligent life ("ETI") will be unable to act virtuously without the grace of God offered in an Incarnation appropriate to its own species. I refer to this as a specific form of the "Cosmic Christ" argument, in that I am calling for the necessity of multiple Incarnations appropriate to each form of ETI. Framing theology this way is, I believe, yet another way of showing the "progressive" nature of specific approaches in theology and science. Specifically, it promises to show not only that redemption theology can and should be in dialogue with cosmology (and thus be progressive in comparison with those many theologies of redemption which do not engage in the dialogue), but even more importantly, such a dialogue will lead to new discoveries not only in theology itself but for its dialogue partner, cosmology—namely that ETI will be as morally ambiguous as humans.[16]

I start with the question whether science gives us any reason to support the idea that life in the universe needs to be redeemed. Here I turn to the work of distinguished evolutionary biologist Francisco Ayala who argues, from a Darwinian perspective, that while humankind's capacity for reason is adaptive and thus determined by evolution, and while our capacity for moral reasoning is similarly determined by evolution, the norms of morality and their enfleshment in human cultures are not adaptive: they are a "free variable." These moral norms come from sources such as culture, and in particular philosophy and religion. I then extrapolate this argument to wherever evolution has brought about intelligent life in the universe and

---

16. See Robert John Russell, "Life in the Universe: Philosophical and Theological Issues," in *First Steps in the Origin of Life in the Universe: Proceedings of the Sixth Trieste Conference on Chemical Evolution*, edited by Julián Chela-Flores, Tobias Owen, and François Raulin (Dordrecht: Kluwer Academic Publishers, 2001) 365–74. See also Robert John Russell, "Many Incarnations or One," in *Astrotheology: Theology Meets Extraterrestrial Life*, edited by Ted Peters with Martinez Hewlett, Joshua Moritz, and Robert John Russell (forthcoming).

predict that it too will have moral capacity, although the norms of morality will be determined by its culture, too.

Now it is an "empirical fact" that we humans are characterized by sin, including the brokenness in our ethical actions that infect the actions of individuals and social systems with personal and institutional estrangement and lead to war, racism, sexism, poverty, and the whole list of atrocities that dominate the daily news. What about with ETI? Some presuppose that ETI will be universally benevolent, a view that is predominant in that part of the scientific community which is engaged in "SETI"—the search for intelligent life in the universe.[17] In contrast, I offer the prediction that such brokenness is not isolated to our species but is characteristic of all ETI capable of reason and moral behavior, and thus they will also require culturally given moral norms. Here I am once again drawing on Ayala's argument for the underdetermination of moral norms by nature and their source in culture.[18] In essence I suggest that ETI will be neither totally benign nor totally malevolent. Instead, my empirical prediction is that ETI will share in the same kind of ambiguity of moral behavior as is found in humankind, even if its manifestation varies immensely. If this is the case, it underscores the universality of the Easter event: God, who is the author of all life in the universe by means of evolutionary biology, is also the redeemer of all life in the universe as symbolized by the phrase "the Cosmic Christ." In essence all ETI will be "fallen" (in planetary- and species-specific ways) and need salvation (again, in planetary- and species-specific ways).

Of course, the key Christological question is whether a single Incarnation on planet Earth can affect the redemption of all fallen ETI in the visible universe, or whether God will graciously provide an Incarnate Christ for every species in the universe capable of rationality and moral capacity. In my view, all ETI will be fallen (as stated above), and God will offer a species-specific Incarnation for all life throughout the universe. However, whether or not such a universal series of Incarnations or a single Incarnation is adequate for universal redemption, my main point here is that I predict all ETI will be fallen and thus will sin in all the personal and social ways that we see on Earth. In making this *empirical* prediction I hope to show that a theology of redemption that incorporates cosmology and the evolution of ETI will be progressive over a theology of redemption that ignores the universal, cosmic scope of a Christian theology of redemption and thus makes no predictions whatsoever regarding ETI—if it even considers the question.

17. See the resources available on the SETI Institute website, http://www.seti.org.

18. See Francisco J. Ayala, "The difference of being human: ethical behavior as an evolutionary byproduct," in *Biology, Ethics, and the Origins of Life*, edited by Holmes Rolston, III (Boston: Jones and Bartlett, 1995) 117–35.

Can a non-interventionist account of divine action, first proposed in the quantum realm, be extended to evolutionary biology and thus be a "progressive" research program in theology and science?

Finally, Murphy has argued that what we often call the "Newtonian mechanistic worldview" consists of three elements: the Laplacian, deterministic view of natural causality embedded in classical mechanics; epistemic reductionism; and ontological materialism in the form of atomism. According to Murphy, this worldview pushed Christian theology into a "forced option": either 1) God really ("objectively") acts in nature, even though this action requires that God intervene miraculously by suspending the regular flow of nature's deterministic causal processes (and thus violate the laws of nature that physics uses to describe them); or 2) God only appears to be acting ("subjectively") in what are in fact the ordinary processes of nature. Conservatives typically opt for the former and liberals the latter.[19] But twentieth-century natural science might offer a way out of this "forced option," if it can provide one or more well-tested *scientific* theories which could be interpreted, *philosophically*, in terms of ontological indeterminism—unlike classical mechanics. Such a possibility could then be the basis for a theological theory of divine action that combines the best of both options: it is objective and it is non-interventionist. This possibility depends, obviously, on an indeterministic philosophy of nature. I have called this possibility "non-interventionist objective divine action" (NIODA).[20]

The task now, as in any genuine research project, is to search out the existing and well-supported theories in physics to see if any, or many, of them are capable of an indeterministic philosophical interpretation. In my view quantum mechanics offers a very promising approach to NIODA (what I will call "QM-NIODA"), perhaps even better than the theories of divine action supported by Ian Barbour, Arthur Peacocke, and John Polkinghorne.[21]

---

19. Nancey Murphy, *Beyond Liberalism and Fundamentalism: How Modern and Postmodern Philosophy Set the Theological Agenda* (Harrisburg, PA: Trinity, 1996) ch. 3.

20. See Russell, *Cosmology from Alpha*, chs. 4–6.

21. Ibid. I offer my reasons for this claim, as well as a defense of the criticisms of QM-NIODA, in *Cosmology from Alpha to Omega*. Some claim that this view amounts to a "gaps" argument; my response is that God created the world *ex nihilo* such that God can act in special ways without intervening in the flow of natural processes. I also argue, against my critics, that it does not restrict divine action to the level of subatomic physics but is consistent with divine action in other levels of nature. It does not presuppose that the laws of nature are ontological and that quantum statistics somehow determine each individual quantum event. And granted that most quantum events "average out" to result in the ordinary processes of nature, it emphasizes that *some* quantum events

I take this to be a clear sign of its "progressive" character in comparison with those of Barbour, Peacocke, and Polkinghorne (using the term "progressive" in a strictly Lakatosian sense, and not as any kind of value judgment).

What makes QM-NIODA particularly attractive from the perspective of a Lakatosian methodology is its surplus predictions in the realm of theistic evolution. To see this, recall that a NIODA view of nature was originally launched on the basis of an indeterministic interpretation of quantum mechanics. Nevertheless, quantum mechanics can be incorporated into the wider framework of molecular and evolutionary biology. Specifically, quantum mechanics is integrally involved in the nature of genetic mutations. In such mutations, the making or breaking of a hydrogen bond, which is intrinsic to such mutations, is a quantum mechanical process. These mutations, in turn, make a crucial contribution to the processes of biological variation that, together with natural selection and many other processes, constitute the neo-Darwinian account of evolutionary biology. In essence, over time evolution expresses the information coded in genetic mutations through phenotypic variation in progeny, with their accompanying relative degrees of fitness. Thus QM-NIODA not only provides a preferable account of divine action in regard to its competitors in physics; it goes beyond physics to have an unanticipated and thus a "novel" impact on evolutionary and molecular biology, and is in this additional sense "progressive." Moreover, it has an advantage compared both to those who deal with divine action but ignore the question of divine action in evolution, or those who incorporate divine action in evolution but fail to tell us what difference, if any, God's action makes during the entire 13.7 billion year history of the evolution of life on earth. In this sense QM-NIODA offers a robust version of "theistic evolution," namely that biological evolution, from the perspective of Christian theology, is "how God creates life."[22] This surplus value offered by QM-NIODA constitutes it, in yet another way, as a progressive Lakatosian research program on non-interventionist divine action.[23]

---

can produce a macroscopic result in the world, such as a single alpha particle setting off a Geiger counter.

22. See Russell, *Cosmology from Alpha*, ch. 6.

23. At the same time, I routinely stress that the success of this account of divine action in nature seems to exacerbate the problem of "natural theodicy" by appearing, at least, to relate God's action to the processes of suffering, disease, death, and extinction which configure the traumatic history of life on earth. Once again, this leads me to probe theological responses to natural theodicy (see my *Cosmology from Alpha*, chs. 7–8) concluding with the unavoidable need to relocate the problem of evil—natural and moral—away from the context of the doctrine of creation (such as theistic evolution) and to the doctrine of redemption and eschatology, particularly the cosmic hope in new creation (see my *Cosmology from Alpha*, chs. 9–10). At this point, however,

Conclusion: Murphy's Lakatos as Springboard for "Creative Mutual Interaction" between Theology and Science

Over the past decade I have repeatedly followed Murphy's lead and used Lakatos's methodology to produce a genuinely *interactive* method in which each side plays a creative and constructive role, offering something of intellectual value to the other. In doing so I have taken the "progressive" dimension of Murphy's approach to its most radical form, especially compared with those who merely bring the results of science into the theological arena: namely that theology can offer science something that *science* will find helpful.

When I was in seminary in the 1960s, it was taken for granted that the most one could hope for in theology and science was a one-way relation: theology's sole role was to interpret science, and if that could be accomplished it would be an enormous step forward indeed! But during my doctoral research in physics a decade later I saw firsthand the multiple ways in which key scientific concepts of nature were often rooted in philosophical systems, as in the thinking of such pioneers such as Niels Bohr, Albert Einstein, Werner Heisenberg, and Erwin Schrödinger. I mused on the story of Fred Hoyle, the outspoken atheist cosmologist, who in the early 1950s had constructed steady state cosmology in which the universe is eternally old with no t=0. He had done so in part to undermine the Big Bang cosmology being invoked by Christians to support the existence of God, including Pope Pius XII. Hoyle became my hero, for he had been willing to take his theology (that is, his atheism) seriously and build a cosmology that to him represented the implications of atheism in the context of science: an eternal universe with no beginning. In my mind he had bridged the worlds of theology and science *precisely* in the way thought impossible by my seminary mentors (and even my physics professors who were open to theological conversation). They all seemed to want to limit the path entirely to one that went *from* science *to* theology! Why, I wondered silently, couldn't others follow Hoyle's example, especially those cosmologists who were theists?

In a variety of writings since then,[24] I have explored the possibility that theology can indeed offer creative suggestions in the form of questions, topics, or conceptions of nature which scientists might find helpful in their research. But how was such an interaction to be formalized? By the end of the 1990s all the pieces were in place: a) Barbour's claim that theological method is analogous to scientific method in which data feed into metaphors and model, and

---

much deeper problems arise from the challenge of cosmology to eschatology.

24. For a summary of these writings, see the introduction to my *Cosmology from Alpha to Omega*.

from there into theories, and that theories offer predictions to be tested and theories of instrumentation by which data is selected[25]; b) Peacocke's epistemic hierarchy in which higher level disciplines describe processes and properties which, while constrained by lower level disciplines, cannot be reduced entire to them ("epistemic emergence")[26]; c) Murphy's claim that Lakatosian research programs can be used in theology as well as in science; and d) my claim that a Lakatosian research program can be used in theology and science in a number of ways, as I suggested above. But it took an educated guess that would only be verified later by its results—an *ansatz*—to unite them all. Graphically, I placed a diagram of theology, with its methodology described basically but with some modifications by Barbour, above a diagram of science, with its methodology again described more directly by Barbour. I then drew eight lines, five of which moved from the science diagram to that of theology, and three of which moved from theology to science. These lines represented the five ways that science can influence theology and the three ways theology can influence science. Together they represent the multiple interactions possible between theology and science.[27]

As I have argued in this essay, the introduction of Lakatos's method as an *interdisciplinary* program for relating theology and science could allow such programs to compete successfully against those theological or scientific programs which do not take the other field into account.

In a *festschrift* like this I feel pulled, almost inexorably, back over the decades and memories since first meeting Nancey. There is so much I could, would, and should say about her impact on my life, starting then and continuing through the present. In this essay I have focused almost entirely on one such impact which is rooted in our first meeting at the GTU and her introducing me to the philosophy of Lakatos. But there are so many more: Her brilliant co-leadership of the CTNS and the Vatican Observatory conferences over twenty-five years; her argument that quantum mechanics offers a basis for divine action in nature; her expansion of the Anthropic Principle to include the evolution of creatures capable of moral agency as part of God's design of the universe; her response to the challenge of natural theodicy as the "unwanted but unavoidable" consequence of God's creating a universe in which intelligent life can evolve; her support for strong emergence and her

---

25. Ian Barbour, *Religion in an Age of Science: The Gifford Lectures, Volume One* (San Francisco: Harper & Row, 1990). Compare his Figure 1 (32) and Figure 2 (36), and my discussion of them in Russell, *Cosmology from Alpha to Omega*.

26. Arthur Peacocke, *Theology for a Scientific Age: Being and Becoming—Natural, Divine, and Human* (Minneapolis: Fortress, 1993); see ch. 12, and esp. Figure 3 on 217.

27. See Figure 4 in Russell, *Cosmology from Alpha*, 23. I explain the figure in more detail there.

use of supervenience and context-sensitive constraints in accounting for top-down/whole-part causality in complex systems and the mind-brain problem; her analysis of the differences between liberals and conservatives in American Protestant Christianity (and the role modern philosophy and mechanistic science played in creating that difference); and so on. She has been a Fellow in Science and Religion here at CTNS. She has served on the CTNS Board of Directors for three decades, including as its Chair. She has been a confidante, a trusted friend, and a supporter of my own academic work, especially when I have felt overwhelmed with funding and the administrative challenges that come with keeping CTNS afloat. And, going back once again to the early years, she is one of the most extraordinary doctoral students—and now accomplished colleagues—I have had. Needless to say, I care for her immensely.

Nancey, your accomplishments ring in my ears with astonishment, your future looms huge with possibilities, and your loving fans (me, foremost!) cheer you on in this *festschrift* celebration. May God bless you deeply with endurance, vision, and joy, now and always.

2

Beyond Liberalism and Fundamentalism for the Theological "Others"
Notes from a Converted Fundamentalist

—RICHARD HEYDUCK

I BEGAN MY CHRISTIAN life as a fundamentalist, though I did not know the term at the time. I did know that the Christianity in the United Methodist churches in which I had been raised was tepid and uninteresting. Fundamentalism, with its stories of the end times (rapture, tribulation, second coming of Jesus) was much more interesting than the jokes and "Chicken Soup for the Soul" sorts of stories I heard in my United Methodist Church. And salvation! I never heard the United Methodists I was around talk about salvation. Sure, we heard about Jesus. He was a nice guy who wanted us to be nice, too. The fundamentalists talked about salvation from sin—it did not take much to convince me that I was a sinner—and eternal life in heaven. They offered more than just a theory, too. According to the preachers I heard, I could not only come to faith in Jesus but I could *know for sure* that I was saved and heaven bound.

I begin with this autobiographical account because it sets up the way Nancey Murphy's account of the possibility of theological change has resonated with my own experience and ecclesial location. Her account of the American theological struggle in *Beyond Liberalism and Fundamentalism*[1] and her development of a postmodern account of religion in

---

1. Nancey Murphy, *Beyond Liberalism and Fundamentalism: How Modern and Postmodern Philosophy Set the Theological Agenda* (Valley Forge, PA: Trinity, 1996).

Anglo-American Postmodernity[2] offered a way for me to think about my own United Methodist tradition in the present and to advance it into the future that evaded fundamentalism without lapsing into liberalism. Murphy's account of fundamentalism and liberalism is a formal account, seeing the two streams of the Western theological tradition as inhabiting the same philosophical space. That that space was distinctly modern meant that each stream was constrained by the resources present in that space.

My awakening to the inadequacy of my fundamentalism happened slowly. It began when I went off to college. College for some can be an occasion of losing faith altogether. As a young Christian I thought taking a course in New Testament my first semester would be an ideal way to grow my faith. Alas, my professor's approach to the New Testament was drawn directly from his own experience in graduate school in the 1950s and came not only with a deep tinge of Bultmann, but also all that one would expect with the methods of higher criticism. Rather than losing my faith, however, I argued with the professor, defending the Bible from what I perceived as attacks. As I did extra reading and research to advance my arguments, I encountered the doctrine of biblical inerrancy for the first time. It became the foundation for my subsequent efforts to defend the faith.

"Inerrancy became my foundation"—only later as I learned my lessons from Nancey Murphy could I recognize the modern philosophy I was drinking in. I was fitting right into the model she developed: epistemology came first if I wanted a secure foundation for Christian faith. I wanted certainty, and an inerrant Bible could give that to me.[3]

My fundamentalism also fit her model in a second way. The United Methodist churches with which I had been associated downplayed or denied the miraculous. Jesus' feeding of the five thousand became an instance of his inspiring stingy people who had food to share with those who did not. Jesus' resurrection was either the instance of his not really being dead in the first place or merely the "rise of Easter faith in the disciples." As Murphy pointed out in *Beyond Liberalism and Fundamentalism*, liberalism had settled for an immanent God, a God who worked through the natural processes of the

---

2. Nancey Murphy, *Anglo-American Postmodernity: Philosophical Perspectives on Science, Religion, and Ethics* (Boulder, CO: Westview, 1997).

3. Not all was smooth fundamentalist sailing, however. As I spent more time reading the Bible for myself rather than just uncritically believing whatever the fundamentalist preachers told me, I discovered that the world portrayed by fundamentalist theology was not the same as that found in the Bible itself. Most obviously, the eschatology of the Bible, insofar as it dealt with something we call "the end times" was nowhere near as clear and distinct as I had been led to believe.

world, the laws and regularities described by modern science.[4] My fundamentalism, to the contrary, insisted that these and other events were actual events in history, occasions of God's supernatural intervention into this world. The contrast between my own convictions and those I saw evidenced around fit nicely with her description.

Issues of language started to come up in my struggle with liberalism. Flowing out of the way I read the biblical depictions of supernatural events, I assumed that the only role of language was to give an accurate report on reality. If language failed to give an accurate report on reality, then it had failed in its specific task *as language*. This exemplifies the third dimension of the philosophical space in which liberalism and fundamentalism contended.[5] I was not perceptive enough to note that my liberal opponents were rooting their approach to language in expressivism, the philosophy of language Murphy found to be predominant in liberal theology.

Murphy's account of the relation between liberalism and fundamentalism built off opposition in these three areas: epistemology, divine action, and the philosophy of language. In epistemology liberals and fundamentalists, good moderns that they were, assumed that real knowledge was built on solid, indubitable foundations. For liberals, those foundations were human experience (whether personal experience or human experience gathered up in science); for fundamentalists the foundation was Scripture. As I mentioned above, the fundamentalists reckoned that divine action occurred as described in its inerrant Scripture—interventions in the world of everyday events. Appealing to their own foundation in experience, liberals were also happy to speak of God's actions; those actions, however, did not contradict or contravene the laws of nature. God's actions were immanent in all of nature.

Complicating the Binary

However, this formal account of fundamentalism is not complete as it stands in *Beyond Liberalism and Fundamentalism*. As Murphy herself notes, fundamentalism and liberalism are *theological* schools. Though the ground in which they grew may have been modern philosophy, they each also entail substantive theological positions. She recognizes that fundamentalism, for example, received its name in the midst of theological controversy. As Murphy says,

---

4. Murphy, *Beyond Liberalism*, 62ff.
5. Ibid., 36ff.

> The fundamentalist movement in the United States can be defined as that which arose in the early twentieth century, stimulated by pamphlets called "The Fundamentals," emphasizing Calvinist orthodoxy along with scriptural inerrancy, substitutionary atonement, and the historicity of miracles, including the virgin-birth of Christ. Evangelicals are sometimes called neo-fundamentalists [usually by liberals], because many are former fundamentalists who have moderated their positions. However the evangelical movement includes a broader range of Christians, such as Mennonites and Pentecostals [and Wesleyans!] who intend to hold a middle position between fundamentalism and liberalism.[6]

Likewise, the liberal theological tradition grew out of Schleiermacher and his successors and came to embody a common set of theological convictions and not only a particular way of relating to modern philosophy.

So far Murphy's account is binary in format: liberals are at one end of each axis, fundamentalists at the other. The first clue pointing to the need for a more complex account is Murphy's mention of evangelicals. Where do evangelicals fit into the schema? What does it mean to say that they are "fundamentalists who have moderated their positions"? Evangelicals, if the Evangelical Theological Society is taken to be an example of this species of Christian, are just as committed to foundationalist epistemology in the form of inerrancy as are fundamentalists.[7] On this point at least, "moderation" seems not to be what has happened. To make sense of this difference, we need more tools than are available in the formal account found in *Beyond Liberalism and Fundamentalism*. One strategy for finding such tools would be to go back to Murphy's first book, *Theology in the Age of Scientific Reasoning*.[8] In that book Nancey presents another formal account of theology, an account that crosses the theological spectrum and is potentially applicable to any kind of theology. Theologies, insofar as they are rational, are structured analogously to Lakatosian research programs. They have a *hard core*, a minimal set of central claims that define the theology, a *negative heuristic*, a "plan or rule to protect the hard core from falsification," and a *positive heuristic* that directs the theology in its growth. Both the negative and positive heuristics do their work through developing *auxiliary hypotheses* which can be either single doctrines subsidiary to the hard core or

---

6. Ibid., 6n8.

7. See "The Constitution of the Evangelical Theological Society," http://www.ets-jets.org/about/constitution#A3.

8. Nancey Murphy, *Theology in the Age of Scientific Reasoning* (Ithaca: Cornell University Press, 1990).

themselves be smaller scale theological research programs that support and extend the larger program.[9] In that book theology structured on these terms is *prescribed* as a way for theology to be considered rational in the context of (at least one) current approach to the rationality of science. But what if Murphy's general picture of the structure of a postmodern rational theology can be not merely a *prescriptive* account, but also a *description* of the way theological research programs actually are?

At first glance, this would not look like a position Murphy would want to take. After all, the origin of her model is the desire to overcome Humean and other modern assumptions that theology is not and cannot be rational, given the then current canons of rationality. Building on a formal account of scientific rationality that allows for holist epistemology—the Lakatosian research program—would seem to require that precisely *that* form of reasoning becomes the determining factor in differentiating rational from non-rational theological programs. But it is not merely "fitting with this form" that makes a theology rational for Murphy. As with Lakatos, the ability for the research program to progress—to produce "novel facts"—is highly important.[10] If it is this additional feature of a research program that can allow the program to be reckoned as rational, then perhaps the Lakatosian *structure* can be counted as descriptive of (theological) research programs, and questions of rationality put to the side. The *form* of the theological program—in our case, whether it be liberal or conservative—is not of primary interest, since both types of theology can be described in terms of such a program. Rather, what is of interest here to me is how the theological program so modeled works over time.[11]

With these additional theoretical insights from Murphy, we might say that for the Evangelical Theological Society the hard core of their theological program is much more minimalistic than for the fundamentalists, including only two doctrines: inerrancy and the Trinity. We could say that where fundamentalism had inerrancy as its positive heuristic, evangelicalism (at

---

9. The whole of *Theology in the Age of Scientific Reasoning* is devoted to explaining how research programs work and what it is like for a theological program to function as one. These particular descriptions are drawn from her final chapter where she summarizes the nature and role of each part. Cf. ibid., 184–86.

10. Ibid., 85ff.; Murphy, *Anglo-American*, 53. See also Imre Lakatos, "Falsification and the Methodology of Scientific Research Programmes," in *Criticism and the Growth of Knowledge: Proceedings of the International Colloquium on the Philosophy of Science*, edited by Imre Lakatos and Alan Musgrave (Cambridge: Cambridge University Press, 1970) 118ff.

11. Murphy specifically notes the importance of how the program works "over time" in Murphy, *Anglo-American*, 53. Her recognition of temporality fits well with MacIntyre's tradition-constituted inquiry explored below.

least as represented by the ETS) has now moved it into the hard core. A theory of Scripture (if we follow the analogy with the philosophy of science, we might call it the theory of instrumentation) has become that which must be defended at all costs.

There are more than doctrinal and philosophical differences between evangelicals and fundamentalists, however. Social differences loom at least as large. In the first place, fundamentalists have a strong tendency toward separationism. They often separated from denominations that they saw as "going liberal," and sought to build enclaves away from worldly influence. Evangelicals, on the other hand, were much less likely to be separationist. Another social difference between the two, and one that likely influenced evangelicals away from separationism, was that evangelicals tended to be more highly educated and philosophically sophisticated. They not only tended to value higher education more than their fundamentalist counterparts, but sought that education at the best institutions in the world. The reality of social differences also plays into the awkwardness of putting groups like the Pentecostals, Mennonites, and Wesleyans on the same map as Fundamentalists and Liberals. I will return to this below.

What about liberals? If we can broadly conceive a liberal theological research program, what might its distinctive feature be? In line with Alasdair MacIntyre's famous jibe from the 1960s, the tradition's propensity to give "atheists less and less to disbelieve,"[12] the liberal tradition may also (and more completely than evangelicals?) evacuate its hard core of substance. Instead, the general positive heuristic becomes a variant of Schleiermacher's appeal to religion's "cultured despisers." This move is exemplified not only in Schleiermacher, but also in the Tillichian practice of "correlation." A postmodern theology may, then, take a step away from the evangelical and liberal strategies of constricting the hard core of its program, in favor of more robust and substantive accounts.[13]

In the rest of this chapter I will further flesh out this picture by adding two more dimensions from Murphy's later work: an appropriation of Alasdair MacIntyre's work on tradition and James McClendon's concept of the "baptist vision." These additions to her account of contemporary Western

12. Alasdair MacIntyre and Paul Ricoeur, *The Religious Significance of Atheism* (New York: Columbia University Press, 1969) 24ff.

13. A possible example of this move can be found in the project of "canonical theism" exemplified in works like William Abraham, Jason Vickers, and Natalie Van Kirk, eds., *Canonical Theism: A Proposal for Theology and the Church* (Grand Rapids: Eerdmans, 2008). I also wonder if the role of the positive heuristic in a research program might move beyond extending the program's hard core, to the reflexive role of defining the *purpose and role* of the hard core. Or is such a task the work of a meta research program about research programs?

Christianity will enable us to better understand outliers like Mennonites, Pentecostals, and the Evangelical tradition (the ETS notwithstanding).

Alasdair MacIntyre on Traditions

In each of her first three books, Murphy makes increasing use of MacIntyre's work on traditions of inquiry. Her references to his work are fewest in the first of these, where we find only three.[14] References increase significantly in *Beyond Liberalism and Fundamentalism* (where his work is treated mostly for its epistemological significance) and even more in *Anglo-American Postmodernity*. Murphy has already accounted for MacIntyre's contributions to postmodern *epistemology*, so in what follows I will take his work in another direction.

MacIntyre offers two definitions of "tradition": first, and briefly, in *After Virtue*, we find, "A living tradition is an historically extended, socially embodied argument, and an argument precisely in part about the goods which constitute that tradition."[15] Later and more substantially, MacIntyre defines it this way:

> A tradition is an argument extended through time in which certain fundamental agreements are defined and redefined in terms of two kinds of conflict: those with critics and enemies external to the tradition who reject all or at least key parts of those fundamental agreements, and those internal, interpretive debates through which the meaning and rationale of the fundamental agreements come to be expressed and by whose progress a tradition is constituted.[16]

The first and most obvious way to take this definition is as a descriptive thesis about the way traditions—or as he observes in the context of the earlier version in *After Virtue*, traditions that are "in good order"—come into existence and have their being. Not every tradition, if we can personify this complex social phenomenon, is willing to identify itself as a tradition. I will develop this important point below.

---

14. Murphy, *Theology in the Age*, 14, 162, 201. The first reference is to MacIntyre's aforementioned identification of current theology (in context, the liberal theology of the 1950s) as "giving the atheist less and less to disbelieve."

15. Alasdair MacIntyre, *After Virtue: A Study in Moral Theory*, 2nd ed. (Notre Dame: University of Notre Dame Press, [1981] 1984) 222.

16. Alasdair MacIntyre, *Whose Justice? Which Rationality?* (Notre Dame: University of Notre Dame Press, 1988) 12.

A tradition is a *socially embodied* argument. This fits perfectly with Murphy's use of McClendon (covered in the next section). Traditions exist only through people living in community and interacting together. A tradition is also an *argument*. It is formulated by people using words. There is not mere obviousness and agreement, or an edict from above. A tradition involves claims and counter claims. A tradition is *extended through time*. Traditions are dynamic, not static. Any given tradition is not now exactly what it was or what it will be.[17] These elements of a tradition give it its stability; these are the "fundamental agreements" that make it *this* tradition and not some other.

Changes in a tradition occur as the fundamental agreements undergo conflict as old questions revive and new questions arise. Participants in the tradition desire to move the tradition forward both in terms of social space in general and in relation to particular neighboring and competing traditions. There will be differing understandings of what the tradition is, what it stands for, what it is trying to accomplish and how it should go about accomplishing its goals. These are what MacIntyre calls "internal, interpretive debates." Finally, a tradition is always butting up against other traditions, producing what MacIntyre terms "external conflict." Some of these traditions will be seen as direct competitors, while others will be seen in such a way that co-existence might be possible.

As historical phenomena, traditions will have both fundamental continuity and discontinuity over time. They will have continuity in the sense that, generally speaking, each tradition is at all points precisely *this* tradition and not some other. They will have discontinuity because the internal interpretive debates and the competitive debates with other traditions are in constant flux. This continuity and discontinuity are in tension. A significant generator of internal interpretive debates is the question of change itself, particularly how much and in what ways the tradition can change and still be counted as the same tradition. In the Reformation era, for example, the debates between Protestants and Catholics were not primarily over which had the better interpretation of the faith but which was the *true* approach. For a more recent example we can look to early twentieth-century America. In the Fundamentalist controversy J. Gresham Machen's argument was not that Liberal Christians were mistaken *Christians*, that is, mistaken participants in the Christian tradition, but that in their innovations they had left the Christian faith altogether and formed a new and different religion.[18]

---

17. In *After Virtue*, MacIntyre observes that arguments can continue through "many generations." MacIntyre, *After Virtue*, 222.

18. J. Gresham Machen, *Christianity and Liberalism* (Grand Rapids: Eerdmans, 1923).

It is at this point that we can bring the question of the "stray" ecclesial groups back into the conversation (the Mennonites, Pentecostals, Evangelicals, etc.). According to MacIntyre, the central agreements of a tradition are defined and redefined through two kinds of conflict, internal and external. In the former, fundamentalists debated each other within their tradition, and liberals debated each other within their tradition. Significantly, to at least a degree, American fundamentalists and liberals took each other as significant *others*, setting the other as their primary external dialog partner. The two traditions thus find themselves playing in the same modern philosophical and theological playground, as Murphy observes, defining their positions against each other. The Mennonites originated in an earlier era and were never mainstream enough in American culture to take either the fundamentalists or the liberals as the *other*. As a distinct cultural minority, the other against which the Mennonites defined themselves was American society as a whole. Likewise, the Pentecostals, though having much in common theologically with fundamentalists, were driven by the life-changing experience of the Holy Spirit (their positive heuristic?). Pentecostals would then identify the other as the world (which did not have the Spirit) or as the other churches, whether liberal or fundamentalist, that while Christian in form, lacked the fullness of the gospel.

James Wm. McClendon, Jr. and "The baptist vision"

Murphy's postmodern account of religion also relies on James McClendon's concept of the "baptist vision."[19] Her use of the concept is in the context of discerning appropriate hermeneutic practices for reading Scripture. Understanding a text (whether the Bible or any other) requires not only access to the text and understanding of the language and rhetorical strategies used in the text, but also that the reader be in some way part of the audience intended by the text. Attention to the community of interpretation is an important part of her postmodern philosophy of language, moving beyond the dichotomy between representationalism and expressivism in modern philosophy.

McClendon introduces the "baptist vision" in the first volume of his systematic theology, developing it further in the second volume. He is a baptist,[20] writing a systematic theology for Baptists (though using a Methodist publisher!); as such, identifying what it is that makes baptists *baptist* is

---

19. Murphy, *Anglo-American*, 147–49.

20. McClendon takes himself to be writing for the broad baptist tradition and not for any particular Baptist denomination, so he uses the word in lower case.

important to his task. Baptists tend to be non-creedal, so he looks for "the guiding stimulus by which a people . . . shape their life and thought as that people. . . . I mean by it the continually emerging theme and tonic structure of their common life."[21] It is a *vision*, not merely a set of beliefs. Some of the possibilities for what uniquely marks baptist theology include biblicism, mission, liberty, discipleship, and community; each one is an important element of the baptist tradition.[22] He eventually finds the first of these, biblicism, to be the window to what he is looking for, though biblicism alone is insufficient. The baptist approach to Scripture is not a narrow epistemological principle as with fundamentalism's doctrine of inerrancy[23]; rather, the baptist approach to Scripture also requires the addition of eschatological and communal dimensions. McClendon puts it this way: "Scripture in this vision effects a link between the church of the apostles and our own. So the vision can be expressed as a hermeneutical motto, which is shared awareness of *the present Christian community as the primitive community and the eschatological community*."[24] He continues in the second volume:

> The baptist vision is the way the Bible is read by those who (1) accept the plain sense of Scripture as its dominant sense and recognize their continuity with the story it tells, and who (2) acknowledge that finding the point of that story leads them to its application, and who also (3) see past and present and future linked by a "this is that" and "then is now" vision, a trope of mystical identity binding the story now to the story then, and the story then and now to God's future yet to come.[25]

The baptist vision is much more than a hermeneutical principle to give us truths to build our doctrinal edifice. It helps us read Scripture by creating and molding the community of disciples, figuring disciples *now* to be part of the same community of disciples *then*. This eschatological dimension points toward the nickname McClendon uses for the baptist vision: "This is that." This phrase, drawn from Peter's address to the Jerusalem crowds on the day of Pentecost (Acts 2:16), provides a way for Peter to identify the Pentecostal audience with the original audience of Joel's prophecy.

---

21. James Wm. McClendon, Jr., *Ethics: Systematic Theology, Volume I* (Nashville: Abingdon, 1986) 27–28.

22. Ibid., 28.

23. Even so, it is true that some baptists are fundamentalists and adhere to a doctrine of inerrancy.

24. Ibid., 31.

25. McClendon, *Doctrine: Systematic Theology, Volume 2* (Nashville: Abingdon, 1994) 45.

McClendon's baptist vision then gives us[26] three important features. First, it gives us a non-modern way to read Scripture. Epistemologically it rejects foundationalism. In terms of the philosophy of language, it goes beyond both representationalism and expressivism. Second, it is inherently social. As a vision that forms and nourishes the life of a people, individualism is impossible. Reading Scripture is always a communal act; and it is never a mere isolated individual reading the text, "Just me and my Bible." Appropriating Scripture in terms of the baptist vision requires an imaginative return to the first community of disciples and an equally imaginative projection forward as the last community that reaps the promises of God in Christ. Thirdly, the baptist vision is thoroughly historical. If it were merely biblicist, it could lapse into a fundamentalism that aims to mine the facts from the depths of the text. But the Bible is not an inert object that can be mined; the kinds of truth sought there are not mere objects waiting for the finding and eventual arrangement in a structure of dogmatic theology. The people now are the people then, a status won through the hard work of maintaining continuity as the people of Jesus (in the midst of constant danger and threat), addressed and commanded by the biblical text.

In these latter two points, McClendon's baptist vision is similar to MacIntyre's tradition. Both the baptist vision and traditions of inquiry are rooted in particular communities. They are operative through *people*, not just through minds or ideas. They are also both profoundly historical: they take place through time. In spite of these similarities, the baptist vision gives us something MacIntyre's theory of traditions does not. On MacIntyre's account, traditions are arguments happening through time, defined and redefined through internal and external conflicts. One could read this as simply a description of the evolution of ideas. Ideas change over time as they encounter new environments, just as organisms change through time as they encounter new environments. Change is basic. The problem on this view is continuity, or more specifically in a theological context, faithfulness or fidelity. In the theory of biological evolution there is a point at which a species has changed sufficiently that it is no longer the same species, and this happening is of no concern. To say it again, change is basic. It is a given. Theology, too, finds change a fundamental reality. But theology also wants to conserve *something*. There is a something or a someone to whom the theological community aims to be faithful. As McClendon puts it in his

---

26. Some might protest about my use of "us." After all, I am not even a baptist, so how can I appeal to the *baptist* vision as relevant beyond that tradition? For a full account of why I think I can do this, see Richard Heyduck, *The Recovery of Doctrine in the Contemporary Church: An Essay in Philosophical Ecclesiology* (Waco, TX: Baylor University Press, 2002) 159ff.

formulation of the baptist vision, the community now is the community then. The community, therefore, is not free to just follow things wherever they might lead. There will be boundaries that make the community what or who it is, and not some other community. This diachronic unity will be a function of God's address through Scripture and the community's determination to be the same community addressed now as in the original writing.

Applying MacIntyre and McClendon to Liberalism and Fundamentalism

The advantage of having a foundationalist epistemology is that it is designed to provide clarity and certainty. When we have an answer we can count on that answer being secure now and remaining secure into the future. MacIntyre's theory of traditions has the smell of relativism: knowledge and truth, insofar as they are not built on a foundation, are not secure, not reliable. From a fundamentalist point of view, this would be reason enough to reject MacIntyre. Obviously, given its relativistic tendencies and rejection of foundationalism, it must just be another version of liberalism. Fundamentalists also usually deny the temporality of their tradition: they are the ones who believed exactly what the first followers believed and what true followers of Jesus have always believed. It is liberals who have changed; if something is true at one time, it is true at all times, so any change must be a deviation away from the truth.

But liberals are better at seeing their tradition *as* a tradition, right? Well, not according to MacIntyre. In *Three Rival Versions of Moral Enquiry*, one of his chief criticisms of what he calls the "Encyclopaedist" tradition, a late nineteenth-century variant of the liberal tradition, is that it fails to see itself as a tradition. It is built on reason. Reason is sure, reason is certain, reason does not change. The changes we see in history are not successive accounts of reason, but the march of progress as humans become more rational and find ways to expel unreason from their lives and societies. Reason, bit by bit, accumulates a mass of truths to bequeath to future generations. *Three Rival Versions of Moral Enquiry*, the published version of his Gifford Lectures, undermines the very tradition exemplified by the foundational document of the lecture series. MacIntyre observes that Adam Gifford and his contemporaries in the Encyclopaedist tradition had such a

> unitary conception of rationality and of the rational mind that they took for granted not only that all rational persons conceptualize data in one and the same way and that therefore any attentive and honest observer, unblinded and undistracted by the

prejudices of prior commitment to belief, would report the same data, the same facts, but also that it is the data thus reported and characterized which provide enquiry with its subject matter.[27]

Later, MacIntyre continues his characterization of this "unitary conception of rationality" in the encyclopaedist tradition:

> The encyclopaedist aims at providing timeless, universal, and objective truths as his or her conclusions, but aspires to do so by reasoning which has from the outset the same properties. From the outset all reasoning must be such as would be compelling any to fully rational person whatsoever. Rationality, like truth, is independent of time, place, and historical circumstances.[28]

For the fundamentalist, as we have seen, God's truth is God's truth, eternally the same, and always accessible to readers as we mine truths from God's word, the Bible. For the liberal the idea of an inerrant sourcebook for truth is incredible: it does not pass the test of reason. But as MacIntyre would have it, where the fundamentalist is unconditionally committed to an unhistorical, noncontextualized Bible, the typical modern liberal is just as unconditionally committed to an unhistorical, noncontextualized Reason.

Given the picture of a postmodern philosophical approach that we have found in Murphy, McClendon, and MacIntyre thus far, what possibilities are there for moving further "beyond liberalism and fundamentalism?" In the first place, keeping Murphy's focus in place, we are not dealing with abstractions—with liberalism and fundamentalism bereft of connection with any tradition. Fundamentalism and liberalism as she deals with them are two *subtraditions* in the *Christian* tradition. Their origins may lie in modernity, which may, in turn, incline them to deny being traditions. Fundamentalism has its atemporal objective truth of Scripture, liberalism its atemporal universal rationality. Moving beyond the modern framework in which fundamentalism and liberalism are mired will require a new stance toward history.

Even if we find a way to move beyond the modern framework in which these two subtraditions have found their home, it is unrealistic to expect that they will suddenly drop their opposition to each other and merge into a common, shared, and unified Christian tradition. As I noted above, during the time they have been separate traditions, more than their commitment to contrasting elements of modern philosophy have come to define them.

---

27. Alasdair MacIntyre, *Three Rival Versions of Moral Enquiry: Encyclopaedia, Genealogy, and Tradition* (Notre Dame: University of Notre Dame Press, 1990) 16.

28. Ibid., 65.

Their modern philosophical commitments may have formed them in distinctive ways, but the traditions have also taken substantive opposing theological positions. To use MacIntyre's language, these theological positions have become "agreements defined and redefined," partly through internal conflict, disputation with those counted as members of the same tradition, and partly through external conflict, disputation with those counted as members of opposing traditions.

One way to move beyond the modern philosophical space is illustrated in George Lindbeck's famous account of "postliberalism" in *The Nature of Doctrine*. Lindbeck clearly rejects and moves beyond the theories of doctrine rooted in modern philosophy. The theory of doctrine associated with fundamentalism he calls the "cognitive propositionalist" position; the theory associated with liberalism he calls "experiential expressivist."[29] Using some of the same postmodern philosophers that Nancey Murphy relies upon, especially Ludwig Wittgenstein and J. L. Austin, Lindbeck proposes these two models be replaced by a "cultural linguistic" model of doctrine. This is not the place for a full critique of Lindbeck's position, but I will mention one major weakness that ties in with the approach I am developing here.[30] A cultural linguistic approach to doctrine gets at some important aspects of doctrine, but its main weakness is that it misses the historical dimension that we find in both MacIntyre's account of traditions and McClendon's baptist vision. The timelessness of the cultural linguistic model leaves us still in the modern philosophical space.

Consider the doctrine of Scripture. Fundamentalism's epistemological foundationalism, expressed in the doctrine of inerrancy, butts up against liberalism's epistemological commitment to universal homogenous Reason expressed through biblical criticism.[31] Liberal biblical scholarship, taking the Bible as it is, cannot help but find errors. Fundamentalist biblical scholarship, faced with the results of liberal biblical scholarship, either rejects those results as the findings of unbelievers or adopts strategies to harmonize the "errors" away. Once this is done, the issue becomes simple: If you are not an inerrantist, then you are a liberal. If you do not play the error-finding game, then you must be a fundamentalist. The positions are binary opposites, defined against each other.

---

29. George Lindbeck, *The Nature of Doctrine: Religion and Theology in a Postliberal Age* (Philadelphia: Westminster, 1984) 33.
30. For a fuller account, see my *Recovery of Doctrine*, which is framed as a dialog with Lindbeck. My response to his philosophy of language is in chapter 2.
31. For the modern commitment to procedural rationality, see Heyduck, *Recovery of Doctrine*, 15ff.

Let us consider another aspect of the doctrine of Scripture—its connection to history. The fundamentalist will commonly assume, given the tradition's commitment to a representationalist understanding of the nature of language, that the historical accounts in Scripture are to be taken as functionally equivalent to modern works of history. When they describe an event as having happened in a particular way, well, that is the way it happened. It is a fact, just like all the other propositions we find in Scripture.

Liberals also turn to history, and like the fundamentalists, to a modern conception of history. They come to Scripture already knowing what is possible and what is right, so they are equipped, as good moderns, to stand over Scripture and judge it. MacIntyre describes one representative of this tradition as having a

> general insistence not only upon treating the writers of the Hebrew Bible just like any other source of evidence but also upon categorizing and conceptualizing their material in the terms of what he took to be enlightened modernity rather than in their own terms, so that the Bible is judged by the standards of that modernity in a way which effectively prevents it from standing in judgment upon that modernity.[32]

This liberal approach is not only contrary to MacIntyre's approach, which sees all traditions in terms of their history, and thus time-bound; it is also runs contrary to McClendon's insights in the baptist vision. Whereas the baptist vision thinks in terms of "this is that," the modern view can be called "that is this." The modern can say, "*We* have reached the pinnacle of reason. Since reason is universal and essentially unchanging, we have insight into other eras that those eras themselves lacked. What we see there ('that') is explainable in terms of what we see today ('this')."

But what if, like Murphy, we eschew the foundationalism of modern epistemology? If we do not play on the field of foundationalism, we can avoid playing the games of inerrancy and errancy. Such a move will be unintelligible to those of either camp who are mired in modern philosophical commitments. Liberals will see any move that does not identify errors as such as residually (even hopelessly) fundamentalist, while their opponents will likewise see any unwillingness to claim freedom from error as the sure sign of at least incipient liberalism. If it is possible for erstwhile liberals,

---

32. MacIntyre, *Three Rival Versions*, 179. Theologian Julian Hartt describes the phenomenon this way: "The thing that 'really happened' is something subsumable under categories of explanation taken for granted in the present. Thus the real event is something conceivable in a nexus intelligible to the present state of consciousness." Julian N. Hartt, *A Christian Critique of Culture: An Essay in Practical Theology* (New York: Harper & Row, 1967) 278.

like those who follow Lindbeck's route, to become postmodern by leaving behind the modern philosophical space, then perhaps it is also possible for those who were once deemed fundamentalists, whether by themselves or by others, to pay heed to Murphy, MacIntyre, and McClendon and transition from a modern to a postmodern philosophical space. In such a case, if we may call these *evangelicals*, these people have not "moderated" their position (i.e., made a move within modern space *away* from fundamentalism and *toward* liberalism, which is how some fundamentalists might describe the change), but have moved to a new space altogether.

Liberals and fundamentalists who move from modernity and postmodernity can also take up a different stance toward the historicity of Scripture. Contrary to the liberals, what we see "back then" is not just a strange and distant version of what we see today. Contrary to the fundamentalists, what we see "back then" are not just events to be reported. Instead, following McClendon, we can imagine ourselves as the same community of disciples that we see on the pages of Scripture, working out our understanding of and obedience to God in new situations and contexts. And following MacIntyre, we can interpret ourselves as members of a tradition that traces its beginnings back to the biblical era, as those who have carried on the tradition and seek to extend it into new conflicts. What we learn from MacIntyre and McClendon converges at this point. Rather than treating history as objective, as a storehouse of truths with the fundamentalists, or as a tool for critiquing Scripture with the liberals, McClendon would have us ask how we can *participate* in history as the current manifestation of the same community.

Another problem with which we must deal is that these phenomena I have been calling "philosophy" and "theology" do not operate in neatly defined spheres. In fact, Murphy's whole argument in *Beyond Liberalism and Fundamentalism* is that the two bear on each other deeply. The confusion lies even deeper. Those we denote "liberals" and "fundamentalists" are not just members of communities that bear those labels. They are also, as are the rest of us, members of other communities: neighborhoods, political associations, cultural groups, and the like. As those who are members of a particular theological community associate together, they may also find themselves in *political* association together, and with others. In recent years, for example, fundamentalists have also been adherents of a different, conservative political tradition. We may talk about our communities as if they are hermetically sealed from each other, but inasmuch as each tradition is carried on by people who inhabit it and participate in a multifaceted world, these traditions find common points in other traditions and people. It is possible then, that in terms of theology, our tradition may have moved beyond modern philosophical space into postmodern space, but that in terms of politics, we remain as modern as ever. There is no way to get around the fact that we are members of multiple communities that overlap to some degree.

Former members of the liberal and fundamentalist traditions may, in the course of continued conflict, develop new names for their traditions. We have already seen that evangelicalism can be seen as a successor tradition to fundamentalism.[33] Some may resolve to stand against this change. "Surely," they might say, "your proposed transition to postmodern philosophical space is no improvement if conflict continues. What we want out of our effort to move beyond liberalism and fundamentalism is to be beyond *conflict*." And yet, the thought that we can surpass conflict is the desire to rest on certainty: the certainty of indubitable knowledge or utter reliable rational procedures. Both are at home in modernity, not postmodernity. MacIntyre teaches us that conflict is inevitable. The good news is that conflict need be neither violent nor acrimonious, whether we are engaging in the internal conflict among friends or the external conflict with those who account themselves our foes.

Supposing that we can treat Christianity as a MacIntyrean tradition, a tradition large enough to have multiple subtraditions (including the two we began with, liberalism and fundamentalism), what does that do for our attempt to transcend liberalism and fundamentalism and to make sense of Christian theological traditions that do not neatly fall into a modern philosophical schematization? Remember, MacIntyre's is a descriptive thesis (as I suggested that Murphy's Lakatosian hypothesis about theology could be taken). He is not saying that traditions *ought* to behave in a particular way: he is saying that they *do* behave this way. Given this descriptive thesis, one of the reasons the conflict between liberals and fundamentalists in Christianity seems insurmountable is that sharing a commitment to modern philosophy, they fail to understand themselves *as* traditions. They are simply "rational" or "true" or "academically respectable" or "rational" or "biblical." All of these qualities are, on the modern way of thinking, univocal. If each of these qualitative evaluations is, however, only applicable within a given tradition, the fact that conflict is built into the very nature of a tradition will mean that none of these evaluations can be applied simply or totally to any one theology without conflict.

---

33. Of course, this is historically complicated. "Evangelical" has meant different things in different contexts and cultures. British evangelicalism, for example, largely followed a different path, keeping it relatively free of some of the features of American fundamentalism. Coming to maturity in an earlier era, British evangelicalism defined itself against a different other than American fundamentalism and its successor, (American) evangelicalism.

Conclusion

My claim has been that a postmodern understanding of religion as we find developed in Nancey Murphy's work not only gives us a better understanding of how religion and theology function but also offers a way beyond the impasse between liberalism and fundamentalism, on the one hand, and a better account of theological traditions that do not fit neatly within the conceptual space of modern philosophy, on the other. This postmodern approach, characterized most prominently by shifts in epistemology, philosophy of language, historicity, and sociality, gives us resources to understand how to best characterize a shift beyond liberalism and fundamentalism in the Christian tradition and to imagine potentially healthy engagement between various Christian theological traditions. Indeed, it is just this kind of healthy interaction within a new, postmodern "space" that is made possible by Nancey's work, and which may offer significant help in resolving—or perhaps, dissolving—many of the conflicts that currently infect Western Christianity.

3

Postmodern Insularity? Epistemological Holism and Its Discontents

—Ryan Andrew Newson

NANCEY MURPHY HAS BEEN an important figure in orienting Christians (especially Anabaptists and evangelicals) to what is now widely recognized as a "postmodern" shift in the Western intellectual world. In particular, Murphy situates herself within the *Anglo-American* postmodern tradition, which she sharply distinguishes from both generalized conceptions of postmodernity that refer to a cultural "mood," as well as the philosophical tradition associated with Jean-François Lyotard and Jacques Derrida, which she argues betrays hyper-modern tendencies rather than anything truly postmodern.[1] For Murphy, this shift is marked not by uniformity, but a variegated group of philosophers and theologians asking new questions (in epistemology, linguistics, and metaphysics) not beholden to Enlightenment categories and assumptions—thinkers who get out of modern intellectual space altogether, without reverting to premodern categories.[2] To have left this space is to *begin* the conversation about where to go next; it is to enter an argument with people who agree that alternatives are needed and on some key elements that will mark these alternatives, but who can still profoundly disagree on how to "go on."[3] Put differently, there is not one thing called "postmodern-

---

1. Nancey Murphy, *Anglo-American Postmodernity: Philosophical Perspectives on Science, Religion, and Ethics* (Boulder, CO: Westview, 1997).

2. Cf. Nancey Murphy and James Wm. McClendon, Jr., "Distinguishing Modern and Postmodern Theologies," *Modern Theology* 5:3 (April 1989) 191, 198–99.

3. For a similar take regarding postmodern thinkers having deep agreements amidst obvious disagreements, see Richard J. Bernstein, *Beyond Objectivism and*

ism," but postmodernisms, and Murphy has entered this fray on a variety of topics as a radical reformation philosophical theologian, with gusto.

In this essay, I engage one argument that has occurred surrounding the postmodern epistemological holism that Murphy skillfully defends. Certain theologians, sympathetic to the postmodern shifts Murphy advocates, nonetheless wonder whether her appropriation of Imre Lakatos and particularly Alasdair MacIntyre is the best option for the practice of Christian theology in the coming century, at the very least raising questions about its theological import. Indeed, Murphy draws friendly fire on this point, some of which is more helpful, or more accurate, than others. The critiques I am interested in center on the question of "insularity," in two senses: one, that Murphy's epistemology fosters a sort of theoretical insularity, such that *only* a traditions' internal standards are relevant to theological justification.[4] As William Schweiker says of so-called "traditionalist postmoderns" (including MacIntyre), it is to be "satisfied with explicating the beliefs about human existence and moral virtue found in their specific moral community."[5] Second, others are concerned that Murphy's epistemological tools may lead to insularity "on the ground," in Christian communities. Colloquially, the concern is that *this* postmodern epistemology carries the (perhaps accidental, unintended) consequence of forming a people who need not listen to others; who are given warrant to get on with their ecclesial practice while ignoring what is happening outside one's moral community; or who come to characterize the theological task as *first* an internal matter, and *second* something interactive.

While I am unconvinced that either is a good or necessary interpretation of MacIntyre's work,[6] or provides reasons to abandon Murphy's epistemological project altogether, the motive behind the latter concern is important: what is the character of the Christian community produced by this approach, and what are some of its potential dangers? Might it produce communities so confident in their tradition's resources that it loses the motivation, or even ability, to listen to countering perspectives? To address this concern, I will first provide an overview of Murphy's epistemological

---

Relativism: Science, Hermeneutics, and Praxis (Philadelphia: University of Pennsylvania Press, 1983) 206.

4. Cf. Philip Clayton, "Shaping the Field of Theology and Science: A Critique of Nancey Murphy," *Zygon* 34:4 (December 1999) 613–14. See also Philip Clayton, "On Holisms: Insular, Inclusivist, and Postmodern," *Zygon* 33:3 (September 1998) 467–74.

5. William Schweiker, *Power, Value, and Conviction: Theological Ethics in the Postmodern Age* (Cleveland: Pilgrim, 1998) 93.

6. See Ryan Andrew Newson, "Alasdair MacIntyre and Radically Dialogical Politics," *Political Theology* (in press, 2016).

approach and its usefulness in theology. This will lead, secondly, to answering several criticisms of Murphy's approach that fall under the "theoretical insularity" umbrella, which I argue turn out to be based on misunderstandings or mischaracterizations of the philosophy in question. Finally, I will address the question of whether or not Murphy's epistemology potentially fosters a "closedness" in Christian communities. While acknowledging the tension at play here (which Murphy herself notes), and that it provides a prophetic reminder to those indebted to Murphy's paradigm, I argue that Murphy can incorporate this critique in good MacIntyrean fashion, while also offering her own corrective to her interlocutors. As it turns out, the impetus behind this critique, as well as Murphy's recognition and appropriation thereof, is found in the tensional edge between MacIntyre and radical reformation convictions.

Postmodern Epistemology, in the Anglo-American Fashion

"What we say will be easy, but to know why we say it will be very difficult."[7] In a fashion true to Murphy, I begin by carefully describing her advocacy of postmodern theological reason. My goal is to clear a path to rightly understanding Murphy's project. The challenge, of course, is not just the what, but the *why*—and to understand why Murphy argues what she does, one must understand the problem that lies behind her work.

"Anything Goes" and the Foundationalist Temptation

Murphy begins by acknowledging what she takes to be a given of human existence: that we are historically contingent beings, and that there are a variety of ways that humans can "cut up" the world, despite frequent philosophical attempts to hide this fact. If Christian theology is to be truthful, it must not run from contingency, particularly if contingency is but a mark of our status as creatures, as James K. A. Smith reminds us.[8] Murphy's teacher Paul Feyerabend famously encapsulated this epistemological plurality with the phrase "anything goes," by which he meant that in actual historical practice one can see multiple approaches to inquiry at play.[9] "Anything

---

7. Ludwig Wittgenstein, *Wittgenstein's Lectures: Cambridge, 1932–1935*, edited by Alice Ambrose (Totowa, NJ: Rowman and Littlefield, 1979) 77.

8. James K. A. Smith, *Who's Afraid of Relativism? Community, Contingency, and Creaturehood* (Grand Rapids: Baker, 2014).

9. Feyerabend tries to make this claim *plausible* through historical examples in

goes" was not a "theory" or "principle," Feyerabend maintained, but "the terrified exclamation of a rationalist who takes a closer look at history."[10] Feyerabend's exclamation provides the sometimes overlooked context for Murphy's work, and while an absolute relativism born of this pluralism is a live threat that Murphy seeks to combat, her task is never to circumvent Feyerabend's insights, but to navigate a way through them.

This is possible because Feyerabend fills the role of gadfly to any rationalist who would listen, showing through multiple investigations that scientific inquiry proceeds without any methodological formula that one must apply with bloodless precision; epistemologically, he is an anarchist. Although some see here nothing more than an advocate of Pyrrhic skepticism,[11] Feyerabend is better understood as continuing in the investigatory mode of Ludwig Wittgenstein, or even Socrates: not an advocate of any one "school," but someone constantly jarring his hearers out of intellectual complacency, revealing the flaws and contradictions in inherited habits of thought.[12] Feyerabend's epistemological anarchy, then, clarified the pretensions of a *particular kind* of rationalism to Murphy—one that saw its logical relations as fixed and universal.[13] Put differently, it revealed the paucity of foundationalism.

In the barest terms, foundationalism is a theory that holds knowledge properly so-called is a collection of justified true beliefs, which are built upon and justified with respect to a chain of justifications eventually ending with some properly basic belief or beliefs—the chain cannot move in a circle, or go on forever.[14] The operative picture here is of knowledge as a building requiring secure foundations. Classically, only foundations that were

---

Against Method, 4th ed. (New York: Verso, [1975] 2010).

10. Ibid., xvii.

11. Cf. the imaginative but very informative "dialogue" between Lakatos and Feyerabend in Matteo Motterlini, ed., *For and Against Method* (Chicago: University of Chicago Press, 1999) 13.

12. For this interpretation of Socrates, see Alasdair MacIntyre, *A Short History of Ethics*, 2nd ed. (Notre Dame: University of Notre Dame Press, [1966] 1998) 19–24. Murphy argues that this mode does not make Feyerabend a relativist as this term is usually understood, although he certainly thinks that our concepts and beliefs are "relative to" particular conceptual frameworks; cf. Murphy, *Anglo-American*, 50n3.

13. Murphy credits Feyerabend, Lakatos, and Thomas Kuhn for developing a dynamic theory of *development* for philosophy of science; *Anglo-American*, 70.

14. Ibid., 9. Cf. Richard Rorty, *Philosophy and the Mirror of Nature* (Princeton: Princeton University Press, 1979) 155–64. For a defense of "infinitism," where an infinite justificatory regress is the marker of justification and knowledge, see Peter Klein, "Human Knowledge and the Infinite Regress of Reasons," *Philosophical Perspectives* 13 (1999) 297–325.

universally acknowledgeable (given an individual with enough time and intellectual ability to investigate) and *indubitable* were suitable to this task. As a theory, then, foundationalism perpetuates an ideal of human knowledge that is "focused on the general, the universal, the timeless, the theoretical—in contrast to the local, the particular, the timely, the practical,"[15] and which tempts adherents with a solution to the plurality pointed out by Feyerabend. I cannot cover every detail of Murphy's demolition of the foundationalist picture[16]; I mention three issues that cause Murphy to resist this picture's temptations.

First, no indubitable or universal foundations have yet been found that could serve in the capacity required by this theory, and the two most popular candidates (bare sense data and necessary truths of logic) can only work against the background of some larger assumed framework. Toying with the building metaphor, Murphy argues that any "foundation" is also supported by elements that are at the top of the structure, such that the foundation is now partially supported by the balcony.[17] Further, even *if* a candidate is found that *may* function in this way, it will necessarily be of such generality that it will be useless for justifying any *interesting* claims; conversely, anything able to justify interesting theological claims (or others besides) will be found to be dubitable. This she whimsically deems "Murphy's Second Law."[18] In short, even if I grant an indubitable universality to $2 + 2 = 4$, or my "impression of greenness," *what follows*, theologically?

Second, Murphy is suspicious of the overly individualized (indeed, "cranialized") focus of foundationalism, which circumscribes the epistemological question to what the conscientious individual can be certain of—to what takes place inside one's own head. This hyper-individualism came to mark conservative *and* liberal theology in the modern period, and is a point I return to below. In a nutshell, Murphy's objection to this is that it rests on a deficient *picture* of both human nature and human knowledge that withers

---

15. Murphy, *Anglo-American*, 10; citing Stephen Toulmin, *Cosmopolis: The Hidden Agenda of Modernity* (Chicago: University of Chicago Press, 1990) ch. 1.

16. Cf. Nancey Murphy, *Beyond Liberalism and Fundamentalism: How Modern and Postmodern Philosophy Set the Theological Agenda* (Harrisburg, PA: Trinity, 1996) chs. 1, 4.

17. Murphy, *Beyond*, 91. Wittgenstein made the same observation; cf. Ludwig Wittgenstein, *On Certainty*, edited by G. E. M. Anscombe and G. H. von Wright, translated by Denis Paul and G. E. M. Anscombe, in *Major Works: Selected Philosophical Writings* (New York: HarperCollins, [1969] 2009) §248. The "analytic-synthetic" distinction, along with reductionism, was classically dismantled by W. V. O. Quine, "Two Dogmas of Empiricism," *Philosophical Review* 40 (1951) 20–43.

18. Murphy, *Beyond*, 90; cf. Murphy, *Anglo-American*, 26–27.

once it is made explicit, and especially when compared to more robust accounts thereof.

Finally, Murphy notes that the chain of justifications on the foundationalist model goes in one direction: from the bottom up, from foundations to justified true beliefs and generalized theories.[19] Murphy, as we will see, sees justifying connections moving up and down and in multiple directions, rather than the neater image provided by foundationalists. This is important, for sophisticated defenders of foundationalism (notably, Alvin Plantinga) have abandoned the principle of indubitability, arguing that foundations need only be properly basic and warranted based on the information available to and social upbringing of the person in question (typically without denying the possibility that indubitable facts may exist).[20] While helpfully recognizing the trouble with indubitability *and* the live possibility of disagreement being a manifestation of differing starting points—even different rationalities—without abandoning the pursuit of truth, these philosophers nonetheless maintain foundationalism's unidirectional trajectory (as well as its individual focus).

Note that Murphy's goal is not to disprove foundationalism, but to reveal contradictions that suggest an alternative is needed, and to show how detrimental foundationalist logic has been to the health of Christian theology. Foundationalism led to an obsession with theological prolegomena, paralyzed by the fear that one's theological supports may be wobbly upon further inspection, or else that one's chain of justification may not go as far "up" as one thinks. Further, the entire theological enterprise came to be viewed as rationally suspect (at best), a source of embarrassment in modern intellectual circles.[21] Happily, Murphy shows theologians a more promising answer to Feyerabend's "anything goes" than foundationalism, which begins by eschewing the foundationalist picture entirely (rather than tweaking it here or there), including its propensity for reductionism, individualism, generalizability, and unidirectional justification.

---

19. Often called the "layer cake" model; Nancey C. Murphy, *Reasoning and Rhetoric in Religion* (Harrisburg, PA: Trinity, 1994) 200.

20. Alvin Plantinga details so-called "Reformed Epistemology" in *Warrant: The Current Debate* (Oxford: Oxford University Press, 1993); *Warrant and Proper Function* (Oxford: Oxford University Press, 1993); and *Warranted Christian Belief* (Oxford: Oxford University Press, 2000). For a helpful summary, see Michael Peterson et al., *Reason and Religious Belief*, 4th ed. (New York: Oxford University Press, 2009) 128–34.

21. Nancey Murphy, *Theology in the Age of Scientific Reasoning* (Ithaca, NY: Cornell University Press, 1990) ch. 1.

Toward a Postmodern Optimism

For an alternative "sly and sophisticated" enough to incorporate Feyerabend's work without shifting to antirationalism, Murphy begins with W. V. O. Quine. For Murphy, Quine represents one end of a spectrum: he rejects foundationalism and its inordinate fear of skepticism, but leads people straight to the problem of relativism. Quine famously replaced the foundationalist picture with the web, wherein *all* knowledge mutually interacted and supported one another, contained only by the boundaries of experience.[22] No one doubts (let alone rejects) all their beliefs at one time (*contra* Descartes), but can replace them piece by piece, as one would repair a raft at sea. Often, Quine's picture is too easily dismissed as nothing more than a sophisticated defense of circular reasoning from persons already assuming the truth of foundationalism. But one must remember that Quine is doing descriptive work; he isn't saying knowledge *should* go this way, but that it *does* go this way. If Quine is correct, it is true even for foundationalists (and vice versa, of course). However, Quine's model seems to entail that one might hold a false belief as part of a web that remains coherent overall, which is problematic if knowledge is justified by coherence alone. If a belief is toward the outside of the web, for instance, it might be replaced easily without effecting any change in the web's coherence. Coherence as such, it would seem, is insufficient.[23] Further, Quine fosters a pessimism concerning the ability to judge between different "webs." Quine, of course, saw human knowledge as a single totality, and one of Murphy's contributions is the recognition that a smaller community might possess a web at odds with another community's. Once this is recognized, Quine's theory creates an intractable version of relativism (perhaps the fear of skepticism, socialized), as the existence of multiple, coherent, incommensurable webs leads to the question, "How ought one judge between them?" Trained by Feyerabend, Murphy (more than Quine) sees the actuality of multiple "webs," such that "if Quine himself is not worried about relativism, perhaps, we think, he should be!"[24]

For Murphy, all postmodern epistemologists by definition reject foundationalism and recognize the complex interactivity of our beliefs. While

---

22. W. V. O. Quine and J. S. Ullian, *The Web of Belief* (New York: Random House, 1979).

23. Ernest Sosa, "Raft and the Pyramid: Coherence Versus Foundations in the Theory of Knowledge," in *Midwest Studies in Epistemology* 5, edited by P. A. French, T. E. Uehling, Jr., and H. K. Wettstein (Minneapolis: University of Minnesota Press, 1980) 3–26.

24. Murphy, *Anglo-American*, 51.

no "serious" philosopher defends absolute relativism, there is a spectrum of those who entertain pessimism about our ability to adjudicate between "webs" (Quine), and those who are *optimistic* about this possibility.[25] Without rejecting the truth in Quine's work, Murphy moves toward the optimistic end of this postmodern spectrum with the help of Lakatos and MacIntyre. In her first book, Murphy utilized Lakatos's conception of a "research program" in service to a better account of theological rationality. In philosophy of science, Lakatos sought to articulate the way scientific inquiry and progress actually happened, and provided the ability to adjudicate between competing research programs—precisely where Quine failed. For Lakatos, a research program is constituted by a collection of theories that are mutually supportive in the way Quine specified, but with three improvements. First, research programs are not formless webs, but are oriented around a "hard core" theory that organizes the whole.[26] This "core" is surrounded by auxiliary hypotheses, outgrowths of the central theory that give it backing and which can change more readily than the hard core. The image is of "a series of complex theories whose core remains the same while auxiliary hypotheses are successively modified, replaced, or amplified in order to account for problematic observations."[27] Of course, this isn't to say that a hard core can *never* change—only that it will not change *easily*, and that changing it will mean change for the entire program. Second, Lakatos does not envision scientific history as a succession narrative of one paradigm to the next (Kuhn), but a disjointed process where different research programs are variously emerging, waning, competing, and evolving in no *automatic* order.[28] For Lakatos, research programs are constellatory dances, ever shifting as new information is encountered; the only static program is a dead program. (More on this below.) Finally, Lakatos provides clues for judging between two research programs: which one is worth continuing and which ought to be abandoned. If a research program is "progressive" (growing, able to make accurate predictions about heretofore unexpected phenomena while preserving the core theory), it is to be preferred to a "degenerative" program (stagnant, with faulty or no predictive power, only changing through ad hoc modifications that protect the core theory from defeat—usually through

---

25. Ibid., 50.
26. Murphy, *Theology*, 58–65.
27. Murphy, *Anglo-American*, 52.
28. This prompted Feyerabend to accuse Lakatos of epistemological anarchism in disguise! Paul Feyerabend, "Consolations for the Specialist," in *Criticism and Growth of Knowledge*, edited by Imre Lakatos and A. Musgrave (Cambridge: Cambridge University Press, 1970) 215–16.

face-saving adjustments or linguistic trickery). Crucially, such assessment happens *over time*, rather than in any single moment.[29]

However, questions lingered with Lakatos's approach, pointed out by none other than Feyerabend. Feyerabend argued that while Lakatos offered a magnificently adaptable theory of rationality, he could not answer why a research program that is degenerative right now—is "behind in the race"—might not, given enough time, come back into favor, or "come back" to win.[30] It is here that Murphy utilizes MacIntyre as an epistemologist who overcomes this failure in Lakatos's work, situating him in the Anglo-American philosophical tradition.[31] One can only understand Murphy's unique use of MacIntyre, and what she so appreciates about his work, in this context. MacIntyre famously argues not that everyone *should* adhere to some tradition in order to proceed rationally, but that everyone *does* inhabit some tradition; there is no traditionless place from which to reason: "To be outside all traditions is to be a stranger to enquiry; it is to be in a state of intellectual and moral destitution."[32] Further, a MacIntyrean "tradition" is not the sort of thing people typically mean by this term, but a socially embodied *argument* extended through time, in part over the goods constituting that tradition, and which is oriented by a community's authoritative texts, practices, and narratives that give each community of inquiry its character.[33] Murphy's primary interest in MacIntyre is his account of assessing two traditions of inquiry with incommensurate conceptions of reality. For MacIntyre, if one can construct a narrative that is able to explain why another tradition, on its own grounds, cannot incorporate some new piece of information, while simultaneously showing why one's own tradition can (*and* can explain how it erred in the first place), then one has good reason to consider one's own tradition rationally superior.[34] To grossly simplify a

29. Murphy, *Anglo-American*, 52–53.

30. Ibid., 53; Murphy, *Theology*, 73–74.

31. Note that Murphy situates MacIntyre in a different tradition than his explicit Aristotelian-Thomism—hers is an odd MacIntyre. Murphy argues that MacIntyre's Aristotelianism is more intelligible against this backdrop, and that it is *possible* to distinguish (though not sever) MacIntyre's criteria for inter-traditioned adjudication from his Thomist conception of truth, which taken alone may appear philosophically nostalgic; Murphy, *Anglo-American*, 60–61, 125.

32. Alasdair MacIntyre, *Whose Justice? Which Rationality?* (Notre Dame: University of Notre Dame Press, 1988) 367.

33. Ibid., 12; Alasdair MacIntyre, *After Virtue: A Study in Moral Theory*, 2nd ed. (Notre Dame: University of Notre Dame Press, [1981] 1984) 222.

34. Alasdair MacIntyre, "Epistemological Crises, Dramatic Narrative, and the Philosophy of Science," in Gary Gutting, ed., *Paradigms and Revolutions* (Notre Dame: University of Notre Dame Press, 1980) 54–74; MacIntyre, *Whose Justice?*, 166–67;

complex argument, MacIntyre takes Quine's web and, with Lakatos, adds the element of time, through which inter-traditioned justification is (sometimes) possible. Granted, this retains a degree of non-vicious relativism (or better, humility), in that a tradition can only be said to be vindicated up to a certain point (the "best so far")[35]; but given our reluctance to admit the depth of our differences, even if "[t]he most one can hope for is to render our disagreements more constructive,"[36] this will have been no small achievement.

Methodological Insularity? Points of Clarification

Having laid the groundwork for understanding her "optimistic" postmodern epistemology, I can now clarify Murphy's approach in light of some friendly criticisms that do not stick. The concern about a postmodern insularity can take a number of different forms, but a common strand in the critiques found in this section is a fear of a "theoretical," *methodological* insularity.

Is Holistic Justification Enough?

To begin, some have questioned whether Murphy has accomplished what she thinks she has accomplished. Philip Clayton and Steven Knapp, who defend a similar understanding of nonfoundational justification,[37] question whether her version of holism is adequate, particularly regarding the relationship between theology and science. These friendly interlocutors note Murphy's insistence that no *one* connection between a theological web of beliefs and science will provide justification for the former within the Western scientific worldview. Instead Murphy highlights the *variety* of kinds of connections possible between the two,[38] which when taken together, she insists, may provide sufficient enough warrant for holding that a particular tradition is justified and "progressive" in the Lakatosian sense. Clayton and Knapp, however, remain unconvinced. If any one type of justificatory

---

Murphy, *Anglo-American*, 57–62.

35. MacIntyre, *After Virtue*, 277.

36. Alasdair MacIntyre, *Three Rival Versions of Moral Enquiry* (Notre Dame: University of Notre Dame Press, 1990) 8.

37. Philip Clayton and Steven Knapp, "Rationality and Christian Self-Conceptions," in *Religion and Science: History, Method, Dialogue*, edited by W. Mark Richardson and Wesley J. Wildman (New York: Routledge, 1996) 131–42.

38. Nancey Murphy, "Postmodern Apologetics: Or Why Theologians *Must* Pay Attention to Science," in *Religion and Science*, 119.

connection is considered on its own (say, the "mutual implication" between a theological conviction and contemporary science), it shows itself to be insufficient to provide justification of the tradition under consideration. Murphy's model, they continue, would seem only to help corroborate an already-worked-out Christian tradition, rather than justify the veracity of that tradition as such.[39] While some of Murphy's tools are helpful to true justification, they conclude, only those which connect Christian theology to "standards of the broader community" are ultimately of any use, "not because they have merely been in some way 'connected' or 'related' to the broader community's beliefs."[40]

However, that Clayton and Knapp focus on any one type of connection leads them astray. Inherent to the holist model is that no single connection will provide justification (or risk its forfeiture). But as such connections compound, whole traditions do begin to look more coherent, more *justified*, in a given time and place (never once and for all). What frustrates Clayton and Knapp, it seems, is Murphy's refusal to specify precisely what kinds of connections will always be most important to this task. But knowing when it is okay to "go on"—when justification has occurred—is necessarily open-ended. Further, for Murphy, *both* standards that relate to other traditions *and* those that connect to one's own community matter to justification; she refuses to grant any "broader community" automatic epistemic priority. Finally, their critique is predicated on viewing Murphy's position, and postmodern epistemology broadly, in individualist terms. How can justification "work" for the individual making such connections? Murphy, however, has sought to shift the focus from whether an individual is justified in believing some such thing, to whether something *is justifiable*. "When we speak of the web of beliefs," she writes, "we must not think of it as the beliefs of one or several individuals, but rather of the community."[41]

---

39. Philip Clayton and Steven Knapp, "Is Holistic Justification Enough?" in *Religion and Science*, 164.

40. Ibid., 165. It is in this sense that Clayton has advocated for a "modern Lakatos," whereby general standards of rational progress can be used to adjudicate between paradigms; cf. Clayton, "On Holisms," 473–74. For Clayton, the recognition of tradition-dependence seems to entail, or strongly imply, *total* incommensurability and thus insularity—an entailment that Murphy explicitly rejects.

41. Murphy, "Postmodern Apologetics," 119. Cf. her "On the Nature of Theology," in *Religion and Science*, 155.

Prioritization of Epistemology?

The above assessment is a reminder that Murphy's use of "epistemology" is not meant to reinforce modernity's elevation of epistemology as the preeminent discipline that necessarily precedes all else—the guarantor of individual certainty. If this were Murphy's task, then to be sure, the concerns of someone like Chris Huebner would apply to Murphy. Huebner (an important interpreter of John Howard Yoder, one of Murphy's primary theological influences) argues that using Murphy's epistemological approach to understand purposely occasional thinkers like Yoder imposes an order on what is intentionally "rough," and thus contradicts the truly postmodern character of his work. Indeed, Yoder explicitly disavowed what he called "methodologism," the overriding preoccupation with clarifying one's preliminary points, questions, and universally-agreed-upon premises, such that one's subsequent inquiry (if it ever happened) was already "settled."[42] For Yoder, this was the epistemological equivalent of "grabbing the mike," and is a particular temptation for foundationalists.[43] Against methodologism, Yoder maintained that there is no "scratch" from which to begin the theological task: one always begins in the middle, with life already underway. For Huebner, then, Murphy's postmodern epistemology, especially its indication of a "core" organizing Yoder's thought,[44] does not take seriously enough, and perhaps negates, the importance of Yoder's intentionally "unsystematic" approach. "In effect, she cancels Yoder's understanding of the priority of ecclesiology to epistemology by reasserting the Enlightenment dogma of epistemological primacy."[45] And again, Murphy "defends Yoder's politically non-Constantinian understanding of pacifism by drawing on the methodologically Constantinian resources of system and theory, thereby reintroducing the dualism between the political and methodological into his work."[46]

Granted, Huebner's concern here is faithful interpretation of Yoder rather than Murphy's own project, and I agree with his compelling

---

42. John Howard Yoder, "Walk and Word: The Alternatives to Methodologism," in *Theology Without Foundations: Religious Practice and the Future of Theological Truth*, edited by Stanley Hauerwas, Nancey Murphy, and Mark Nation (Nashville: Abingdon, 1994) 77–90.

43. John Howard Yoder, *For the Nations: Essays Public and Evangelical* (Grand Rapids: Eerdmans, 1997) 19n9.

44. Nancey Murphy and George F. R. Ellis, *On the Moral Nature of the Universe: Theology, Cosmology, and Ethics* (Minneapolis: Fortress, 1996) 178–201.

45. Chris K. Huebner, *A Precarious Peace: Yoderian Explorations of Theology, Knowledge, and Identity* (Scottdale, PA: Herald, 2006) 107.

46. Ibid.

argument for "dialogical vulnerability." I only wish to resist a subtext in his critique: that Murphy's approach prioritizes epistemology in a way that is quintessentially modern, negating the patiently receptive mode of inquiry that Yoder exemplifies. Granted, one cannot divorce the "how" and the "what" in Yoder's work (for instance), but this does not mean that Yoder's work therefore lacks any coherence.[47] Indeed, Yoder's objection to methodologism would not seem to be the mere existence of orienting convictions or a "hard core"—the Lordship of the crucified Jesus surely serves as such for him—but the presumption that this could serve as an indubitable, universally accessible foundation in the way of Descartes's *cogito*. To (rightly) reject the way this *could* function does not mean all such "hard cores" necessarily serve to prioritize epistemology. Rather, on Murphy's view, only those that presume indubitability, foster individual certainty, or seek to control how inquiry *must* proceed from first principles are suspect. In any case, to critique and move past modern epistemology, one must still use the word; one is not thereby committed to every presumption that Enlightenment epistemology is heir to, not least its prioritization as the discipline to precede all disciplines.[48]

First-Order, Second-Order

This leads to a third point of clarification: Murphy's careful distinction between religion and theology—or better, first-order and second-order theology.[49] Murphy's postmodern epistemology is not mere throat clearing, for its usefulness comes after a community already exists that produces groups of people interested in doing this second-order work, reflecting on the first-order beliefs, practices, and "theories" of the church. This is not to divorce the two activities; ideally, second-order reflection grows from and rationally reflects upon first-order theology and the convictions of some community. But it is to *distinguish* second-order theology's methods and standards of coherence from first-order work.

---

47. As Hauerwas writes, "Yoder's account of the vulnerability of the church is based . . . on the nonnegotiable lordship of Christ"; Stanley Hauerwas and Romand Coles, *Christianity, Democracy, and the Radical Ordinary* (Eugene, OR: Cascade, 2008) 30.

48. For Murphy's explicit rejection of this prioritization, see her "Missiology in the Postmodern West: A Radical Reformation Perspective," in *To Stake a Claim: Mission and the Western Crisis of Knowledge*, edited by J. Andrew Kirk and Kevin J. Vanhoozer (Maryknoll, NY: Orbis, 1999) 107.

49. See James Wm. McClendon, Jr., *Doctrine: Systematic Theology, Volume 2* (Nashville: Abingdon, 1994) 24, 33.

It is only in this way that Murphy's analogizing scientific and theological methodologies can be understood. Murphy does not claim that Christian practice is analogous to science; but *doing* (second-order) theology, she thinks, is indeed analogous to *doing* science. The similarities are in "the conditions for rational *theologizing*, rather than for religious belief."[50] Murphy distinguishes, then, the content of theological reflection (primarily, God) from the *form of reflection* possible for humans, which *can* be analogized to other modes of rational reflection. But further, Murphy is "cognitivist" in her conception of theology: theological claims have propositional content about reality (rather than serve as "expressions" of feelings) such that it is possible to rationally reflect on them in this way.[51]

To be sure, it is unlikely that first-order theology will see the need to construe itself using Murphy's resources, if everything is going well. This is similar to linguistic analysis: when everyday ("first-order") language is working well, only the oddball bothers to analyze a conversation using J. L. Austin's categories in real time. ("Because your request to pass the bread meets the illocutionary, locutionary, and perlocutionary conditions required for felicitous speech, I will indeed do as you ask!") Only the person reflecting on language after the fact, or the person prompted to reflect on language when it goes wrong, needs such analysis, at which point it may be incredibly helpful. So the question, "But why must theology genuflect at the bar of science?" misses the point. Murphy does not grant automatic veridical status to the Western scientific worldview[52]; but she *does* argue that in our particular context, an important challenge to the very possibility of second-order theology is its reasonability, or the presumed lack thereof. In this cultural moment, there is need to show theology to be a rational (or better, non-arbitrary) discipline, and she gives herself to this task.

Of course, some may worry that allowing theology (first *or* second-order) to interact with science admits too much fluidity in the discipline, for scientific theories can change over time. But for Murphy, this is an unavoidable and central feature of theology, which "ought to be expected to change along with the rest of our dim and faltering knowledge. . . . So the task of relating theology to science will never be finished—it is bound to be an ongoing job, and there will surely be disappointments, but has not that been the lot of theologians and apologists from the beginning?"[53] Here we

---

50. Murphy, "On the Nature," 155.

51. Murphy and Ellis, *Moral Nature*, 235. Thus does Murphy uniquely refer to experiences of God as "data"; see Murphy, *Theology in the Age*.

52. Cf. Clayton and Knapp, "Is Holistic," 162–63.

53. Murphy, "Postmodern Apologetics," 119.

see methodologism's opposite, and which echoes Yoder's own description of theology *not* as a chain of boxes that are passed on over time with no change, but a river that shifts and adapts in each new generation, even as it continually circles back to reinterpret its central message, *Jesus is Lord*.[54]

Is "Hard Core" Just a Fancy Term for Foundation?

Finally, certain sympathetic interpreters have charged that Murphy actually supports a closet foundationalism, or that her view only "works" because she assumes some version of critical realism. F. LeRon Shults, for instance, argues that Murphy's willingness to start with the particularity of the Christian form of life is foundationalist, "immunizing our most basic epistemic and hermeneutic assumptions."[55] To argue that Christian communities determine what is part of its "hard core," for Shults, is a "centripetal" foundationalism, "placing the foundations in the 'center' instead of the 'base.'"[56] To be sure, genuine *post*foundationalism will not attempt to *immunize* a "hard core" from all challenge, but will actively seek interdisciplinary, "transcommunal" criteria of judgment. But first, it should be clear from section 1 that calling a "hard core" a foundation simply for it being *central* is a mistake, as it ignores other key elements of the foundationalist picture. This mistake is common; Murphy's "hard core" indeed adds organization to a Quinean web, but foundationalism is not just about some beliefs being more important than others; it is about the nature of their relations, not least the *one way* direction of justification.

Second, Shults has imported the notion of insularity, immunity, or indubitability into his description of Murphy. While he recognizes (in a footnote) that Murphy actually *is* interested in justifying convictions in wider settings, Shults still worries that Murphy insulates core religious convictions from outside challenge, fostering a crypto-fideism.[57] Bluntly, this reflects a deep misunderstanding of Lakatos and MacIntyre. To suggest that a "hard core" is indubitable or immune to criticism is to miss the whole point of Lakatos's work, which is to show how, in science, change and progress actually go. For Lakatos, no "hard core" is insular or immune to change; every

---

54. John Howard Yoder, *Preface to Theology* (Grand Rapids: Brazos, 2002) 258.

55. F. LeRon Shults, *The Postfoundationalist Task of Theology: Wolfhart Pannenberg and the New Theological Rationality* (Grand Rapids: Eerdmans, 1999) 65.

56. Ibid., 64. Shults is utilizing the work of his doctoral advisor; see Wentzel van Huyssteen, "Is the Postmodernist Always a Postfoundationalist?" *Theology Today* 50:3 (October 1993) 373–86.

57. Shults, *Postfoundationalist*, 64, n79.

research program is *constantly* rotating and changing, and while Murphy explicitly argues that "immunity from challenge" indeed marks the persistent foundationalist imagination,[58] such immunity is not a part of her proposal. Descriptively, her point is that change at *that* level of a "web" does not happen easily, or without change to the entire research program—but of course it is possible. Indeed, this is precisely why Murphy appreciates MacIntyre, as the notion of change over time and growth through welcoming outside challenge is even more explicit in his work; Murphy surely assumes that this marks theological approaches indebted to their work, too.

Insularity, Confidence, and the Radical Reformation

While the notion that Murphy's approach creates a first-order, methodological insularity is mistaken, it does echo a different, related theo-ethical challenge that Murphy *ought* to heed, using resources from her Anabaptist tradition. Granted the promise in Murphy's theological appropriation of Anglo-American postmodern resources, and granted that interactivity (both inside and outside the Christian tradition) marks her theology, a separate concern is with the potential liabilities of this appropriation for Christians *on the ground*. The issue is not whether the epistemology is insular, but whether this second-order approach might require nuancing and correcting by first-order theologians. For many Anabaptist readers, this concern has centered on MacIntyre's epistemology in particular needing "conversion"; otherwise, Christians may find themselves closed to neighbor (let alone enemy) in a manner contrary to the call of the gospel. This is not a necessary liability, as I will show, but its existence as a potential danger is important to acknowledge if it is to be counteracted.

The Worry: Unreceptive Overconfidence

This concern is best articulated by political philosopher Romand Coles. Coles rightly reads MacIntyre as a "postmodern" philosopher, highlighting the radical (rather than socially conservative) implications of MacIntyre's work. Coles sees MacIntyre resisting Rawlsian liberalism, both epistemologically and politically, *not* because liberalism fosters "too much" difference, but precisely because liberalism allows only the "simulacrum" of difference, thus leaving the average citizen unable to differentiate between healthy and

---

58. Murphy, *Anglo-American*, 93, n13.

unhealthy kinds of heterogeneity.[59] Coles's interpretation of this representative of Anglo-American postmodern philosophy is sympathetic, then, since for MacIntyre, "contingency, conflict, difference, heterogeneous traditions, and a version of dialogical enlightenment and politics are central."[60] However, Coles cautions those who would follow MacIntyre (such as Murphy) to be careful in their use—*not* because MacIntyre advocates authoritarian sectarianism, a closet "foundationalism," or because of any stated issue with tradition-constituted reason, but for fear that MacIntyrean resources may be used to engender too strong a form of "confidence" in one's tradition, such that in actual, ordinary communities of practice, receptivity to adherents of other traditions is blocked.[61] Recall Murphy's spectrum of postmodern epistemologists, marking those who are more and less optimistic about the possibility of overcoming relativism; in her words, it represents a range of those who have "more or less confidence concerning our ability to adjudicate among competing theories or traditions."[62]

Distinct from the positions considered above, the critique here isn't that MacIntyrean resources automatically cause epistemological isolationism (at least of one's most deeply held convictions). It's that, perhaps despite one's best intentions, use of MacIntyre might foster an *over*confidence that allows Christian congregations to get on with their business *before* reaching out to their neighbors. This critique is bolstered by Coles's appreciation of radical reformation theology as refracted through Yoder. For Coles, Yoder's work is beneficial precisely because it countenances a patient receptivity to neighbor and enemy—which Yoder's "patience as method" explicitly defends.[63] Coles is deeply impressed by Yoder's insistence that faithful churches are vulnerably open to those outside, not because it is "nice" or politically correct, but because as a sociality the church owes its existence to the One who was *most* open to others, even to the point of death.[64]

Another way to put the same worry is that MacIntyre's project, particularly in its focus on practices, can lead to a subtle prioritization wherein communities try to get their internal practices settled *before* moving to engagement with others and service to the world. Coles doesn't want to

---

59. Romand Coles, *Beyond Gated Politics* (Minneapolis: University of Minnesota Press, 2005) 82, 89–90.

60. Ibid., 80.

61. Ibid., 99–107.

62. Murphy, *Anglo-American*, 50.

63. John Howard Yoder, "'Patience' as Method in Moral Reasoning: Is an Ethic of Discipleship 'Absolute'?" in *The Wisdom of the Cross*, edited by Stanley Hauerwas et al. (Grand Rapids: Eerdmans, 1999) 24–42.

64. Coles, *Beyond*, ch. 4.

deny the importance of formative practices or even the reality of central convictions to this task, but to recognize that they are "partly constituted by the borders themselves," re-picturing the church not as gathered "*prior to encountering others*," but as "a people equiprimordially gathered and formed precisely at the borders of the encounter."[65] Such wouldn't neglect the cruciality of ecclesial practices, nor view encounter with those outside as "secondary"; *nor* would it erase the reality of boundaries (between church and world, for instance). But it would make them of a different kind—porous and permeable rather than rigid.[66]

Of course, Coles is clear that MacIntyre's project *need* not lead to squelching vulnerable receptivity to others,[67] which is to say that it depends how MacIntyre is used as to whether or not this fear becomes reality. But *this* critique is more able to "stick," grounded as it is in accurate assessment of and sensitivity to MacIntyre's radical potentiality.

The Tension: Radical Reformation Convictions and Postmodern Epistemology

A way to narrate the tension I am identifying here is between radical reformation theological convictions and the tools of Anglo-American philosophy. As theologian Craig Hovey notes, MacIntyre himself relies on a strong distinction between those inside and those outside one's own community in order to defend the act of lying or killing to protect the community's integrity. Hovey, a holder of Anabaptist convictions, argues that MacIntyre can make this *strong* distinction because he works with a notion of "practice" that has no explicit place for subverting categories like "inside" and "outside," "stranger" and "friend" (a subversion inherent to the gospel); Christians can only maintain this strong distinction by neglecting the question of *which* practices are constitutive of the Christian life, and which ought to be eschewed. Put differently, MacIntyre's strong appeal to those inside and those outside one's community works because he avoids getting "closer to the ground than practices-in-general."[68] To paraphrase, then, MacIntyre

---

65. Romand Coles, "Gentled Into Being," in *Christianity, Democracy*, 212.

66. Romand Coles, "The Pregnant Reticence of Rowan Williams," in *Christianity, Democracy*, 190–91.

67. Coles, *Beyond*, 107.

68. Craig Hovey, *Bearing True Witness: Truthfulness in Christian Practice* (Grand Rapids: Eerdmans, 2011) 228. Hovey points out that MacIntyre's argument about lying is incoherent from his own virtue-based perspective; ibid., 223.

needs "converting" by Anabaptists; specificity—of *which* tradition, *which* community—matters.[69]

Murphy is not unaware of these tensions, immersed as she is in the Brethren tradition. In fact, Murphy identifies two weaknesses in MacIntyre's epistemological account (which remains, she says, the best so far) born of these convictions. First, Murphy claims that MacIntyre is overly optimistic in his evaluation of social practices, viewing them as inherently bent toward human flourishing in a way that Anabaptists cannot. Following Jim McClendon, she argues instead that practices should be seen as *powerful*—necessary for human flourishing, but also open to corruption and capable of dominating humanity.[70] Second and relatedly, Murphy claims that MacIntyre is unable to provide conclusive reasons to reject the Genealogical tradition precisely because of his generalized (and "typically Catholic") conception of tradition. In response, Murphy proposes an extension of MacIntyre, synthesizing (as well as correcting and supplementing) his philosophy with radical reformation social analysis, focusing on *particular* "Christian epistemic practices"—"communal practices aimed at the pursuit of truth"[71]—to aid MacIntyre's project.

Overconfidence versus Competence

This suggests to me that there is precedent in Murphy's own research program to heed warnings *of a certain sort* about the potential consequences of MacIntyre's work: in particular, those warnings warranted by radical reformation theology. After all, given that MacIntyre works with Aristotelian categories, Anabaptists must remain attuned to the ways Jesus radically refashions and even "explodes" these categories in ways that Aristotle would find objectionable.[72] Put differently, there is room for gift exchange between Coles and Murphy.

And so, I propose that Murphy add Coles's concerns to her list of ways that first-order radical reformation theology constrains uses of MacIntyre's work, without leading to its abandonment. Murphy can accept that on the ground, radical Christians should be wary of a "first, second" approach to "Christian epistemic practices." This isn't to say that Christians should be

---

69. A specificity, of course, that MacIntyre the philosopher has not *tried* to provide.

70. Murphy, "Missiology," 116. Cf. James Wm. McClendon, Jr., *Ethics: Systematic Theology, Volume 1*, rev. ed. (Nashville: Abingdon, [1986] 2002) 178–82.

71. Murphy, "Missiology," 116.

72. Stanley Hauerwas, "The Politics of Gentleness," in *Christianity, Democracy*, 206.

automatically wary of "hard cores" (an impossibility), but it is to say that our core convictions are formed *as* we engage others, which, after all, is always already underway. Indispensable Christian epistemic practices such as communal discernment, prophetic utterance, scriptural interpretation all curdle if they cause communal insulation from others. Indeed, the original use these practices were put to in Anabaptist history was *engaged struggle* to be "in but not of the world"—to serve the world without acquiescing to it—not isolation.[73] But the danger must be acknowledged.

Similarly, Coles is right to warn against overconfidence. Again, while no necessary consequence of MacIntyre's work, radical reformation openness offers a healthy correction to the *possibility* of overconfidence. "Listening to the least of the brethren (and sisters),"[74] for example, is an important Christian practice, but one that may fall by the wayside if we are *so* confident in our own voices that we see no *need* to listen to our brothers and sisters, let alone the least of them. The middle way here is between what Anglo-American postmodernity is rightly working against—what some have recently called "moral incompetence"[75]—and the opposite error, overconfidence. The mean is a receptive competence.

Murphy can and should envelope this critique (in good MacIntyrean fashion), but she also offers a gift of her own: in Coles's lauding of Yoder, he nonetheless expresses worry about Yoder's "jealousy" for Jesus. His worry is that Yoder's insistence on Jesus' centrality may end up stealing energy from the receptivity that he so clearly manifests.[76] And indeed, this is a constant refrain in Coles's work: for his money, a modicum of "ateleology" is always needed for communities to remain open to radical transformation, especially in our liberal (and post-liberal) political context. He is *religiously* ateleological; whenever a single voice grows too loud, Coles will be there to express concern.

Murphy's exchange is that for people like Yoder, it is precisely *because* Jesus is the center of a particular "research program" or "tradition" that he is patiently receptive to strangers. Jesus does not steal these energies, but creates them. So while Coles remains reticent about the image of "centers"

---

73. For an incredibly helpful, nuanced defense of this counterintuitive claim, see Gerald Biesecker-Mast, *Separation and the Sword in Anabaptist Persuasion: Radical Confessional Rhetoric from Schleitheim to Dordrecht* (Telford, PA: Cascadia, 2006).

74. Murphy, "Missiology," 118.

75. Willis Jenkins, "Atmospheric Powers, Global Injustice, and Moral Incompetence: Challenges to Doing Social Ethics From Below," *Journal of the Society of Christian Ethics* 34:1 (2013) 65–82.

76. Coles, *Beyond*, 129, 135–36.

or "concentric circles,"[77] or even a central melody with which people harmonize (because it presumes we "already know" the tune),[78] Murphy can appreciate his critique but respond that Christians cannot help but confess that the central *logic* of God has been revealed in the crucified Jesus—which after all, is *kenotic love*.[79] What new improvisations spring from this song are genuinely open, but the notion of harmony or "center" need not manifest Coles's fears of hegemonic overconfidence. It depends on what that "logic" looks like, and kenotic enemy love does not fit the bill.

Holding Coles and Murphy together, then, is worth the effort. Doubt—or better, humility—is indeed important to keep churches from closing in on themselves; all should work against fostering a *communio incurvatus in se*. But doubt is always parasitic on some tradition (one cannot doubt from nowhere), and "ateleology" ought not be prioritized or recommended as though one *should* feel incompetence.

Conclusion

Throughout, I have presumed that Murphy's embodiment of Anglo-American postmodern epistemology has withstood every critique thus far, and is worth appropriating by the coming generation of theologians. I have argued that one line of critique of Murphy's philosophical hero, MacIntyre, should be accepted—that radical Christians indeed should push back on (or "convert") MacIntyre in specific ways—but that this does not thereby warrant abandonment of Murphy's project. Of course, one cannot say that this will always remain the case, especially given theology's ever-changing character; the most one can claim is that this is "the best so far." But I am convinced that when it is surpassed in content, it will be as Christians carry on in the spirit of Nancey's work, honoring the Spirit of the Crucified Lord towards whom she has consistently directed the church's attention.

---

77. Coles, "Gentled," 211.
78. Coles, "Pregnant," 188.
79. Murphy and Ellis, *Moral Nature*, chs. 6, 8.

# SECTION II

Theological Anthropology

4

Beyond the Isolated Self
Extended Mind and Spirituality

—Warren S. Brown and Brad D. Strawn

A PERENNIAL CHALLENGE IN neuroscience, psychology, and philosophy has been how human minds can describe minds. Implicit in this concern is the question of the nature of humanity itself, and for Christians, the role of spirituality in this conversation. As a neuroscientist and a psychologist, our question is even more specific: what do the cognitive neurosciences have to offer these discussions?

The problem of human nature has been a topic of cultural, philosophical, and theological discourse for centuries, ebbing and flowing in its importance as information and theories surrounding such questions have changed. Over the last century, focus on these questions has progressively intensified as the neurobiological sciences have flourished, resulting in an exponential increase in the amount that is known about human neurophysiology, cognition, and psychology. The rapidly unfolding view of the neuropsychology of personhood provides important new perspectives, but also raises new issues.

This paper will provide an overview of some positions and movements in this conversation. Specifically, we will summarize the movements from dualism, to physicalism and embodiment, to embeddedness, to embodied cognition, and finally to extended cognition—each move fostered by ongoing research and theory development in the cognitive and brain sciences. Given that extended cognition (also called externalism) is a view that has been given little if any attention in Christian thinking, we will particularly focus on this view and its implications for theological anthropology and Christian spirituality.

Dualism

For most of its history, the Western Christian world has been dominated by the view that persons have a dual (two-part) nature—body and soul. This position (*dualism*) asserts that humans are composites of two different parts, a material body and a non-material mind or soul (these latter two terms being generally synonymous in dualist thinking). In most versions of dualism, these two parts are not equals. Rather, the soul/mind is considered to be superior to the body and to rule over it. The soul/mind is the source of human rationality, sociality, and spirituality, as well as the locus of personal identity. In addition, the soul is immortal, while the body is mortal and transitory.[1]

This sort of dualism is difficult to maintain in the light of modern neuroscience in that there is scarcely any human capacity that has not already been shown to emerge from identifiable patterns of brain activity.[2] In addition, dualism raises the problem of how a non-material soul would interact with a physical body.[3] We have argued elsewhere that dualism is also problematic for reasons of its impact on our understanding of human life, practical theology, and the role of communities.[4] If the soul is superior

---

1. Dualism, as a position on human nature, has been well-described and critiqued by Nancey Murphy in her introduction and chapter in Warren S. Brown, Nancey Murphy, and Newton Malony, eds. *Whatever Happened to the Soul? Scientific and Theological Portraits of Human Nature* (Minneapolis: Fortress, 1998) 1–29, 127–48. As Nancey has shown us, contemporary versions of dualism are the result of a particular philosophical, theological inheritance: they do not drop from the sky. See also Nancey Murphy, *Beyond Liberalism and Fundamentalism: How Modern and Postmodern Philosophy Set the Theological Agenda* (Harrisburg, PA: Trinity, 1996) 150.

2. Cf. Nancey Murphy and Warren S. Brown, *Did My Neurons Make Me Do It? Philosophical and Neurobiological Perspectives on Moral Responsibility and Free Will* (New York: Oxford University Press, 2007); Nancey Murphy, *Bodies and Souls, or Spirited Bodies?* (Cambridge: Cambridge University Press, 2006); Malcolm Jeeves and Warren S. Brown, *Neuroscience, Psychology, and Religion: Illusions, Delusions, and Realities about Human Nature.* (West Conshohocken, PA: Templeton, 2009); and Warren S. Brown, "The Brain, Religion, and Baseball: Comments on the Potential for a Neurology of Religion," in *Where God and Science Meet: How Brain and Evolutionary Studies Alter Our Understanding of Religion, Volume 2, The Neurology of Religious Experience*, edited by Patrick McNamara (Westport, CT: Praeger, 2006) 229–44.

3. Nancey addresses this problem in Murphy, *Beyond Liberalism*, 66.

4. Warren S. Brown and Brad D. Strawn, *The Physical Nature of Christian Life: Neuroscience, Psychology and the Church* (Cambridge: Cambridge University Press,

to the body and rules over it, and if it is the soul that is eternal, then each person must focus on caring for and nurturing their soul, first and foremost. One's body and outward behavior are secondary priorities. Only if time and energy permit should attention be paid to the physical, economic, and social well-being of other persons.

Physicalism, Embodiment, and Embeddedness

Our focus is not on undermining dualism here (that work has been done elsewhere), but beginning with its presumed difficulties, on exploring alternatives equally faithful to the Christian tradition. In psychology, philosophy, and theology there are a number of alternatives to dualism that seem to capture much of the fundamental nature of human beings and personhood, but that also have the advantage of being more resonant with neuroscience and neuropsychology. These models are expressed in terms such as Nonreductive Physicalism, Emergent Monism, Dual Aspect Monism, and Emergent Holistic Dualism, among others. Very generally, these alternative positions take more seriously the embodiment of human nature and, thus, the relevance of cognitive science and human neurobiology. In these alternative formulations, the concept of neurobiological emergence plays a central role. For example, Nonreductive Physicalism asserts the fundamental physical nature of humankind (i.e., embodiment), but with the strong qualifier "nonreductive" suggesting that the hypercomplex physical system that is a human being has properties of the whole that are emergent, and therefore not reducible to the properties of its elemental constituent parts such as molecules, cells, neurons, neural systems, the brain.[5]

However, what emerges in the hypercomplex physical system of a human being is conditioned by the physical, cultural, and social environment in which it is embedded. Mind emerges from environmental interactions during human development. This is particularly true of human cognition. The human cerebral cortex is slower to develop than that of other primates.

2012); Warren S. Brown, Sarah D. Marion, and Brad D. Strawn "Human Relationality, Spiritual Formation, and Wesleyan Communities," in *Wesleyan Theology and Social Science: The Dance of Practical Divinity and Discovery*, edited by M. Kathryn Armistead, Brad D. Strawn, and Ronald W. Wright (Newcastle: Cambridge Scholars Publishing, 2010) 95–112.

5. Cf. Murphy, *Bodies and Souls*; Murphy and Brown, *Did My Neurons?*; and Jeeves and Brown, *Neuroscience, Psychology, and Religion*; see also Joel B. Green, *Body, Soul, and Human Life: The Nature of Humanity in the Bible* (Grand Rapids: Baker, 2008) and Joel B. Green, ed. *What About the Soul? Neuroscience and Christian Anthropology* (Nashville: Abingdon, 2004).

Slow physical development of the brain implies greater openness in its structure and connectivity to influences from the environment in which the child is embedded. Thus, while genetics certainly plays a general role, the specific patterns of functional connectivity within and between many brain systems come about in direct response to environmental challenges and interactions (i.e., embeddedness).[6]

The best explanation of how higher-order properties (like mind) emerge in a hypercomplex system (like the human brain and body) in response to environmental challenges can be found in theory and research on complex dynamical systems. This body of work provides a reasonable explanation of how new adaptive properties emerge within complex systems from processes of self-organization that are forced by the need to meet environmental challenges (physical, cultural, or social). When the system as currently constituted faces a new adaptive challenge, the elements within the system reorganize their patterns of interactivity to meet the challenge. New patterns of organization embody higher-order emergent properties that reflect adaptations to the system's (person's) current environmental embeddedness.

Complex Emergent Developmental Linguistic Relational Neurophysiologicalism

While we embrace the basic motivation and premises of human embodiment and embeddedness, we have been critical of the conceptual simplicity of the expressions of these positions. It is all too easy to debate the relative truth or value of sparsely labeled positions (e.g., Nonreductive Physicalism, or Emergent Monism) without having to come to grips with so much of what is critical in the emergence of human personhood. We (and, of course, Nancey Murphy) have advocated for Nonreductive Physicalism as an adequate view of the basic nature of humankind. However, even this label (which we endorse) limits the imagination and concatenates discussion. For example, what *sort* of physical creature is being referenced, and what specific *properties* of this physical creature allow its non-reductive characteristics to emerge?

As an alternative, we have proposed a more complex, and therefore we believe richer and more robust, position: Complex Emergent Developmental Linguistic Relational Neurophysiologicalism (CEDLRN, if you like

---

6. Cf. Steven R. Quartz and Terrence J. Sejnowski, *Liars, Lovers, and Heroes: What the New Brain Science Reveals about How We Become Who We Are* (New York: William Morrow, 2002).

acronyms). While admittedly cumbersome and not easily remembered, this descriptor of our position has the value of making explicit more of the richness and complexity necessary for an adequate model of human nature. Nothing less will do. From this viewpoint, personhood is constituted by emergent properties which are the product of self-organizing processes within the hypercomplex neurophysiological systems of human beings. These properties emerge progressively over a long period of developmental, linguistic, and relational history.[7]

We have argued that we must not be content to merely philosophize about physicalism without being cognizant of the unique characteristics of neurophysiology. What is more, the human brain is the most complex neurophysiological system known. This functional and structural complexity must be explicitly acknowledged and understood as having the properties of a complex dynamical system—a system that is subject to processes of self-organization from which emerge high-level, causal, agentive functional properties. Adequate understanding of human nature must also take into account the progressive processes of self-organizing neurocognitive development that are characteristic of human children, as well as the dramatic enhancement of psychosocial capacities and human agency contributed by the acquisition of language. Finally, the deeply formative influences of interpersonal relatedness and socio-cultural embeddedness must be explicitly taken into account.

It is our position that progress cannot be made in theories of human nature without this sort of explicit recognition of the depth and richness of what it means to be a human being and to become a person. Given the state of understanding of complex systems, human cognition, neuroscience, child developmental, semantics, and relational psychology, it is time to move the discussion of human nature past the sparse models currently employed.

Embodied Cognition

Over the last few decades there has been an increasingly important movement in the philosophy of mind called *Embodied Cognition*.[8] According to this view, the content and processes of mind are not like those of a computer. That is, the mind is not a processor of abstract symbols or representations

---

7. Warren S. Brown and Brad D. Strawn, "Self-Organizing Personhood: Complex Emergent Developmental Linguistic Relational Neurophysiologicalism", in *The Ashgate Research Companion to Theological Anthropology*, edited by Joshua Ryan Farris and Charles Taliaferro (Burlington, VT: Ashgate, 2015).

8. For example, see John A. Teske, "From Embodied to Extended Cognition," *Zygon* 48 (2013) 759–87.

that are only remotely coupled with input/output streams. Rather minds work by simulating motor outputs and re-experiencing their likely consequences. The processes of thinking are simulations of potential actions in the world, rather than the manipulation of abstract representations. Similarly, the content of thinking is assembled from records of the sensory-motor consequences of past action. Therefore, the nature of the body determines the nature of mind. Even when working offline (that is, thinking without acting) the mental processes are constituted by the virtual re-enactments of schemas of actions and consequences. The brain is constantly interactive with all of the peripheral systems that control and sense the entire body, and not distanced from these through processes of encoding of information into abstract representations for off-line symbolic manipulation.

Embodied cognition makes the following claims:

1. *Cognition is for action.* The basic problem of mind is what to do next—how to adjust ongoing behavior to be more effective; whether to shift to another behavior; what to do in the immediate or distant future; what can and should be said.

2. *Cognition is situated.* Actions (current, remembered, or anticipated) which constitute mind cannot be extracted from situational contexts. The content of mind is what one can do in particular situations and, thus, the processes of mind are always in some sense situated. Knowing is inseparable from doing in particular physical, social, cultural contexts. Mind is built upon sensory-motor contingencies between agent and world.[9]

3. *Cognition is time-pressured.* Thinking is on-the-fly, rather than atemporally dis-engaged retrieval and manipulation of stored abstract, symbolic knowledge. The basic problem of mind is what to do *now or next*, even if current thinking is primarily internal and decoupled (for now) from direct physical activity.

4. *Action (and therefore cognition) is enmeshed in recurrent situational feedback.* Mind is what is going on *between* the body and the world, not what is going on in disengaged abstract space in the head. Thus, mind is engaged in cycles of action and feedback. The ongoingness of mind cannot be stopped as if awaiting the next conscious decision

---

9. The theory that mind is constituted by sensory-motor contingency between agent and world is sometimes referred to as "enactivism"; see J. K. O'Regan and and A. Noë, "A Sensorimotor Account of Vision and Visual Consciousness," *Behavioral and Brain Sciences* 24:5 (2001).

regarding what to do. Consciousness can be shifted to internal modes of action-simulation, but never ceases to be ongoing.

5. *Off-line cognition is body-based (simulation).* To seemingly "stop and think," or ruminate, or meditate is to run emulations and simulations of physical and social engagements and interactions. Running behavioral simulations in our sensory-motor neural systems constitutes "off-line" thought.[10]

6. *Meaning of language is rooted in sensory-motor experiences.* Semantic content is constituted by *linguistic* interactions with the social world. For a word to have meaning is for it to have some linkage to action-in-the-world—that is, meaning is primarily constituted in prior language interactions with persons in particular contexts. The "intentionality" of a word is how it is used in embodied social interactions—that is, the stored memories of interactions involving the word.[11]

7. *Mind is primarily constituted in communities of practice.* Human communities provide contexts for social, cultural, and linguistic interactional learning. Communities embody understandings of how the physical and social world functions and can be successfully manipulated. Knowing is expressed in, and constituted by, the agent's ability to act as an increasingly competent participant in a community of practice.[12]

8. *Emotions are indices of the dynamics of bodily attunement with the environment.* Ease, distress, frustration, anger, joy, happiness, positive or negative feedback are all means of attuning the body to the contingencies of the current (and sometimes imagined) physical and social context. Emotions are not primarily inner subjective experiences, although these often accompany.

---

10. The idea of thought as simulation is often referred to as "grounded cognition"; see Lawrence W. Barsalou, "Grounded Cognition," *Annual Review of Psychology* 59 (January 2008) 617–45.

11. George Lakoff and Mark Johnson, *Philosophy in the Flesh: The Embodied Mind and Its Challenge to Western Thought* (New York: Basic, 1999).

12. This is a point Nancey has returned to again and again in her work, and is very much confirmed by the notion of embodied cognition; for example, see Nancey Murphy and George F. R. Ellis, *On the Moral Nature of the Universe: Theology, Cosmology, and Ethics* (Minneapolis: Fortress, 1996) 110; and Nancey Murphy, Brad J. Kallenberg, and Mark Thiessen Nation, eds., *Virtues and Practices in the Christian Tradition: Christian Ethics after MacIntyre* (Harrisburg, PA: Trinity, 1997) ch. 2 and her introduction to ch. 6.

9. *Some cognitive work is off-loaded into the environment.* If mind is constituted by situated sensory-motor interactions, then situations themselves, and the artifacts they contain, become a part (a catalyst and necessary element) of intelligent, high-level cognitive activity. Philosopher of mind Andy Clark has commented that "we make the world smart so that we can be dumb in peace"—e.g., a smart phone.[13] We pursue this idea further in what follows regarding "extended cognition."

Theories of embodied cognition thus make it clear that we think with records of experiences gained as our bodies interact with the world. Human nature is emergent from more than just a complex brain, but from entire bodily systems involved in behavioral interactions with the world and their consequences in ongoing sensory feedback as to the outcomes of such actions. Thus, as culture and its social and physical artifacts proliferate and become increasingly complex, the developmentally self-organizing mental capacities of persons get more diverse and complex.

Extended Cognition

Included in the description of the tenets of embodied cognition is the claim that some cognitive work is off-loaded into the environment. The claim of Extended Cognition is that what is taken to be mental or cognitive must include not just the brain and the body, but also those physical, cultural or social aspects of the environment that are, at the moment, enmeshed in the current, ongoing mental transactions. While mind is embodied more than just "embrained," it is also extended beyond the body in varying times and manners. This theory of mind is also labeled "externalism," recognizing the important role in cognitive processes played by things external to the body. Thus, it is not simply that persons are embedded within cultural and social contexts, the contents and implications of which become internalized in ways that shape the nature of mental processes. Rather the claim of situated and extended cognition is that important aspects of mental processing take place in reciprocally interactive exchanges with certain artifacts or persons within the current context, such that mind cannot be understood as simply internal.[14]

13. Andy Clark, *Being There: Putting Brain, Body, and World Together Again* (Cambridge, MA: MIT Press, 1997) 180.

14. Andy Clark, *Supersizing the Mind: Embodiment, Action, and Cognitive Extension* (New York: Oxford University Press, 2008). See also Teske, "From Embodied to Extended Cognition."

It is not that all aspects of the current environment are objects of extended mental processes. Rather, at any particular moment, and depending on the current mental problem to be solved, different aspects of the physical or social environment may become enmeshed in an ongoing feedback loop with the brain and body such as to constitute an extended cognitive processing system. Thus, activity that we would label as "intelligent" does not occur exclusively in the brain/body, but includes also the interactive loop between the person and immediately incorporated aspects of the external world. Within such a temporarily assembled system, one cannot readily identify the boundaries of the mind at work as occurring solely in the brain and body, but rather "mind" encompasses the external artifacts or situations. For example, during a problem-solving interaction involving two persons, both individuals become enmeshed in an ongoing reciprocal interaction such that, as solutions emerge, there is no clear demarcation between the two persons that would allow location of the solution in one brain/mind. The mind at work was extended beyond either participant into the interactive space. By virtue of the interaction, a more powerful and imaginative (supersized) processor emerged that had greater capacity to solve the problem at hand than either isolated mind.

Philosopher of mind Andy Clark, in his book provocatively titled *Supersizing the Mind*, provides a simple example of extended cognition in the form of Otto's notebook.[15] In this illustration, Otto's memory is failing significantly. So, Otto uses a notebook to write down things he needs to remember—shopping lists, appointments, jobs around the house, people's names, etc.—and uses this to enhance his significantly weakened memory. Clark argues that Otto's notebook works as a part of his cognitive systems in such a way that its contributions to mental processing cannot be readily distinguished from his brain-based memory. What is more, Otto credits items in the notebook as real records of things remembered in the same way he credits (when he can) things emerging from his brain-based memory systems. Otto's weak memory has been "supersized" by the extension of his memory system into the world of artifacts in the same manner that our problem-solving conversation enhanced cognitive processing by its extension into interpersonal space.

---

15. Clark utilizes Otto's notebook as an illustration throughout *Supersizing the Mind*, an idea he further engages in Andy Clark and David J. Chalmers, "The Extended Mind," *Analysis* 58:1 (1998) 7–19; reprinted in *Philosophy of Mind: Classical and Contemporary Readings*, edited by David J. Chalmers (New York: Oxford University Press, 2002). This coauthored essay is included as an appendix in *Supersizing the Mind* (220–32) and is the version we refer to in this essay.

Clark argues that cognitive extension involves *interfaces*. An interface is a point of connection between the human body and the external artifact or person. This idea is best understood in the context of tool use. For example, a hammer, when in use, is no longer a separate object, but during use becomes a part of the body via the interface of hand and grip, creating "a whole new agent-world circuit."[16] Similarly, in the problem-solving conversation, social interactions involving the interfaces of language, gestures, tone-of-voice, and facial expressions allow for extension of two minds into a shared and supersized cognitive space. In the case of Otto's notebook, eye, hand, and pencil interface with the notebook allowing it to be incorporated into the memory system.

The concepts of cognitive extension and interface are supported by findings in neuroscience. It has been demonstrated that the human brain does not just "use" tools as external artifacts, but, over time, the brain begins to experience and represent the tool as part of the body itself, much as a prosthesis becomes a part of the brain's body map. This is what Andy Clark calls *incorporation*, rather than simple use.[17] Due to the plasticity of the brain, one's body schema is changed by the ongoing incorporation of tools or other artifacts. In the case of a hammer, through the hand-grip interface, the tool becomes a part of the brain's body schema. Hammering instantiates an action-feedback loop not different in principle from a brain-body loop, extending the body schema to include the hammer. Such extension enhances what can be physically imagined and accomplished.

Otto is interfaced with his notebook in such a way that the notebook is incorporated into what we must credit as Otto's memory. Thus, Clark and Chalmers suggest that the notebook should be endowed with "epistemic credit" for the resulting cognitive processes of Otto's memory. They argue, "If, as we confront some task, a part of the world functions as a process, which *were it done in the head*, we would have no hesitation in recognizing it as part of the cognitive process, then that part of the world is (so we claim) part of the cognitive process. Cognitive processes ain't (all) in the head!"[18] Therefore, Otto's notebook is an example of the extension of mind outside of the person as aspects of the environment—whether physical artifacts or other persons—become incorporated into the cognitive task at hand.

For these reasons, Clark argues that, due to processes of extension and incorporation, humans are not simply embodied, but *profoundly embodied*. He states,

16. Clark, *Supersizing the Mind*, 31.
17. Ibid., 37–39.
18. Clark and Chalmers, "Extended Mind," 222.

... biological systems (and especially we primates) seem to be specifically designed to constantly search for opportunities to make the most of body and world, checking for what is available, and then (at various timescales and with varying degrees of difficulty) integrating new resources very deeply, creating whole new agent-world circuits in the process. A profoundly embodied creature or robot is thus one that is highly engineered to be able to learn to make maximal problem-simplifying use of an open-ended variety of internal, bodily, or external sources of order.[19]

Supersizing Spirituality

Within Christian discussions about human nature, the biggest problem with crediting the claims of non-reductive physicalism and embodiment is not so much about the nature of mind as it is about the nature of spirituality.[20] Does spirituality not require the existence of a non-material, spiritual soul within each person? We have explored elsewhere the nature of Christian life when viewed from the point of view of the embodiment of personhood.[21] We argued that "spirituality" should be reckoned as an awareness of the presence of God's spirit, rather than the cultivation of an inner non-material spirit or soul that is, by definition, private—separated from the external and social world. From the point of view of physicalism and embodiment, the world of spirituality moves outward by means of actions and interactions of the entire person with the world in a manner that encompasses the Spirit of God.

If the mind and soul are embodied and contextually embedded, and if spirituality is, in fact, a disposition to be aware of God's presence in the world, then we might also consider the possibility of extended spirituality. That is, we might think about spirituality as a property not bound to individual persons, but as extended beyond the person into the interpersonal. Viewed from this perspective, spirituality is extended (at least in some contexts) beyond the individual into the external context of enmeshments within reciprocal and communal religious/spiritual practices. For example, when persons are involved in congregational worship or corporate prayer, it becomes unclear who owns the spirituality in play. Much as Otto's notebook supersized his weakened memory, and an interaction with another person

19. Clark, *Supersizing the Mind*, 42.
20. Nancey specifically addresses this throughout Murphy, *Bodies and Souls*.
21. Brown and Strawn, *Physical Nature of Christian Life*.

can supersize problem-solving, so we might also consider interpersonally and congregationally extended spiritual life as supersizing the spirituality possible in an isolated person. Compared to supersized spirituality of corporate prayer and worship, individual, private, and exclusively internal spirituality would appear undersized, dwarfed, and even puny. Through such extension, spirituality would no longer be trapped inside an autonomous, private, self-focused world of heroic individualism. Rather, much of spirituality would occur in the space of engagement with other persons, and thus exist as extended into the congregational environment, with the supersizing potentialities of being drawn beyond the limitations of the self.

Ecclesiology: From Puny to Supersized Spirituality

What would be the implications for the life of the church if we took into account the possibility that spirituality can exist in extra-personally extended interactions? What if what we refer to as spiritual is not just embodied within individuals? If spirituality is a property that emerges and exists in inter-individual space, at least during times of reciprocal and corporate activity such as worship, prayer, study, conversation, and work, then we might need to think differently about ecclesiology. The spirituality at play would be located outside of individuals, and would be more than the sum of the individual spiritualities of the participants.

Recently it has become popular to say, "I am spiritual but not religious." People who say this typically mean that they perceive themselves to have a form of inner, private spirituality, but that they do not engage in the life of traditionally organized religious practices. The argument we are making here would suggest that such individual and privatized spirituality is dwarfed and puny compared to what might be the case when spiritual life is enhanced by incorporation into some form of congregational worship.

The idea of extensions of individual worship by corporate activity would seem to be obvious. In many faiths, religious worship is done corporately suggesting an awareness of the power of extension of worship into the larger group. Jesus taught that "where two or three are gathered in my name, there am I in the midst of them" (Matt 18:20, RSV), suggesting something uniquely powerful about groups over individuals. However, as society and the church become ever more individualistic in their understanding of spirituality and faith (for example, the current movement toward more ascetic spirituality[22]), many parishioners have a difficult time giving an ac-

---

22. For examples of ascetic spirituality see Dallas Willard, *The Spirit of the Disciplines: Understanding How God Changes Lives* (San Francisco: HarperCollins, 1988);

count for why the corporate activity of the church is important and what role it plays in Christian life. It may be seen as a "spiritual refueling stop," or as an institution for religious education, or simply as source of accountability for one's individual spiritual quest. Most evangelical Christians today believe that spiritual life and the real work of Christian formation occur entirely within an inner, private, and individual relationship with Christ. This relationship is proclaimed by the church and incubated by the warmth of worship, but is nevertheless a private matter.

In contrast to this individualist view, we have previously argued that all of personhood—including one's faith—is developed in and through relationships with others, and thus the church is the context for the formation of one's spirituality and Christian character.[23] But the idea of extended spirituality broadens this view in arguing that spirituality often reaches beyond what exits within an individual person, existing (at least at times) in the situated and extended interactions occurring in worship and corporate Christian life. In this way, ideas of the nature of Christian life move from a self-focused, internal, private spirituality to an embodied and embedded Christian formation that is, nevertheless, somewhat dwarfed by the limitations of individual persons, and on to a more robust spirituality that extends into interpersonal interactive space.[24]

The process of thinking about spirituality and Christian life as extended leads us down interesting pathways. For example, many of the "tools" of Christian worship become not just external props, or emotionally evocative instigators, or educational inputs to be managed (like inputs to a computer). Rather, liturgy and its interactive elements serve to extend spiritual life beyond the capacities of individual participants, much as a conversation can extend the problem-solving capacities of individuals. During times of worship, participants *interface* with such corporate "tools" as oral Bible readings, corporate prayer, singing, teaching, and Eucharist. Engagement with such "tools" extends the spirituality of individual persons into the interactive worship space, making worship larger, richer, and more robust.

As we have seen, extension through interfaces leads to *incorporation* of the properties of extended space or tool into the sphere of the cognitive processing of an individual. When extension occurs into social space, we

---

and Richard Foster, *Celebration of Discipline: The Path to Spiritual Growth*, 25th Anniversary Edition (San Francisco: HarperCollins, 1998).

23. See Brown and Strawn, *Physical Nature of Christian Life*, chs. 7–9.

24. Nancey has explored the importance of communal discernment as an important but neglected practice in modern Christianity; see Nancey Murphy, *Theology in the Age of Scientific Reasoning* (Ithaca, NY: Cornell University Press, 1990) ch. 5; and in Murphy and Ellis, *Moral Nature*, 191–92.

can talk of *reciprocal incorporation*, with each person interfacing with and incorporating the space created by the interactive environment. The contributions of each individual enhances the quality of the ongoing interactions, while incorporation of the shared interactive space enhances (supersizes) the cognition of each participant. Similarly, reciprocal incorporation during corporate religious activity can enhance (supersized) spirituality. Corporate worship, for example, serves as an extension incorporated into the spiritual experience of each individual, as each individual contributes to the shared interactive space. What is more, it is through incorporation taking place during participation in Christian worship and life together that new embodied action schemas (action programs) come to be formed in individual persons.

Thus, elements of Christian worship, including all the liturgical aspects of a service (e.g., gathering of the church, proclamation and praise, responses and offerings, taking of the Eucharist, benediction and sending forth) are not simply ways to organize and direct individual spiritual experiences and promote individual Christian formation. As worshippers engage them, these tools can cease to be external events which separate congregants simultaneously "use," but rather worship and congregational life can become a new emergent in the form of a larger and more robust form of spiritual life that is incorporated by each participant.

However, our argument about spirituality becoming extended and supersized during corporate worship is contingent on the degree to which worshippers become actively incorporated into a shared liturgical space, rather than remaining isolated from interaction. Without interaction and consequent incorporation, worship is merely used remotely. Without incorporation nothing is supersized. While it is beyond the scope of this paper, further exploration is needed in order to adequately comprehend the issues around incorporation versus use in corporate worship.

Ideas of extended and situated cognition also reflect interestingly on a property of Christian faith that is of central importance in the theology of the church—that of belief. Clark and Chalmers also suggest that "*beliefs* can be constituted partly by features of the environment when those features play the right sort of role in driving cognitive processes."[25] We have already encountered their illustration of Otto's failing memory and his use of a notebook to enhance his faulty memory. These writers argue that the notebook should be given "epistemic credit" as a functional part of Otto's memory. Otto writes down all new information in his notebook and when he needs it he looks it up. Whereas a person with intact memory would sim-

---

25. Clark and Chalmers, "Extended Mind," 226.

ply consult their memory, Otto consults his notebook. While a person with intact memory believes, based on retrieval from biological memory, that a museum (for example) is located on a particular street, Otto also believes but it just happens that this belief is not in his head but in his notebook. Clark and Chalmers note that some might argue that Otto simply believes that the museum is located at the address *in* his notebook, and that the belief disappears as soon as he closes his notebook. But this is to miss how Otto actually lives, how he uses his notebook and how persons with normal memories utilize memory. In fact, both Otto's and a normal person's memory "disappear" when not in use. "In both cases the information is reliably there when needed, available to consciousness and available to guide action, in just the way that we expect a belief to be."[26] Furthermore the notebook is continuous for Otto just like a normal biological memory would be. It is just that this belief is not in Otto's head. "The moral is that when it comes to belief, there is nothing sacred about skull and skin. What makes some information count as a belief is the role it plays, and there is no reason why the relevant role can be played only from inside the body."[27]

In many respects, the church plays a similar role as Otto's notebook when it comes to religious belief. Much of the corporate life of the church must be given "epistemic credit" in the belief systems of Christians. What we believe often does not appear until some life activity demands it, at which point we reference what we have experienced in our life in the church among other believers. Clark and Chalmers would call this *socially extended cognition*, when one's "mental states are partly constituted by the states of other thinkers"—other thinkers who may be physically present, or written into the notebooks of our memories.[28] In an ecclesial body, the church's corporate beliefs can play the same role in the life of individuals as Otto's notebook. The church *holds* my beliefs, is the place where I go to be *reminded* of what I believe, even believes for me when I can't believe myself. And these beliefs are held, repeated, and referenced over and over via elements such as liturgical readings, creeds, songs, sermons, and the like.

Finally, Clark and Chalmers point out that language is especially important in extending human cognition. They argue that it is language that allows coupling to take place. "Without language, we might be much more akin to discrete Cartesian 'inner' minds, in which high-level cognition relies largely on internal resources. But the advent of language has allowed us to

---

26. Ibid., 227.
27. Ibid., 228.
28. Ibid., 231.

spread this burden into the world."[29] Particularly in the context of worship and corporate Christian life, much further work will be necessary to come to grips with language that can robustly promote engagement and interface in such a way as to enhance incorporation, versus language use that reinforces disengagement and isolation.

Extending Theology into the Mind of Nancey Murphy

This essay is written in celebration of the work of philosopher and theologian Nancey Murphy. For Christian theological anthropology, as well as for wider philosophical discussions, her work has been seminal in providing a rationale for thinking differently about the nature of human persons (e.g., nonreductive physicalism and emergence), as well as a catalyst for further exploration of new and exciting ways of understanding human nature and Christian life. Arguments for nonreductive physicalism have helped us distance ourselves far enough from the world of Cartesian dualism to be able to consider the nature of human embodiment, the power of social embeddedness, and the critical role of the body in all mental life, as well as the implications of these for Christian life. As another example of the thinking that Nancey has provoked, we have attempted in this essay to move even further into concepts of extended cognition and the degree to which the external world of artifacts and social engagement become functional parts of our minds, as well as our spiritual and religious lives.

---

29. Ibid., 232.

5

Practicing Religious Conversion
What Nancey Murphy Taught Me About Spiritual Development in a Physical World[1]

—Paul N. Markham

Religious conversion is a topic of broad interest. Not only do biblical scholars and theologians study the phenomenon, but social and cognitive scientists also show a great interest in exploring this notable experience. Conversion is often cited as the central point of religious identity—the *moment* or the *process* through which one becomes committed to a particular religious ideology and way of life. In the evangelical Christian tradition, the experience is often connected to Jesus's instruction to Nicodemus when he claims that "Very truly, I tell you, no one can see the kingdom of God without being born from above" (John 3:3, NRSV). Thus, the conversion experience is taken to be of central importance to soteriology (doctrinal issues concerning salvation) as well as a proper understanding of Christian discipleship. In addition to the theological and sociological explorations of religious conversion, researchers within the biological neurosciences have produced interesting work related to this experience. These scientific perspectives provide support for a process-oriented view of conversion that moves beyond basic religious experience and takes seriously socio-moral reorientation. Neuroscientific studies help us understand how significant religious change is constituted by complex neurobiological processes taking shape within personal, social, cultural, and religious contexts.

1. An earlier version of this chapter appeared in *Sacred Tribes Journal* 5:1 (2010) 5–24.

Nancey Murphy has cultivated an international dialogue at the intersection of science and religion. She represents the very best in what it means to take seriously the spiritual dimension of the human experience as well as insights that arise from rigorous scientific investigation. In the early days of my graduate education, Nancey's "nonreductive physicalism" challenged my view of human nature and pushed me to inextricably link my interest in *spiritual* development with a firm social ethic that emphasized the development of whole people. Since my time as Nancey's student, I have worked in ministry, higher education, and philanthropy. Through all these roles, I have maintained a constant commitment to social and moral development, which I learned from Nancey's life of intellectual curiosity and engagement with her students. I owe Nancey a great deal and hope this chapter will stand as a small sign of her legacy.

Conversion, Religious Studies, and Sociology

Conversion connotes a turning or reversal of course. The Hebrew term, *shubh*, refers primarily to the orientation of a people or the corporate response to a divine initiative. In the Old Testament, the term designates both a movement *from* and a turning *to*. In this way, conversion is understood to be an explicitly goal-oriented change toward God's will for God's people (cf. John 3:7–10). Here, the issue is not response to individual sin, but repetitive rejection of God's covenant by the people of Israel. Therefore, "conversion" in the Old Testament is not used in an evangelistic sense to refer to change in religion or personal faith; the primary concern, rather, is the maintenance of covenantal relationship.

As in Greek literature more widely, so in the New Testament, the concept of conversion is typically associated with the terms *metanoeo* ("to change one's course") or *epistrepho* ("to turn around"). On the basis of word-usage alone, however, a whole range of issues important to the interpreter remain ambiguous. Is "conversion" an event, a process, or both? Is conversion a cognitive or a moral category, or both? What is the relationship between "rejection of one way of life for another" and "embracing more fully the life one has chosen"?

Conversion in the New Testament often entails the recognition of and participation in the kingdom of God. Mark's summary of Jesus's proclamation is programmatic in this sense: "The time is fulfilled, and the kingdom of God has come near; repent, and believe in the good news" (Mark 1:15, NRSV). Transformation of this nature has both personal and social ramifications. The Gospels and Acts include a number of "conversion accounts," such as the conversions of Levi (Luke 5:27–32) and Paul (Acts 9:1–20), and texts in which the demands of repentance are highlighted (especially Luke 3:1–17), but we find in the New Testament no normative conversion scheme or formula. What we do find is that, from the standpoint of the overarching theme of soteriology, human response, which includes *metanoia*, is necessary for individuals to appropriate for themselves God's offer of salvation; and, that conversion refers to a change of thinking and believing that is itself inseparably tied to behavioral transformations (e.g., Luke 3:7–14).

These behavioral changes, which include welcoming into the community those whom God has accepted, are necessary for and instrumental in the establishment of the Christian community as recounted in Acts. In many cases, the emphasis of the conversion account is less on a crisis event, and more on a sustained participation with a divinely ordained community. Indeed, in Luke-Acts, where the language of conversion especially congregates, the purpose of Jesus's coming was "to guide our feet into the way of peace" (Luke 1:79), the gospel is the "way of salvation" (Acts 16:22), and the community of Jesus's followers are known as followers of "the Way" (Acts 9:2; 19:9, 23; 22:4; 24:14, 22), with the result that conversion is cast in the form of a "journey."

In biblical and theological studies, conversion has increasingly been understood in sociological terms. Donald Gelpi, for example, presents conversion as a "social process" consisting of seven stages: (1) settlement within a particular social context that sets the tone for the conversion experience, (2) experience of personal crisis, (3) personal crisis leads to religious quest, (4) religious quest leads to a connection with an advocate of a particular religious tradition, (5) interaction within the religious community, (6) religious commitment, and finally (7) recognition of the consequences of the religious commitment.[2] In this case, conversion is noted not only for producing interior change related to belief and conviction, but also for generating a significant ethical predisposition toward social transformation. Bernard Lonergan has spoken similarly of the multi-dimensional character of religious conversion by identifying the intellectual, religious, and moral elements of the overall phenomenon.[3] Indeed, Gelpi expanded Lonergan's typology to include the *socio-political* dimension that emphasizes a particularly important aspect of the conversion experience related to social transformation.

This social transformation is intimately connected with Jesus's proclamation of the kingdom of God. In this context, there is a tension between

---

2. Donald L. Gelpi, *The Conversion Experience: A Reflective Process for RCIA Participants and Others* (New York: Paulist, 1998).

3. Cf. Bernard Lonergan, *Method in Theology* (Toronto: University of Toronto Press, 1990).

God's role in the conversion experience and the subsequent mandate for the convert. Not only is there a change in religious allegiance, but there is also an acquired transformation in motivating desires. As one's life comes to be characterized by Christian virtues, the primary concern for the convert becomes the love of God and the love of neighbor, especially the neighbor in need. Therefore, to experience Christian conversion is not simply a juridical fact; rather, it is a holistic experience taking place within the context of a particular religious tradition that is marked by the acquisition of virtues having both internal and external significance.

Conversion and American Evangelicalism

In *The Unsettling of America*, Wendell Berry writes,

> For many of the churchly, the life of the spirit is reduced to a dull preoccupation with getting to heaven. At best, the world is no more than an embarrassment and a trial to the spirit which is otherwise radically separated from it. . . . As far as this sort of "religion" is concerned, the body is no more than the lustreless container of the soul, a mere "package" that will nevertheless light up in eternity, forever cool and shiny as a neon cross. This separation of the soul from the body and from the world is no disease of the fringe, no aberration, but a fracture that runs through the mentality of institutionalized religion like a geologic fault. And this rift in the mentality of religion continues to characterize the modern mind, no matter how secular or worldly it becomes. . . . And yet, what is the burden of the Bible if not a sense of the mutuality of influence, rising out of an essential unity, among soul and body and community and world?[4]

This excerpt from Berry points out a common characteristic of many Western religious traditions. Elsewhere, I have argued at length that this perspective suffers from an inadequate view of Christian spirituality.[5] This is particularly true of American evangelicalism, in which a number of strict dichotomies have developed—body and soul, heaven and hell, religious and secular, etc. Often times, spirituality is closely connected with a privatized and individualized form of religious experience that is primarily about self-

---

4. Wendell Berry, *Recollected Essays, 1965–1980* (San Francisco: North Point, 1981) 283–84.

5. Paul N. Markham, *Rewired: Exploring Religious Conversion* (Eugene, OR: Pickwick, 2007).

transformation and the purification of the inner life. In this case, the "self" becomes an essence that lives *inside* of us, consisting of personal thoughts, feelings, and reflections. For instance, as Owen Thomas has argued, "In the tradition of writing about the Christian life or spirituality, commonly known as ascetical theology, down to the present burgeoning of this literature, a pervasive emphasis and focus has been on the inner or interior life as distinct from the outer, bodily, and communal life."[6]

The dualistic interpretation of spirituality has far-reaching implications regarding Christian community orthopraxis and on how Christians conceive conversion, particularly within American evangelicalism. For many evangelicals, conversion is primarily presumed to occur instantaneously as God responds to prayerful petition. Conversion is then understood as receiving Jesus Christ as one's *personal* Lord and Savior and is subsequently characterized as a "personal relationship with God."[7] Conversion in this context is considered to be a change that occurs within the soul—hence the popular phrase "salvation of the soul."

In a sobering appraisal of North American evangelical Christianity, Mark Baker notes that evangelicals tend to read the Bible through an individualistic and spiritualized lens. This reading places the salvation of the soul at the center of the Christian faith. Such an understanding leads many evangelicals to interpret all aspects of Christian life in relation to this central idea. Baker comments that,

> Rather than seeing their individual salvation as part of a larger theme, like the kingdom of God, people attempt to understand the kingdom of God as a subcategory of individual salvation. They might only equate the kingdom of God with heaven or as something within the individual Christian. What cannot be brought into line with the central theme of future individual salvation is left as optional or secondary in the Christian life. As long as this lens is in place, much of the biblical holistic gospel will either be spiritualized, rejected or considered an appendix to the gospel.[8]

---

6. Owen C. Thomas, "Interiority and Christian Spirituality," *The Journal of Religion* 80:1 (2000) 41.

7. Cf. Larry Richards, *Born to Grow* (Wheaton: Scripture, 1977) 11.

8. Mark D. Baker, *Religious No More: Building Communities of Grace and Freedom* (Downers Grove: InterVarsity, 1999) 57. Evangelical historian Nathan Hatch shows the connection between American revivalism in the eighteenth and nineteenth centuries and the emergence of American individualism. For instance, Hatch notes that many early American evangelical leaders saw religion as "a matter between God and individuals"; cf. Nathan O. Hatch, *The Democratization of American Christianity* (New Haven: Yale University Press, 1989) 112.

The issue is not that individualism produces a society of social hermits. On the contrary, communities do form, but these are communities where the individual is primary to the group. C. Norman Kraus observes that in individualistic societies, "Community is seen as a contractual association of independent individuals.... The group [becomes] a collection of individuals created *by* individuals *for* their own individual advantages."[9] This condition creates a Christian culture that views the church as a community offering care for individual souls rather than serving the role of the visible kingdom of God in the world.

In a helpful analysis of American evangelicalism, James Davison Hunter notes the increasing methodization and standardization of spirituality within the evangelical tradition. Although Protestantism in the eighteenth and nineteenth centuries did display certain propensities for the rationalization of spirituality, Hunter notes that

> What is different about contemporary American Evangelicalism is the intensification of this propensity to unprecedented proportions. This intensification comes about as an adaptation to modern rationality. Thus one may note the increasing tendency to translate the specifically religious components of the Evangelical worldview, previously understood to be plain, self-evident, and without need of elaboration, into rigorously standardized prescriptions.[10]

In this way, the spiritual aspects of evangelical life are often interpreted in terms of "guidelines" or "laws." The means by which one enters the Christian faith can be systematized in this fashion. For example, in *How To Be Born Again*, Billy Graham offers the following "Four Steps to Peace with God":

> First, you must recognize what God did: that He loved you so much He gave His Son to die on the cross. Second, you must repent for your sins. It's not enough to be sorry; repentance is that turnabout from sin that is emphasized. Third, you must receive Jesus Christ as Savior and Lord. This means that you cease trying to save yourself and accept Christ without reservation. Fourth, you must confess Christ publicly. *This confession is a sign that you have been converted.*[11]

---

9. C. Norman Kraus, *The Community of the Spirit* (Scottdale: Herald, 1993) 32.

10. James D. Hunter, *American Evangelicalism: Conservative Religion and the Quandry of Modernity* (New Brunswick: Rutgers University Press, 1983) 74–75.

11. Billy Graham, *How to Be Born Again* (Waco: Word, 1977) 167–68. Italics added to emphasize the past tense "have been converted." This is an important feature of this notion of conversion—it is an instantaneous event that can be connected to a single

A similar methodological presentation can be seen in the writing of Bill Bright. Bright claims that "just as there are physical laws that govern the material universe, so are there spiritual laws which govern your relationship with God."[12] Conversion then occurs through acknowledging the validity of the *Four Spiritual Laws*,[13] and then by responding to specific instructions on how to "receive Jesus Christ as Savior and Lord"—an instruction also known as the *Sinner's Prayer*."[14]

This understanding of Christian conversion has not been left unchallenged, however. For instance, Lesslie Newbigin was a harsh critic of dualistic and individualistic characterizations of Christian life. Newbigin asserted that:

> The hope set before us in the gospel is fundamentally corporate, not individualistic. . . . This purely individualistic conception of the Kingdom robs human history as a whole of its meaning. According to this view, the significance of life in this world is exhaustively defined as the training of individual souls for heaven. Thus there can be no connected purpose running through history as a whole, but only a series of disconnected purposes for each individual life. History, on this view, would have no goal, no *telos*.[15]

---

moment in time. The case can be made that the fourth step is Graham's way of insuring that conversion is not a solely an *interior* experience. The point that I wish to emphasize here is that the coming forward in the mass revivals, for instance, is a way to publicly express that conversion has already occurred. The public proclamation (external) is simply a witness to the completed conversion moment (internal).

12. See the introduction to Bill Bright, *Four Spiritual Laws* (San Bernardino: Campus Crusade for Christ, 1965).

13. Law One: "God loves you, and offers a wonderful plan for your life." Law Two: "Man is sinful and separated from God. Therefore, he cannot know and experience God's love and plan for his life." Law Three: "Jesus Christ is God's only provision for man's sin. Through him you can know and experience God's love and plan for your life." Law Four: "We must individually receive Jesus Christ as Savior and Lord; then we can know and experience God's love and plan for our lives." Ibid.

14. "Lord Jesus, I need you. Thank You for dying on the cross for my sins. I open the door of my life and receive You as my Savior and Lord. Thank You for forgiving my sins and giving me eternal life. Take control of the throne of my life. Make me the kind of person You want me to be." Graham, *How to Be*, 287.

15. Lesslie Newbigin and Geoffrey Wainwright, *Signs Amid the Rubble: The Purposes of God in Human History* (Grand Rapids: Eerdmans, 2003) 24. Newbigin understands that, as a social philosophy, individualism stresses personal morality over social ethics and views individual transformation as the key to social change (mission)—a position that he is bound to reject. For more, see Dennis P. Hollinger, *Individualism and Social Ethics: An Evangelical Syncretism* (Lanham: University Press of America, 1983) 44.

The model of conversion that I present in this chapter is intended to reflect Newbigin's sentiment and to avoid the short-comings pointed out above. The neuroscientific research I will present below challenges the notion that conversion is an isolated affair of the individual "inner self" and supports a view of religious conversion as a significant social reorientation commensurate with a transformation of identity.

Conversion and the Neurosciences

It is important to note that the distinction between "inner" and "outer" is not equivalent to the distinction between soul and body. It is feasible that one could be a body-soul dualist and avoid an excessively inward-oriented spirituality. Furthermore, it is also possible for one with a physicalist anthropology to ignore the responsibilities of "Kingdom work" by retreating to solitude, self-examination, and contemplation. The type of religious conversion described here should not be understood as merely "salvation of the soul," but as the holistic process of socio-moral transformation of a person within the context of a religious community. Conversion, in this sense, is not simply about a "correct" system of beliefs, but *necessarily* involves a transformation in socio-moral attitude and behavior.

While I reject the notion that humans lack freedom in the sense of classic behaviorism, I do embrace the idea that we are socially determined selves—that is, that there is no "me" without "you." Such a conviction renders the Christian life less about proper belief and more about vital relationships. I argue that religious conversion should be considered a *process* of moral formation that (1) involves normal human biological capacities, (2) is characterized by a change in socio-moral attitude and behavior, (3) is best understood as the acquisition of virtues intrinsic to a particular religious tradition, and in a theological sense, (4) should be viewed as the co-operant result of divine grace and human participation. To speak of religious conversion as a biological process deserves further elaboration.

As I mentioned above, it is common among many religious adherents to imagine a separation between the spiritual and the physical; however, neuroscientists are, at a rapid rate, presenting data indicating that many of the faculties once attributed to the mind or soul can now be explained as complex functions of the human brain. There are a number of such examples available from within the field of neuroscience. Many scholars with interest in both science and theology consider the cognitive sciences to have great potential for advances in theological thought. Gregory Peterson suggests that "all forms of theology stand to be affected by a serious dialogue with the cognitive sciences. Insofar as methodology and content are connected, the content of the cognitive sciences can affect the way we go about *doing* theology."[16] Of particular interest to this chapter are neuroscientific investigations of moral attitude and behavior.

Human moral behavior—how we relate in a social context—is of great concern to religious adherents. At the center of the Christian faith rests a mandate for proper relation toward God and creation. Such "spiritual" relationships have traditionally been viewed as faculties of the soul. This area of human experience, once left completely to the realm of religious thought (and later included within the scope of psychology), has now been taken under investigation by neuroscientists.

Researchers are uncovering intrinsic links between biology and morality. Research from neuroscience has demonstrated that moral reasoning and behavior is dependent upon the proper function of various subsystems within the brain, particularly in the prefrontal cortex.[17] This aspect of human functioning, once inaccessible to science, can now be investigated via various experimental techniques.[18] Some neuroscientists believe that these new technological advances will unlock the deepest secrets of the human species and eventually render the insights gained from religion obsolete.[19] The point of a neurobiological explanation of religious conversion is not to argue against the existence of a soul per se; rather, the aim is to emphasize the embodied nature of human existence.

In this case, becoming a Christian convert necessarily involves the formation of socio-moral attitude and behavior characteristic of a particular religious tradition. In simple terms, conversion is a *visible* process. This is a clear challenge to the notion that individual Christian faith is developed by adopting beliefs that then lead to an alternate form of social life. Conversion,

---

16. Gregory R. Peterson, *Minding God: Theology and the Cognitive Sciences* (Minneapolis: Fortress, 2003) 12.

17. Leslie Brothers is credited for being a catalyst for much of the present work regarding neuroscience and social interaction. See Leslie Brothers, "The Social Brain: A Project for Integrating Primate Behaviour and Neurophysiology in a New Domain," *Concepts in Neuroscience* 1 (1990) 27–51.

18. Neuroscientists use a number of experimental techniques to gather relevant data. The most common and reliable techniques involve neuroimaging.

19. Truett Allison says that "as we learn more about the development and operation of the system for social cognition . . . it is likely, perhaps even desirable, that the domain of understanding provided by neuroscience, evolutionary psychology, and cultural anthropology will expand, while the domain that is properly a function of ethics and religion will shrink." See Truett Allison, "Neuroscience and Morality," *Neuroscientist* 7:5 (2001) 360–64.

from a biological perspective, requires that religious *character* be formed through social contexts that constitute self-identity.

Human beings have acquired a level of biological complexity that allows for the emergence of "higher order" capacities such as morality and moral behavior that are honed through a process of symbolic interaction.[20] The complex evolution of the human brain has led to capacities particular to human behavior, and thus the emergence of scientific disciplines, which focus on the brain and cognition. Various disciplines within the cognitive sciences are dedicated to investigating human cognition. At an increasing rate, brain sciences are permeating many scientific disciplines resulting in the emergence of new fields of investigation—such as neuropsychology, social cognitive neuroscience, and even neurotheology. These all point to the significance of the human brain in complex functioning.

My most basic claim is that religious conversion must somehow involve our physical or *embodied* selves—that is, it must in some way be a change recognizable at a biological level of investigation. We must have a way of conceiving of moral sentiment and action within a biological framework and understand the inextricable connection between biology and moral character. In other words, I am suggesting that conversion be seen as occurring in a "normative" fashion such that biological constraints must be considered.

A biologically rooted view of conversion involves the consideration of three interrelated levels: (1) the *phenomenal level* (the occurrence of religious conversion), (2) the *cognitive level* (the components of a moral cognition), and (3) the *neural level* (the biological correlates of moral cognition).[21] Here, "moral cognition" generally refers to what researchers in the field of social cognitive neuroscience refer to as *social cognition*. The two are equivalent insofar as they both deal with the neural underpinnings of human socio-moral behavior.

---

20. For an excellent resource on the issue see Terrence W. Deacon, *The Symbolic Species: The Co-Evolution of Language and the Brain* (New York: W. W. Norton Company, 1998).

21. While I assume it to be true that *some* relationship exists between various brain areas and moral cognition, I am quick to point out that identifying such neural mechanisms is difficult. I hold that the exercise of moral sentiment and judgment in humans requires multiple cognitive processes and is ultimately an affair of the entire brain and body. In other words, I do not claim that moral cognition is "in the head" or is the result of any particular module within the brain; this would be an example of what Nancey, expanding on a phrase from Daniel Dennett, has called "Cartesian materialism"; cf. Nancey Murphy and Warren S. Brown, *Did My Neurons Make Me Do It? Philosophical and Neurobiological Perspectives on Moral Responsibility and Free Will* (New York: Oxford University Press, 2007) ch. 1.

The "neural correlates" of moral cognition refer to a collection of data that points to particular areas within the brain that appear to be "correlated" with various levels of socio-moral attitude and behavior. Jorge Moll and his colleagues suggest that the present state of neuroscientific research points to the existence of brain networks specialized for the generation of moral emotions.[22] Such emotions are integral to the formation and implementation of moral action.

From this perspective, religious conversion is considered a process-oriented change in socio-moral attitude and behavior. This process of change is commensurate with a reorganization of neurobiological substrate and as such can be characterized as neuroplastic in nature. The ability of the brain and certain parts of the nervous system to respond and adapt to new conditions is called *neural plasticity*.[23]

Specifically, neural plasticity refers to the formation, breakdown, and re-formation of neural synapses, and the subsequent changes in brain function. Synapses are formed or reinforced as an individual experiences or performs particular actions—such actions stimulate simultaneous activity of the presynaptic and postsynaptic neurons. In contrast, synapses dissolve as neural links become less active due to the lack of corresponding experiences or actions. As this process of formation and breakdown occurs, localized subsystems within the brain change and as a result become more or less capable of performing certain tasks.

Research in brain plasticity is well known in the field of neuroscience. In fact, the nineteenth-century scientist Santiago Ramón y Cajal early on described the brain's ability to adapt to environmental change.

> When one reflects on the ability that humans display for modifying and refining mental activity related to a problem under serious examination, it is difficult to avoid concluding that the brain is plastic and goes through a process of anatomical and functional differentiation, adapting itself progressively to the problem. . . . In a certain sense, it would not be paradoxical to

---

22. Jorge Moll et al., "The Neural Correlates of Moral Sensitivity: A Functional Magnetic Resonance Imaging Investigation of Basic and Moral Emotions," *The Journal of Neuroscience* 22:7 (2002) 2730–36. Also see Jorge Moll et al., "Functional Networks in Emotional Moral and Nonmoral Social Judgments," *NeuroImage* 16 (2002) 696–703.

23. I use the term *neuroplasticity* or *neural plasticity* in a *descriptive* fashion. By this, I mean that I am characterizing the change by using this term. I am thereby not implying any causal explanation. In other words, I am not saying that neural plasticity *causes* conversion, nor am I saying that neural plasticity *is* conversion in the sense of a type-identity relationship. I am simply saying that a physicalist account of the person requires that a psychological change be commensurate with a change in brain state. I am using the term "neural plasticity" to describe this relationship.

> say that the person who initiates the solution to a problem is different from the one who solves it.[24]

It is obvious that human beings are able to adapt to a multitude of environmental fluctuations. While there has long been research showing neural plasticity and neurogenesis in various areas of the somatosensory and visual cortices, hippocampus, and the like, little research has been done on neural plasticity and changes in personality. Jim Grigsby and David Stevens discuss synaptic (neural) plasticity in such a context. They claim that,

> Personality is shaped by the interaction of constitutional processes and the experiences of individuals in unique environments. In other words, we are, at least in part, who we learn to be. As a result of these experiences, learning drives the acquisition and refinement of a wide repertoire of enduring perceptions, attitudes, thoughts, and behaviors. The relative permanence of learning and memory reflects the operation of processes that modify the microscopic structure of the brain, yielding changes in different aspects of functioning over time as a result of the individual's interactions with the world. These experience-dependent changes in brain structure and functioning are known by the general term *synaptic plasticity*.[25]

While it is unclear precisely how neuroplastic changes occur in the brain, there is wide agreement that a structural change of some kind occurs at the synaptic level in response to experience.[26] The effect of physical experiences alters the probability that an action potential from a presynaptic neuron will lead to a discharge in a postsynaptic neuron. Grigsby and Stevens continue by saying that,

> On a functional level, the effect of synaptic plasticity is a change in probabilities. Learning induces structural changes that make it either more or less likely that stimulation of a given neuron or

---

24. Santiago Ramón y Cajal, *Advice for a Young Investigator*, translated by Neely Swanson and Larry W. Swanson (Cambridge, MA: MIT Press, 1999) 35.

25. Jim Grigsby and David Stevens, *Neurodynamics of Personality* (New York: Guilford, 2000) 39.

26. One of the most popular notions of how learning (neural plasticity) occurs in the brain was offered a number of years ago by Donald Hebb. He suggested that "the persistence or repetition of a reverberatory activity (or 'trace') tends to induce lasting cellular changes that add to its stability.... When an axon of cell A is near enough to excite a cell B and repeatedly or persistently takes part in firing it, some growth process or metabolic change takes place in one or both cells such that A's efficiency, as one of the cells firing B, is increased." Donald O. Hebb, *The Organization of Behaviour: A Neuropsychological Theory* (New York: Wiley, 1949) 62.

(more accurately) a population of neurons will cause the stimulated neurons to fire. . . . The probabilities are determined to a large extent by the overall state of the individual at any given time. Changing one's state can reset the probabilities for almost all kinds of behavioural, perceptual, cognitive, and mnestic activity.[27]

In other words, the repetition of actions realized by particular brain states has the effect of making the same actions more likely to occur in the future. Perhaps the best example of neuroplastic change is the process of *learning*. Take, for example, learning to play the piano or learning to ride a bicycle. To learn either involves a process of trial and error that is usually a slow and tedious business. Such exemplifies the nature of neuroplastic change—a gradual process of training resulting in the reorganization of neurobiological substrate on which particular skills supervene.

Conversion and Moral Learning

Given the above discussion, I claim that religious conversion can be understood—from a neurobiological point of view—as the *learning* of new skills characterized by a tendency toward a particular moral attitude and behavior. Such learning should be considered a process involving neuroplastic changes in the complex neurobiological substrates necessary for a particular type of socio-moral cognition.

This embodied view of conversion dramatically affects the way one approaches moral development in a given religious tradition. The model of conversion that I present here is not understood as an instantaneous change of personality associated with a crisis religious experience; rather, I claim that, when the biological nature of human persons is taken seriously, conversion is best understood as a process of personal moral formation within a communal context. As individuals are exposed to a community that disciplines their socio-moral behavior, their physical neurobiology is changed (or *converted*) as a result.

This is radically different than the notion that humans aspire to principles that lead to a reasoned decision to execute this or that moral judgment. In that case, religious conversion is contingent upon possessing a particular knowledge that guides decision-making. While I do not discount the importance of individual decisions, I do assert that religious life is less about making positive moral decisions than it is about developing enduring dispositions to perceive, feel, think, and act in a manner consistent with

27. Grigsby and Stevens, *Neurodynamics*, 53.

the virtues of a particular religious tradition (e.g., to *be* a loving person). Furthermore, I argue that the goal of a mature conversion experience is to act in these virtuous manners *automatically*, given that the majority of our daily lives are spent doing things automatically, without focused attention. Just as we drive, type, or get dressed with a high level of automaticity, we can also develop habits that predispose us toward certain *moral* attitudes and behaviors. The embodied model of religious conversion that I am espousing depends less on "making up one's mind" to be a convert than it does on the development of habits that supervene on the creation of certain neurobiological states—morality isn't just an idea, it is an anatomy.

In an evangelical Christian context, all of this is to stress the importance of the shared life that we call "church." This community is all too often considered to be a helpful gathering for the convert to learn the vital teachings of the Christian faith and to exercise post-conversion fellowship. While these are certainly important, it is imperative to stress the role of the church in the conversion process itself. This is certainly not a new idea, given the third-century assertion *extra ecclesiam nulla salus*—"outside the Church there is no salvation." The community of the church provides the context necessary to form the virtues required to become a proper convert of the Christian tradition.

Particular religious communities play a vital role in the formation of the *narrative self*. The basic premise underlying the concept of the "narrative self" is the conviction that narratives or stories are a necessary component to understand the self, social groups, and their histories. It follows that our sense of morality or *character* consists less of rules or principles and more as collections of stories about human possibilities and paradigms for action. These stories allow us to orient ourselves in the world by disclosing who we are, where we have been, and where we are going.

Despite the tendency to regard the self as being detached from societies and personal history, I claim that a more adequate conception of the self "resides in the unity of a narrative which links birth to life to death as narrative beginning to middle to end."[28] In this sense, human actions are not isolated events independent of a person's intentions, beliefs, and historical context; rather, action flows from a position within particular narratives. The idea that particular actions derive their character from larger wholes is a necessary concept if we are to consider how life may be more than simply

---

28. Alasdair MacIntyre, *After Virtue: A Study in Moral Theory* (Notre Dame: University of Notre Dame Press, 1981) 205. I contend that MacIntyre offers the best account of the "narrative self" and his or her status as a moral agent; thus, I will frequently return to his work.

a sequence of individual actions. In this regard, Alasdair MacIntyre claims that,

> Man is in his actions and practice, as well as in his fictions, essentially a story-telling animal. He is not essentially, but becomes through his history, a teller of stories that aspire to truth. But the key question for men is not about their own authorship; I can only answer the question, "What am I to do?" if I can answer the prior question, "Of what story or stories do I find myself a part?"[29]

This sentiment is echoed by cognitive psychologist John Teske. Teske speaks of the "social construction of the human spirit" as a way to talk about the interdependent emergence of individual minds. He claims that "any integrity that we have as spiritual beings is likely also to be an achievement contingent upon the character of our relationships with other persons, and our memberships in larger communities."[30] In this sense, if human lives are historically developed constructions, it is possible to realize the transformation of these lives in various ways by recognizing relevant social interdependencies as a key source of human behavior.

The concept of the "narrative self" suggested by MacIntyre and Teske does justice to the embodied view of human nature that I have espoused throughout this chapter. We are persons only in so far as we exist as narrative selves in complex social networks with other persons. Likewise, our *character* is formed (or transformed) through shared narratives set within a historical framework.

MacIntyre asserts that virtues are understood only within the context of particular narratives and types of *practices*. He defines a practice as:

> any coherent and complex form of socially established cooperative human activity through which goods internal to that form of activity are realized in the course of trying to achieve those standards of excellence which are appropriate to, and practically definitive of, that form of activity, with the result that human

---

29. Ibid., 216. This claim reflects MacIntyre's central argument that the "Enlightenment project" of grounding morality within the individual limits of reason alone has failed miserably. He contends that the way out of this predicament is to return to an Aristotelian ethic of virtue with its particular teleological character. A key aspect of this renewal is found in MacIntyre's treatment of narrative (although the concept of narrative is not explicit in Aristotle's work).

30. John A. Teske et al., "The Social Construction of the Human Spirit," in *The Human Person in Science and Theology* (Grand Rapids: Eerdmans, 2000) 189. By "human spirit" Teske is referring to "that aspect of human mental life by which we can apprehend meanings and purposes extending beyond our individual lives"; ibid., 190.

powers to achieve excellence, and human conceptions of the ends and goods involved, are systematically extended.[31]

Practices provide the context in which virtues can be understood. MacIntyre proposes that a *virtue* be defined as "an acquired human quality the possession and exercise of which tends to enable us to achieve those goods which are internal to practices and the lack of which effectively prevents us from achieving any such goods."[32]

Here, virtues serve as the *intentional* content of practices, which in turn constitute cooperative forms of human inter-relational activity. In other words, virtues can be seen as the motivational force (or skill) behind practices particular to a given tradition. The concept of tradition is also critical to MacIntyre's account of a social or moral agent. The story of one's life (self-identity) is inextricably embedded in a community of collective stories held together by a common understanding—or narrative tradition. MacIntyre claims that,

> A living tradition is then an historically extended, socially embodied argument, and an argument precisely in part about the goods which constitute that tradition.... Hence the individual's search for his or her good is generally and characteristically conducted within a context defined by those traditions of which the individual's life is a part, and this is true both of those goods which are internal to practices and the goods of a single life. ... The narrative phenomenon of embedding is crucial.... The history of each of our lives is generally and characteristically embedded in and made intelligible in terms of the larger and longer histories of a number of traditions.[33]

---

31. MacIntyre, *After Virtue*, 187. It is important to note that practices themselves require moral evaluation based on their contribution to the *telos* of human existence. That is, in terms of a moral theory, any practical "ought" is to be evaluated in light of the ultimate end to which all virtuous action is to achieve. Nancey writes that "the original form of an ethical claim (implicitly, at least) is, 'if you are to achieve your *telos*, then you ought to do (or be) *x*.' This sort of ethical claim can be straightforwardly true or false; the 'ought' is no more mysterious than the 'ought' in 'a watch ought to keep good time.' Furthermore, it can and in fact *must* be derived from certain sorts of 'is' statements: about the nature of ultimate reality, about regularities in human life regarding the achievement of ends as a result of adopting certain means." See Nancey Murphy and Robert John Russell, "Supervenience and the Nonreducibility of Ethics to Biology," in *Evolutionary and Molecular Biology: Scientific Perspectives on Divine Action*, edited by Robert John Russell (Vatican City: Vatican Observatory, 1998) 485.

32. MacIntyre, *After Virtue*, 191.

33. Ibid., 222. MacIntyre further describes a tradition as "an argument extended through time in which certain fundamental agreements are defined and redefined in terms of two kinds of conflict: those with critics and enemies external to the tradition

Only when we know the narrative traditions of which we are a part can we know what we are to do. I suggest that religious communities embody a "narrative tradition" in so far as it satisfies the description offered by MacIntyre. That is, Christianity is a "historically extended, socially embodied argument" whose existence implies that a distinction cannot be made between communal beliefs and practices. These practices require virtues intrinsic to the Christian faith—that is, they require that an individual be a particular "kind of person" characterized by these virtues that are subsequently enacted within the context of a particularly Christian way of relating.

I have argued that much of socio-moral attitude and behavior can be considered intuitive and occurring automatically, particularly in regards to underlying motivations and inclinations, and that this entire realm of socio-moral functioning is dependent upon our biology. In this sense, the formation or transformation of socio-moral attitude and behavior should be seen as a process likened to learning or skill acquisition. Similarly, in their commentary on *Intuitive Ethics*, Jonathan Haidt and Craig Joseph state that

> Virtues are social skills. To possess a virtue is to have disciplined one's faculties so they are fully and properly responsive to one's local sociomoral context. To be kind, for example, is to have a perceptual sensitivity to certain features of situations, including those having to do with the well-being of others, and to be sensitive such that those features have an appropriate impact on one's motivations and other responses. . . . Virtues, on this understanding, are closely connected to the intuitive system. A virtuous person is one who has the proper *automatic* reactions to ethically relevant events and states of affairs.[34]

Thus can it be said that a virtue (or virtuous behavior) supervenes on a particular human biological or psychological (depending on the level of analysis) characteristic (or event). Recall that MacIntyre defines a virtue as an *acquired* human quality; it follows that virtues are not genetically

---

. . . and those internal, interpretive debates through which the meaning and rationale of the fundamental agreements come to be expressed and by whose progress a tradition is constituted." Alasdair MacIntyre, *Whose Justice? Which Rationality?* (Notre Dame: University of Notre Dame Press, 1988) 12.

34. Jonathan Haidt and Craig Joseph, "Intuitive Ethics: How Innately Prepared Intuitions Generate Culturally Variable Virtues," *Daedalus* (2004) 61, emphasis added. Likewise, Greg Jones argues that people "*learn* to acquire and exercise the virtues ingredient in making wise decisions. Such learning occurs in and through social contexts of particular linguistic communities." See L. Gregory Jones, *Transformed Judgment: Toward a Trinitarian Account of the Moral Life* (Notre Dame: University of Notre Dame Press, 1990) 2.

determined traits, but should be seen as habitually cultivated behavioral states based on genetically produced biological propensities.

In this case, acquiring a virtue refers to a complex process involving the re-interpretation of particular biological propensities in relation to a specific tradition-dependent purpose or *telos*. This transformation occurs through social interaction and participation in practices inherent to a particular religious community. Therefore, the process of becoming a religious convert necessarily involves *active* participation that transcends mere intellectual assent and the notion that proper belief leads to proper action.

This conviction is primarily motivated and bolstered by an understanding of the physical nature of humans. In an analysis of ethical training, John Bickle asserts that

> Ethical training in a behavioral vacuum (other than speech production and comprehension) is likely not to have much effect on people's behavior. . . . Better to get people to practice planning and executing the specific motor sequences desired, rather than training them to construct more sophisticated moral narratives. . . . One must perform the appropriate actions repeatedly to acquire the moral virtues. Theory and argument—narratives, both internal and verbally expressed—won't suffice. Our increased knowledge of the diverse neural mechanisms that underlie speech production and comprehension on one hand and planning and motor execution on the other puts us a step ahead of Aristotle toward understanding why theory and arguments (narratives) are less efficient for inculcating virtue than is practice (actually performing the planning and acting).[35]

In essence, "beliefs" are most often implicitly adopted following instantiation into a set of practices that makes belief intelligible in the first place. Our wonderful biological selves make experiential learning critical to moral formation, such that action leads to belief, which then leads to further action, and on and on.

Conclusion

In a spirit true to Nancey, the primary aim of this chapter has been descriptive in nature—to provide a viable explanation for how religious conversion can be understood in the context of increasing scientific discovery about

---

35. John Bickle et al., "Empirical Evidence for a Narrative Concept of Self," in *Narrative and Consciousness: Literature, Psychology, and the Brain* (New York: Oxford University Press, 2003) 82.

the nature of human beings. In addition to this central goal, I have pursued a secondary and more prescriptive goal. The material above emphasizes the physical nature of human beings and describes the extent to which notions of philosophical anthropology deeply affect held concepts of spirituality. The ramifications of this argument extend beyond academic reflection to the intimate practicalities of Christian ministry. If my argument is taken seriously, the business of clergy becomes to ensure the integrity of the community's religious practices and to pursue means of actualizing potentially abstract notions such as peace and love.

This more prescriptive aim is meant to challenge any notions of Christian discipleship (common in many Christian churches) that place a premium on intellectual pursuit over practical experience. While proper ethical reasoning is necessarily an intellectual exercise, the emphasis should be on the *process* by which one is formed in the faith and the *community* in which the formation occurs. The same point can be made regarding many notions of evangelism understood as an act wholly separate from discipleship (in most cases these are sequential in nature—*first* one is "evangelized," and *then* one becomes a disciple). If moral formation is truly a biological process, then development in religious life exists on a continuum determined by particular formative communities. In short, participants are *continually being converted*. Consideration of the physically embodied model of conversion presented in this chapter supports critical reflection on what it means to *act* for peace in a time of war, or to love the poor by *serving* them. Of course, as Nancey has taught me, these are not challenges for individuals, but for communities who are interested in practicing religious conversion in a physical world.

6

Then Sings My Soul

—Brad J. Kallenberg

> What must the world be like, what must I be like, if between me
> and the world the phenomenon of music can occur?
>
> —Victor Zuckerkandl

WELL-MEANING EVANGELICALS UNFAMILIAR WITH Nancey Murphy's philosophical theology frequently worry that her work in philosophy of mind has the effect of depriving us of our souls. When such an objection is voiced after a speaking engagement, Murphy's "reassurance" is predictable: "Don't worry! There is nothing to be lost; we never had souls to begin with!"[1]

Underneath her wry reply is a deep concern that philosophical confusion about "having a soul" is seriously undermining Christian discipleship. For example, it has become second nature for many Christians to hold that the soul is more important than the body; regardless of the state of one's body, the state of one's soul is what really counts. Using this line of reasoning, St. Augustine (d. 430) concluded that the rape of women by invading barbarians did not cost them their chastity. He reasoned that chastity is primarily a property of the soul that becomes the body's by association: "not

---

1. I am extremely thankful for the many helpful comments made by my generous colleagues Aaron James, Colin McGuigan, D. Michael Cox, Elizabeth Farnsworth, Ethan Smith, Jason Hentschel, and Lucas Martin.

only the souls of Christian women who have been forcibly violated during their captivity, but also their bodies, remain holy."[2]

Augustine's conclusion seems forced, to say the least. But the line of reasoning that cannot but bifurcate bodies and souls can be avoided if we reconsider where to imagine the dividing line between the "inner" and the "outer." It is without question that human experience is marked by both "inner" and "outer" aspects. (I cannot feel your pain in the same way you feel it.) The question is *where* best to locate the dividing line. I cannot deny the popularity of the dualistic picture, which sees the dividing line "in here" (pointing to one's head or heart) as it were, between body and mind (or soul). But there is another way to understand the dividing line.

I begin with the suggestion (following Stephen Mulhall[3]) that the primary dividing line between "inner" and "outer" is not between *soul* and *body*. Rather the dividing line is better understood as lying between *body* and *surroundings*. This is not a bright, red line but a fuzzy boundary constituted by a set of "skins." After explaining the concept of "skins," I will argue that both language and technology function as "skins" in distinctive ways. The upshot of my reasoning is that "soul" is not something we have but something we are. The difference in these verbs, "have " and "are," connotes a difference between *substance* and *time*. In surrendering the notion of *souls-as-substance*, Murphy is not obligating herself to deny the notion of *souls-as-timeful*. I end with a comparison of the grammars of "time" and "soul" by considering the nature of music.

An Alternative Model to Dualism: Body-World

In biological terms, we call the surface that demarcates body from world our "skin." If skin is taken to be the dividing line, then everything under the skin is presumed, functionally at least, to be a unity—not two parts, but one. I assume this as my starting point: humans are *bodysouls* (or perhaps "soulish bodies").[4] In short I am proposing that we deliberately abandon anthropological dualism (Figure 1) in favor of anthropological holism (Figure 2):

---

2. St. Augustine, *City of God*, 1.16–19, translated by Gerald G. Walsh, et al., edited by Vernon J. Bourke (Garden City, NY: Doubleday, 1960) 53. For an earlier version of this argument see Brad J. Kallenberg, "Holistic Spirituality as Witness," in *Vital Christianity: Justice, Spirituality, and Christian Practice*, edited by David L. Weaver-Zercher and William H. Willimon (New York & London: T. & T. Clark, 2005).

3. Stephen Mulhall, *Wittgenstein's Private Language: Grammar, Nonsense, and Imagination in Philosophical Investigations §§243–315* (Oxford, UK: Clarendon, 2007).

4. Thus Wittgenstein's observation, "The human body is the best picture of the human soul." Ludwig Wittgenstein, *Philosophical Investigations*, edited by G. E. M.

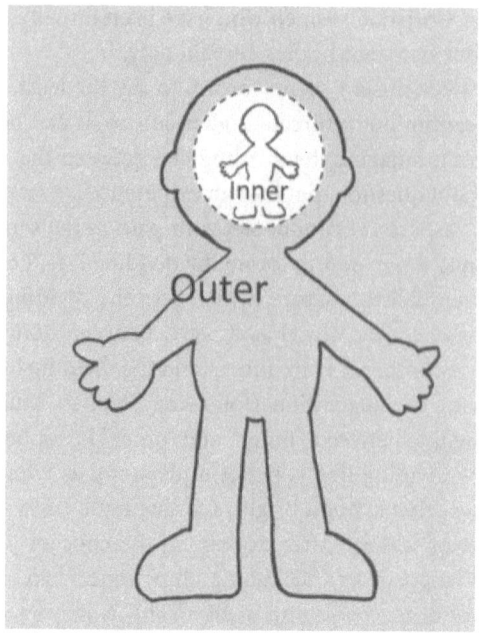

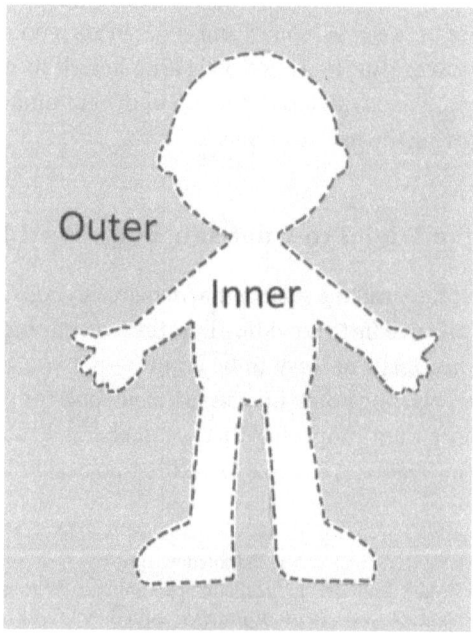

Anscombe and Rush Rhees, translated by G. E. M. Anscombe (New York: Macmillan, 1953) Part II.iv, 178. For contemporary trends in philosophy of mind see Warren S. Brown, Nancey Murphy, and H. Newton Malony, eds., *Whatever Happened to the Soul? Scientific and Theological Portraits of Human Nature* (Minneapolis: Fortress, 1998).

The latter picture makes "skin" the crucial dividing line between the "inner" and the "outer" dimensions of human experience.

The epidermis, of course, is only one of our skins. The epidermis is the interface between us and the *tactile* world. If all we had were tactile sensations, the world would seem to us very thin, for most tactile events take place on or near the surface.[5] The olfactory "world" for human beings is a bit further out. The olfactory skin, as it were, is "thicker." Sometimes, though not always, we can smell something stinky before we step in it. Some smells (e.g., ammonia, fresh brewed coffee, *Pinesol*) fill the entire room. Of course, the human sense of smell is nothing compared to that of a bloodhound, or a shark, or a bear.

The "skins" of our eyes and ears reach much, much farther than our tactile and olfactory skins. Here again our visual and aural worlds are nothing compared to eagles or beagles. But compared to our own tactile and olfactory senses, the "skins" of our seeing and hearing are extremely baggy—the outer extent of "me" has a greater range.

Language as Skin

It is in this spirit that Herbert McCabe writes of language as "skin."[6] As each of our sensory skins are interfaces between a person and his or her respective surroundings, so too is language. Both kinds of skin, sensory and linguistic, are means by which our surroundings are "taken up" by us, become meaningful to us, become significant for us.

When I lived in densely populated southern California, I encountered an astonishing variety of animals while on long trail runs in the foothills: bobcats, rattlesnakes, deer, bear, owls, and, most surprisingly, entire flocks of sheep! Imagine that on one such run, I and the flock of sheep espy a wolf.[7] For both the sheep and I, the wolf is significant; its presence spells danger. The meaningfulness of the wolf is "taken up" by means of sensory skins by both the sheep and me. At the moment of sensory perception the sheep and I share a world of significances, a world of meanings; we are "in communion," we are *co-munus, same world*. Thus we both react as we are apt to do—nostrils flare, muscles tense, eyes widen, head rears, heartbeat quick-

---

5. Exceptions would include temperature gradients which can be detected as we approach hot objects.

6. Herbert McCabe, *Law, Love, and Language* (New York: Continuum, 2004) 74.

7. The illustration is McCabe's; see his "Soul, Life, Machines and Language," in *Faith within Reason*, edited and introduced by Brian Davies; foreword by Denys Turner (London: Continuum, 2007) 123–49.

ens. However, unlike the sheep, I have another skin, the skin of language. The wolf's meaning is also taken up by means of my linguistic skin. Unlike my other skins, which are more or less tight fitting, the "skin" of language is loose fitting, extending much farther than eyesight and earshot—it circles the globe and extends backwards in history. I have listened to tales around campfires, watched NOVA, read scientific accounts, and even heard music recounting the behavior of wolves. In the linguistic world the wolf is also significant. But this is not a world that I can share with the sheep ("Well, Dolly, things are looking baaaaaad for us!"). I have read and heard that the wolf is one of the only other mammals that, like humans, hunts in the daylight and *hunts in packs.* So the sheep, who cannot help but flee directly from the lone wolf will unwittingly run directly into the teeth of the rest of the pack while I, running orthogonally (at 90°), may escape both the scout and its pack.

On McCabe's account, the shared world-of-meanings (*co-munus*) of language is of a higher order than the shared world (*co-munus*) of animal senses. I share the latter with other mammals; I share the former with other language-speakers. There is an asymmetrical relationship between the two. The sensory world is, in an important sense, the "material basis" for the linguistic world.[8] (It is because we naturally squint at bright lights that the word "bright" is used in the way we use it.) Yet the linguistic world is of a higher order than that available to other animals.[9] The linguistic world does not and cannot be reduced to sensory meanings any more than a sphere, which exists in three dimensions, could be exhaustively explained to someone living in "Flatland."[10] Yet in both animal and linguistic worlds, there are sets of interfaces between you and your surroundings. To recall: I am proposing that the crucial dividing line between you and your surroundings is not that between "mind" and "body," a division "in here" (head

---

8. I might have equally said that human language "supervenes" upon bodily senses so long as "supervenience" is understood in a non-reductive way. I'm indebted to the extension Nancey Murphy has given to the philosophy of mind of Jaegwon Kim. See, for example, Nancey Murphy, "Nonreductive Physicalism: Philosophical Issues," in *Whatever Happened to the Soul?*, 127–48; "Supervenience and the Downward Efficacy of the Mental: A Nonreductive Physicalist Account of Human Action," in *Neuroscience and the Person: Scientific Perspectives on Divine Action*, edited by Robert John Russell et al. (Vatican City: Vatican Observatory, 1999) 147–64.

9. Except, perhaps, the dog. Of all mammals, dogs alone have the natural ability to read human faces and follow the gesture of our pointing—even when we point with our eyes! Even Koko the gorilla could not learn to follow this simple gesture of pointing. See Dan Child, "Dogs Decoded," in *NOVA* (9 Nov 2010).

10. Edwin A. Abbot, "Flatland: A Romance of Many Dimensions," Public domain, http://www.math.brown.edu/~banchoff/gc/Flatland/.

or heart), but a set of *skins* between your body and your surroundings. It is this image that will help us get clearer on the possibility of one more skin: Technology.

Technology as Skin

In order for it to function as a skin, Technology must be seen as a vast system in which human beings are today embedded. When attempting to define "Technology" with a capital "T," it is helpful to think in terms of mereological systems, systems of parts whose properties emerge at increasing levels of complexity.[11] To choose a familiar example, the basic building block of material stuff is (say) the atom and each atom possesses certain properties, such as the property of mass. When atoms are bound together in various complex ways, molecules are formed. Molecules also have the property of mass. In fact, molecules have a mass that is additive, simply the sum of the mass of each constituent atom. No surprise here. However, at the level of the molecule, a *new* property emerges—three dimensional shape. Dextrose (or D-glucose) and L-glucose are chemically identical, but stereoisomers of each other; one is "right-handed" with respect to three dimensions and the other "left-handed." The property of dimensionality cannot be reduced to anything at the atomic level; it is an *emergent* property. Large organic molecules join to form organelles, organelles form cells, cells form organs, organs form organisms, organisms form societies, etc. At each level of complexity new properties emerge that cannot be reduced to lower level phenomena.

The same emergence of properties can be observed in the mereological organization of Technology. Every technology can be analyzed into its constituent parts (see Figure 3).

---

11. For Murphy's own employment of this notion see Nancey Murphy and George F. R. Ellis, *On the Moral Nature of the Universe: Theology, Cosmology and Ethics* (Minneapolis: Fortress, 1996).

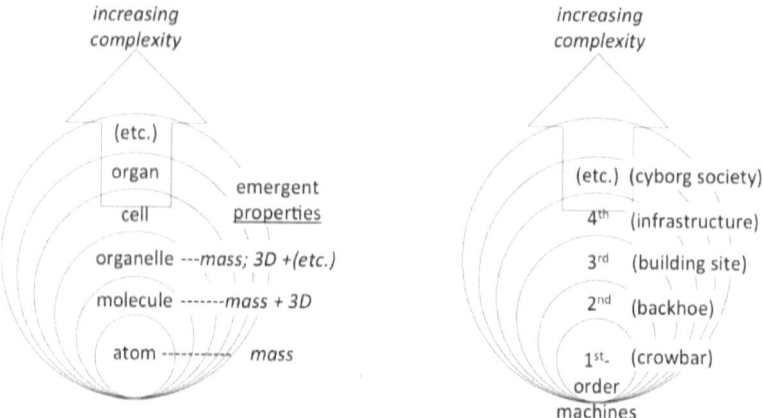

Mereological Hierarchies (Figure 3)

The corollary to atoms are called "first-order machines."[12] The crowbar is a first-order machine with correlative first-order properties (i.e., the principle of the lever). First-order machines can be creatively combined to form second-order machines, and second-order machines can be combined to form third- and fourth-order machines. At some point the vast network of simple properties becomes an infrastructure (indoor plumbing, electricity, cell phone, etc.). Let us not get sidetracked by trying to draw clear boundaries between the orders, but simply admit the point that *new properties may emerge at each level of complexity*. I will capitalize "Technology" as reminder that we are not considering isolated hammers or crowbars but also vast infrastructures and networked industries, the entire mereological system that has made us, together, as a species, a "cyborg society."

The interweaving of emergent properties and human living makes plausible the notion that Technology itself is one of our skins. Human beings have skins we share with animals—in addition to the five senses, animals have the kinesthetic sense (proprioception) and balance (equilibrioception), etc. But human beings also share a linguistic skin with other human speakers. In addition, residents of developed countries share the skin of Technology by which we—together—"take up" meanings, the sharing of which constitute (at least in part) our contemporary social-cyborg world, our world of meanings, our *co-munus*. When my automated email reply announces that I'm blissfully offline for three weeks in July, people trying to reach me take that to be as meaningful (perhaps more so) than were they to walk past my home and notice my car is gone. Many of us are individual

12. This terminology derives from Barry Allen, *Artifice and Design: Art and Technology in Human Experience* (Ithaca, NY: Cornell University Press, 2008).

cyborgs: we have fillings in our teeth, we wear eyeglasses, we ambulate by means of artificial hips and knees, and so on. But *together* we form a cyborg society; we are *social* cyborgs.

Technology as Impeding Christian *Co-munus*

Christian discipleship, which Murphy is intent on preserving in her work (whether directly[13] or indirectly[14]), presupposes the vitality of an extant community. By her lights, the vitality of Christian community is threatened by soul-body dualism. Reconceiving the division between inner and outer as comprised by a set of skins may help repair the distortion wreaked by dualism. However, the skin of Technology itself may be a distortion in the formation of Christian community. To be a community entails, among other things, the sharing of a world of meaning. As I've argued above, creatures come to share a world of meaning by means of "skins." Animals of each genus share a world of significance constituted by meanings taken up by their physical senses. In addition, language speakers share a higher-order world of meanings taken up by the skin of language. We might say that the limits of one's skin(s) is the limit of one's world. But now a puzzle emerges: if the skin of eyesight "takes up" meanings that are ocular, and ears "take up" meanings that are aural, what *kind* of meaning does technological skin "take up" and in what sense might this uptake affect and even distort Christian discipleship?

Technology as a Time Bandit

To recap: thus far I've tried to give an alternative to the dualistic picture of human persons by exploring what changes in our perception of technology follow if we reconceive the boundary between the "inner" and "outer" as lying not "in here," between mind and body, but rather "out here," between body and surroundings. But note: on this alternative picture, everyday phrases such as "he's my soulmate" or "her soul is in a frightful state" are not

---

13. E.g., Nancey Murphy, "Using Macintyre's Method in Christian Ethics," in *Virtues and Practices in the Christian Tradition: Christian Ethics after MacIntyre*, edited by Nancey Murphy, Brad J. Kallenberg, and Mark Thiessen Nation (Valley Forge, PA: Trinity, 1997).

14. E.g., Nancey Murphy and Warren S. Brown, *Did My Neurons Make Me Do It? Philosophical and Neurobiological Perspectives on Moral Responsibility and Free Will* (New York: Oxford University Press, 2007).

barred on the grounds that "soul" has no substantive referent.[15] In point of fact, they are not barred at all. Rather, such phrases make the rich sense they do because soulishness is embodied in our manner (or mode) and ways of being in the world. And it is precisely this notion—"ways of being in the world"—that technology threatens to change. As we shall see below, a cure for our bewitchment is timeful practices, such as music.

What do I mean by "ways of being in the world?" We are bodies. We are solid. We are vulnerable. We are fragile. We are aging. We take up space, and we take up time.[16] Taken together these features mean that our lives can only be recounted in *story* form; we are material critters who can only be one place at a time and who journey from beginnings through middles to endings, each according to her or his own distinctive plot, settings and fellows. For all its benefits, when taken to the extreme, Technology-as-skin inflicts a kind of myopia on account of which we can no longer quite see the *storied* character of creaturely life. *Technology-as-skin obscures the timefulness of the meanings we uptake.* All of our other skins take up meanings that only make sense in time. We see the flight of the baseball *in time*; we hear the progress of a symphony *in time*; we feel the ever-so-slow abatement of the pain of a stubbed toe *in time*; we tell stories that *take time*. But the meanings taken up through our technological skin are liable to be untruthful for *having collapsed temporality into spatiality.*

Bodily (aka creaturely) engagement with our surroundings is simultaneously spatial and temporal. I spot a friend in a crowded room and rush to deliver a hug. That episode is timeful—it has a beginning, a middle and an end. It is also spatial—I cross the room, bumping into other bodies along the way, and deliver an embrace that takes seriously the robustness or fragility of the friend and delivers a bear hug or a light squeeze. This event is at once spatial and timeful. In sharp contrast, Technology has the effect of shifting our attention, sometimes violently so, to objects-in-space to the exclusion of living-in-time.[17] It is not so much that technology-as-skin is

---

15. As Wittgenstein strove to point out, our trouble is that we are forever at risk of assuming a substantive (noun) corresponds to a thing, an object, a *substance*. "The mistake we are liable to make could be expressed thus: We are looking for the use of a sign ["soul"], but we look for it as though it were an object *co-existing* with the sign." Ludwig Wittgenstein, *The Blue and Brown Books* (New York: Harper and Brothers, 1958) 5.

16. This way of speaking is drawn from Rowan Williams, "Art: Taking Time and Making Sense," in *Images of Christ: Religious Iconography in Twentieth-Century British Art. Exhibition Catalogue* (St. Matthews, Northampton, UK: Centenary Art Committee, 1993) 25–27.

17. Edwin Hutchins explains that Micronesian (and pre-modern) navigation takes place not in terms of distance but in terms of time. See Edwin Hutchins, *Cognition in the Wild* (Cambridge, MA: MIT Press, 1996) 65–115.

unable to register the "passing" of time. It is rather that Technology-as-skin distorts our perception of time, often by turning time itself into a "thing" with "thingish" properties. It is no wonder that we Thoroughly Modern Millies have become even more enamored than our medieval forebears by souls-as-thingish. This may strike some as a surprising claim. But consider: for medievals, everything was sacramental; everything was shot through by the presence of God. What held all creation together in their eyes was the forever immanent God (Col 1:17). In contrast, today we assume that what holds everything together is a scientific theory about stuff. In our modern outlook, to be real a thing must be constituted by stuffness and be intelligible against the field of all the stuffs there are in the cosmos.[18] Thus do Christians fight for the recognition of the "soul's reality" as real by asserting its materiality: the soul is a substance, a special "immaterial" substance, but a substance nonetheless.[19] But I digress. I was addressing the issue of our conception of time as itself thingish.

As every child will confirm, "things" have shape and weight and position—all of which can be specified to (virtually) any degree of accuracy we desire.[20] Since the scientific revolution, technological tools have enabled ever-increasing precision in our measurements of these thingish properties. Thus the question seems inevitable: Cannot time itself be quantified with equal precision? We seem happy to imagine so. It is said that the continuous cold Cesium fountain atomic clock (known as the FOCS-1) in Switzerland can be trusted not to lose more than one second every 30 million years! But notice that underneath all the striving for precise measurement of time is the presupposition that time is something material, like a brick. We can talk about the mass of the brick because we all know that bricks do not spontaneously change size, shape, weight or location! Similarly, when we set out to measure time, we presume that time plays fairly, that it doesn't change "shape," "weight" or "location" (note the spatial metaphors), that time is something *regular*, something *divisible* into standard units. But in fact, I wonder whether "regularity" may be an alien property pressed onto time by Technology, first with the invention of the clock and now by the entire Technopoly.[21] To live under regularized time alters the manner, pattern, and rhythm of our proper way of being in God's world.

---

18. On the contrast between the enchanted outlook of medieval and the "buffered selves" of modernity, see Charles Taylor, *A Secular Age* (Cambridge, MA: Harvard University Press, 2007).

19. Sadly, analytic theism has today done the same to God, making God a part of the furniture of the universe as the only conceivable way to champion God's reality.

20. Within quantum limits, of course.

21. Neil Postman, *Technopoly: The Surrender of Culture to Technology*, rev. ed.

Consider the significance of a very recent shift in English-speaking onomatopoeia. When I was a child everybody knew that clocks spoke: the clock says "Tick, tock!" But today, if a clock speaks at all—most are silent—the child learns that it says "tick-tick-tick." This change is significant. The difference between a "tick" and a "tock" is not so much the character of the sound as the position of the pendulum which swings gently back and forth: tick (perhaps to the left) then tock (perhaps to the right). The motion of a pendulum is *reciprocal*. Granted, a pendulum's *period* is entirely regular, and the reciprocity of a pendulum depends only upon the length of the arm (and not its arc). However, the motion itself is not constant. The pendulum accelerates as it heads toward its midpoint, then decelerates. When it reaches its highest point, it stops and reverses direction, accelerating again toward the midpoint. This rhythm of speeding up, slowing down, stopping, and changing directions is repeated over and over. Meanwhile the pendulum is imperceptibly losing energy ("winding down") until it finally ceases movement altogether. Such a rhythm is a paradigm of the ordinary experience of biological bodies. For example, the pendulum mimics the human gait. We lean forward, begin falling, accelerate toward the ground until we catch ourselves with an extended leg. Our body position is righted, we retract the trailing leg and for a brief instant we are at rest before we fall forward again.

Reciprocal rhythms are mirrored everywhere in nature. Twice a day the tides change. The moon that causes the tides itself passes through phases that recur monthly. Once a day the sky passes from night to day. And, perhaps excepting life on the equator, no two successive days are identical in duration. Moreover, because the earth's axis is tipped, its annual journey around the sun produces the reciprocal transition of seasons: planting and growing, then harvest and rest.

Perhaps no one in Newton's day was very much troubled by his suggestion that the world was a clock, because the "clock" in view would have been a pendulum clock, and the innumerable *reciprocal* patterns of the cosmos were manifestly obvious in the metaphor. But the *reciprocal* motion of the pendulum clock has given way to, has been displaced by, *rotary* motion. Henry Ford may have benefitted the workers on the assembly line when he increased their pay and reduced their workday from nine to eight hours. But his motives were more nefarious: an eight-hour shift meant that there could be three shifts in a 24-hour period. Like a flywheel that keeps spinning rather than a pendulum that is punctuated by moments of rest as it slowly winds down, manufacturing could continue unabated by any temporal restrictions. Such changes in manufacturing drove the culture further toward

---

(New York: Vintage, 1993).

the myth of *standardized* time.[22] *Can time be standardized* like the shape of light bulb sockets or the thread count on nuts and bolts?[23]

Perhaps none of my readers is troubled by the standardization of time or the universal applicability of "efficiency" as the criterion by which bodily work in time is assessed. These are not objections I intend to take up here. My point is simply that the kind of meaning we take up by our shared technological skin, and thus the kind of *co-munus* we've become, is distorted because of what technology has done and continues to do to our perception of time. Our other skins do not thus mislead us. Our sensory skins adjust to the rhythms of reciprocal time, informing us when time is swift (as when engaged in an interesting task) or creeps slowly (as when bored) or when it is moving without us (as during sleep) or at a standstill (insomnia). In other words, our sensory skins are able to take up meanings that preserve both the spatiality and temporality of our bodily existence. Even our linguistic skin does *not* threaten to distort the timefulness of bodily existence. Granted, there are biblical expressions that treat time materially ("redeem the time," "count your days," and so on). But Christian language also makes room for time to serve as its own figure. In other words, Christians need not understand time by means of spatial or mechanical or material figures. Time is *sui generis*, therefore, we may only begin to understand it by attending to its intersection with our lives. The best place to begin to attend to that intersection is by attuning ourselves to the way we *speak* of time, what Wittgenstein called the *grammar* of the word.[24] Thus the biblical poets urge us to attend to time's changing rhythms: "there is a time to break down, and a time to build up; a time to weep, and a time to laugh; a time to mourn, and a time to dance . . ."[25] The telling of such times cannot be answered by consulting the atomic clock in Switzerland. Rather, these times come in seasons, in rhythms, and to tell the time one must know what is appropriate and proper ("You give them their food *at the proper time*"[26]). I do not speak

22. For a history of standardization in western engineering see Merritt Roe Smith, "Army Ordnance and the 'American System' of Manufacturing, 1815–1861," in *Military Enterprise and Technological Change: Perspectives on the American Experience*, edited by Merritt Roe Smith (Cambridge, MA: MIT Press, 1985).

23. Bruce Sinclair, "At the Turn of the Screw: William Sellers, the Franklin Institute, and a Standard American Thread," *Technology and Culture* 10:1 (1969) 20–34.

24. "*Essence* is expressed by grammar." In stark contrast to the analytic school, which seeks to understand a thing by reducing it to its constitutive parts, Wittgenstein leans the other way, insisting that what something is is shown by its connections. How we ordinarily speak about time, its grammar, is a record of these connections. Wittgenstein, *Philosophical Investigations*, §371; see also §373.

25. Eccl 3:4.

26. Ps 145:15. See also Eccl 8:5.

hyperbolically. I mean to say that the kind of time learned by immersion into, say, literature and poetry better equips us to live well (i.e., truthfully and faithfully) as bodies in creation than the kind of tin ear toward time that our technological skin gives us. Technologically speaking, the answer to "What time is it?" can receive only one true answer, for example, "12:52 pm EST." But if it is time to mourn (or to dance) then "12:52" wildly misses the point of the question. To say the same thing differently, reciprocal time is inherently storied time, while technological time (aka mechanical or rotary time, i.e., time conceived as discrete, identical, punctiliar units in mere linear sequence) is not essentially story-formed or story-formable. Despite its inherent repetition ("tick," then "tock," then "tick" again), *reciprocal* time consists of beginnings and middles and endings. So, to the extent we (unwittingly) live by technological time our lives are stripped of poetry, leaving us unsung and unstoried.[27]

Music of the Soul

One way to untangle the confusion over the notion of the soul is to reconceive the dividing line between "inner" and "outer." To recap, the alternative to the received account (the Cartesian homunculus; Figure 1) is to understand the boundary as a set of skins by means of which we take up various kinds of meanings. The "thinnest" skin is our epidermis, while the other skins are "thicker"—the skin of hearing being thicker than the skin of smell; the skin of eyesight being thicker than the skin of hearing, and so on. To the extent that the "soul" inevitably (but wrongly) gets identified with the "inner," to understand the division as a set of skins may help one see the soul as itself thicker than our epidermis, lying not inside, but perhaps well *outside* our bodies![28]

A second phase of our conceptual therapy involves loosening the grip that a particular analogy holds over our understanding of time. As physical critters, human beings experience "reality" in terms of both space and time.

---

27. I owe these insights to Aaron James.

28. Wittgenstein often attempted to get readers to see that language does not need to be grounded by something more interior, such as "meaning" or "intention," because there is no way to think the meaning or intention of a sentence without simply repeating the sentence. Ludwig Wittgenstein, *Culture and Value*, edited by G. H. von Wright and Heikki Nyman, translated by Peter Winch, English translation with the amended 2nd ed. (Oxford, UK: Basil Blackwell, 1980) 10e. If, as McCabe suggests, language is a skin, then the work it does is not "inner" in the Cartesian sense ("in one's head" so to speak) but "inner" in the language-as-skin sense—which is to say, interior to the community of language speakers and thus decidedly "outer" on the Cartesian scheme.

For the sake of argument, I will assume Catherine Pickstock's conclusion (without reproducing her argument) that technological progress, especially since the time of Peter Ramus (1515), has resulted in a perceptual outlook in which *temporality* tends strongly to be elided in favor of seeing *spatiality* as absolute.[29] If human temporal sensibilities have atrophied, then when it comes to thinking about the soul, we are left all the more vulnerable to a lopsided conception of the "real" solely in terms of spatiality. Also without argument I will assume that the priority of spatiality in our perception is often manifest as an attunement to, and penchant to think in terms of, materiality: to be counted as real, souls *must* be substantial. I aim to hint in the direction of a challenge to this "must" by supplying one telling counterexample.

I return to the claim made above that time ought to be allowed to serve as its own figure (rather than frame our understanding of time along the lines of nontemporal, mechanical metaphors). The therapy I propose follows Wittgenstein's admonition that we attend to the ordinary activities in which a word is at home in order to understand it. For example, the fact that we understand "cheese" to signify the sort of thing that does not spontaneously change size, weight, or location is shown by the simple activity of our buying cheese by the pound.[30] In the present case, the word is "time" and one of the activities in which "time" is at home is the practice of music.

In his masterful study, *Theology, Music and Time*, Jeremy Begbie suggests that music

> might be of considerable value in a culture which . . . is disaffected with certain alienating and imprisoning conceptions of linear[31] time, which rely on simple and rigid patterns of cause and effect, and which can easily lead to mechanistic notions of progress. . . . But movements such as the Beethoven [String Quartet in F major] so obviously *break through the categories of singular linear narrativity*, yet while being directional, without evoking temporal chaos.[32]

---

29. Catherine Pickstock, *After Writing: On the Liturgical Consummation of Philosophy* (Malden, MA: Blackwell, 1998) 49–94.

30. Wittgenstein, *Philosophical Investigations*, §142.

31. Begbie does not deny that "linear" has its place in music (e.g., "linear pitch set"), but by the term "linear" takes into his sights "simple and rigid patterns of cause and effect, and which can easily lead to mechanistic notions of progress" (117).

32. Jeremy Begbie, *Theology, Music, and Time* (Cambridge: Cambridge University Press, 2000) 117–18. Emphasis added. Hereafter, citations will be in text.

It is important not to miss Begbie's underlying argument. The linear model of time—on which we imagine time as divisible into standard units as though the regularity of these units were guaranteed by a rotary mechanism—is drastically incomplete. In so far as music (itself a rational activity) cannot be rationally accounted for by a one-level linear model of time, then "[m]usic's very rationality challenges the assumption that time must be conceived in *one-level linear terms.*"[33]

There are at least two ways that attention to music might provide therapy for our bewitchment by the mechanical image of time. First, musical time is not one-leveled, but multi-leveled.

Music Is Multi-Leveled

Wittgenstein once stated what should be obvious: "The temporality of the clock and temporality in music . . . are not by any means equivalent concepts."[34] This is because a single piece of music has multiple temporal layers at work. Generally speaking, temporality in music is expressed in terms of *meter* and *rhythm*. When a tune is played, it is possible to identify a time signature simply by observing how a listener claps, or bobs, or nods, or toe taps. This is meter. Interestingly, not only are some beats more accentuated than others, but not every beat of the meter is sounded (played). So meter is intuited (or tacitly detected).[35] Bodies are apparently well suited for detecting meter because meter is reciprocal, like most natural motions of our bodies. Meter washes over us in regular iterations like the breaking of waves upon a seashore.

The second feature of music that conveys temporality is rhythm. Unlike meter, rhythm is explicitly played and therefore always heard.[36] If meter is the regularity of the breakers (regularity being one of the few features that

---

33. Nicholas Wolterstorff, "The Work of Making a Work of Music," in *What Is Music? An Introduction to the Philosophy of Music*, edited by P. J. Alperson (University Park: Pennsylvania University Press, 1987) 103–29.

34. Wittgenstein, *Culture and Value*, 80e.

35. When a beat is played, giving it duration and accent, it is called a *pulse*. One of the most startling pulses in choral music is Brahms' Deutsche Requiem. In the second movement, beginning in bar 22, the simple ¾ time is expressed by a half note rest followed by a quarter note falling on beat three, followed by a half note on beat one of the next measure. The pattern is short-long, 3-1, 3-1, 3-1, 3-1 or unmistakably: lub-dub, lub-dub, lub-dub; a terrified heartbeat expressing the choral text: "*All flesh is grass . . .*" (Isa 40:6).

36. As Begbie explains, "the meter is implied and sensed through the rhythm of tones. Rhythm and meter may coincide very closely, but they can be out of step, sometimes quite radically." Begbie, *Theology, Music, and Time*, 41.

mechanical time *can* capture), rhythm is the "shape" of each incoming wave. The "shape" of each wave may be unique (surfers wait for the "just right" wave to ride), yet the large-scale pattern of their arrivals is regular (41).

Here is where things get interesting: waves are additive. There can be multiple waves simultaneously expressed by a series of incoming musical measures. Said differently, as measures of music strike the listener's ears, multiple waves flood over the listener at once, each wave embodied in measures of music, but the played measures expressing more than one temporal wave at a time. Begbie gives several detailed examples. Consider Chopin's Waltz in A flat major, op. 34, measures 17–24, part of which is reproduced below (42). Each measure consists of three beats. But if one looks carefully, measures 17 and 18 in the treble clef are similar (two dotted half notes) and measures 19 and 20 are similar to one another in a different way (three quarter notes, especially visible in the bass clef). This is a wave structure in its own right. Begbie goes on to point out that this second-order wave is called a "hypermeasure." There is a third-order hypermeasure that links measures 17–20 and 21–24. Begbie identifies a fourth-order hypermeasure consisting of measures 17–24 and 25–32 . . . and so on. These hypermeasures may (or may not, for there is no necessity in music) extend until the entire piece is expressed.

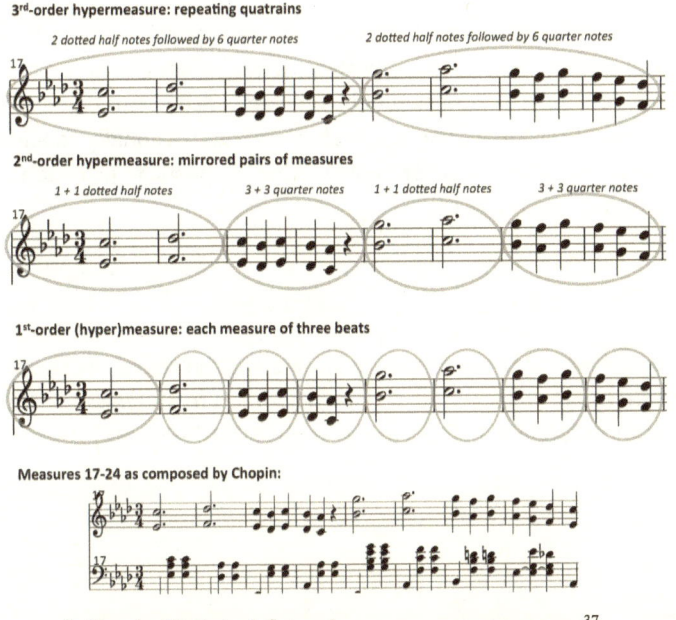

F. Chopin, Waltz in A flat major, op. 34, measures 17–24[37]

37. I have reproduced Begbie's example of Chopin by means of a program called

The patterns exhibited in the example are simple enough for even amateur musicians to recognize. And Begbie provides many other (more complicated) examples.[38] His point is that each temporal pattern falling on our ears is distinct but concurrently enmeshed with other patterns.

This organization of hypermeasures is reminiscent of the mereological hierarchy that we saw in Figure 3 above.

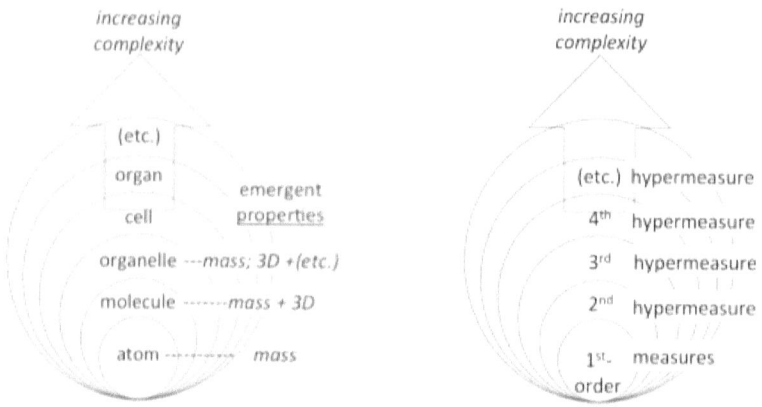

Mereological Hierarchy of Spatial Entities and of Musical Time (Figure 5)

I mean to imply by Figure 5 simply that this hypothesis is worth further study: time may be in one important sense as complexly organized as physical stuff. Such a claim cannot be fully defended in this context, but the comparison is suggestive enough to allow us to provisionally conclude that mechanical time, being flat (one level), is too simplistic to provide adequate description of our world.

Musical Time Is Directional but Not Linear

The second way that music may provide a way out of our conceptual enslavement to mechanical time is that, in addition to understanding musical time as multi-leveled, it is also true that musical time is not linear.

Musecore.

38. See also Jonathan D. Kramer, *The Time of Music: New Meanings, New Temporalities, New Listening Strategies* (New York: Schirmer, 1988).

Musical Expectations

The diverse temporal patterns that constitute multi-leveled hypermeasures are likely to be indistinguishable to the listener (especially on the first hearing) and even to the professional musician (especially on the first playing). That measure 17 in the Chopin waltz begins a fifth-order hypermeasure, as Begbie claims, cannot be assessed at the downbeat of measure 17 but rather in retrospect from further down the line (e.g., from the vantage of measure 32 or later). Of course, even the casual listener may sometimes be surprised and delighted by a sudden musical turn.[39] That is because the patterns of both tone and rhythm and tempo set up tacit expectations which may be fulfilled later on in various ways (musical reprise, musical joke, musical irony, etc.). That expectations are set up early and fulfilled later shows there is undeniable directionality to musical time. Yet while directional, musical time is not linear. Music is not simply one note after the other any more than history is "one damn thing after another" (*pace* Henry Ford). For, in addition to expectations that are set up in the present and fulfilled in the future, there are two other temporal features of musical time that evade capture by the reductionist linearity of the mechanical model.

Endlessness

On the one hand there is an endlessness to musical time. The sameness of mechanical time entails a kind of drudgery, since each successive nanosecond is the same as the last. But a given piece of music is able to gesture, even to yearn beyond the border of the (closing) double bar. My favorite example is Duruflé's Fourth Motet. The choral text is surfeit with praise to the Trinity culminating with a drawn out "Amen." But the last chord doesn't sound right. Since it does not return to the tonic chord of the key, the ear is restless. There is an earlier hint that the tonic will come, but then it never does. The ear waits, even yearns for a future which is unlike the present, a future in which there is closure and fulfillment.

In terms of meter (rather than tone), Begbie gives a complicated example of musical endlessness. The form of the Sonata is *Introduction, Exposition & Development, Recapitulation* (and sometimes a *Reprise*). The long middle section, *Exposition & Development*, is a unit with strong closure. At the moment of closure, the piece is tonically resolved (i.e., it returns to the root note of the key) and in the Sonata form both rhythm (played) and meter (intuited) close in *agreement* (rather than discord) at the end of the

---

39. E.g., Mozart's musical joke, the very last couple bars of K522 -IV Presto.

Exposition & Development. But just then the final section (*Recapitulation*) begins.

> The strong accented metrical beat of the hyper[measure] (the return to the tonic) is followed by weak beats within the recapitulation, but there is not another first beat of comparable strength to complete the wave. Hence the entire movement [i.e., the Sonata as a whole] can be described as a complete hyper[measure] followed by an incomplete one. So, in the field of key, a cadence is a closure, but in the field of meter it occurs *prior to closure* and *demands (metric) resolution*. In one sense [i.e., in terms of tone] the music resolves; in another [i.e., in terms of meter] it strives ahead toward resolution. . . . The music is projected beyond the final cadence into the ensuing silence. (126)

On Begbie's view, this "unfinishedness" makes the Sonata form eschatological by nature. Said differently, the Sonata form (and others) look to a future that is necessarily unlike the present. In stark contrast, mechanical time is marked by perpetual sameness: the future can only be exactly like the present. There is nothing in the mechanical model of time that helps us understand the source and end of temporally transcendent longing.

Temporal Contextuality

Finally, not only does musical time differ from mechanical time in its ability to gesture into a future outside itself, but musical time is also constituted by a present that is only intelligible in light of what precedes and follows, in light of past and future. Wittgenstein asks, "Doesn't the [musical] theme point to anything beyond itself? Oh Yes! But this means: the impression it makes on me is *connected with things in its environment*. . . . A theme, no less than a face, wears an expression."[40] We can read the expression (the look) of our friends because we connect it with previous interactions, we connect it with the whole of their lives with us up till now. We understand today's expression in light of what life together was like yesterday. But that isn't all. We are sometimes compelled to reinterpret today's looks and expressions in light of what happens *tomorrow*. What holds for a facial expression, a line of poetry, a sentence in a play or story, or a comment spoken over dinner also holds for music: the intelligibility of the present is a function of *both* what precedes and follows. Begbie observes that in Beethoven's String Quartet no. 7 in F major, op. 59, no. 1, the return to the tonic is "spread out, dissipated,

---

40. Wittgenstein, *Culture and Value*, 51–52.

over five timepoints" (103). Each of the five only makes sense in light of the others and all five together only make sense in light of the whole. (Which is why we are drawn to listen to music again and again and again.) Mechanical time can make no sense of such temporal loopiness. For mechanical time, the past is gone, the future is not yet, and the present has no duration. But in musical time

> We are not given an evaporating present but a present through which the past is directed towards the future, or—to put it another way—with phenomena which in their physicality are intrinsically and very closely bound to earlier and later musical occurrences. (67)

Conclusion

The task of this paper was to sketch two lines of a defense for Murphy's oft-misunderstood position that humans have no souls. Her claim is not so much a denial as a grammatical remark: the word "soul" does not refer to the sort of thing we possess; souls are not "things" at all. I have argued that readers will perpetually misunderstand Murphy so long as they (1) insist on a particular way of drawing the boundary between "inner" and "outer" and (2) unwittingly kowtow to a mechanical model of time. In the first instance, I deflated the insistence by proposing that the division between "inner" and "outer" is better conceived as constituted by a series of "skins." In the second instance, I shed light on the inability of the mechanical model of time to account for the nature of that noblest of human activities, the making of music. This second move aimed to counter our need to locate the soul "somewhere" by restoring attunement with temporality over the totalizing lure of spatiality.

In closing, I return to the epigram: "What must the world be like, what must I be like, if between me and the world the phenomenon of music can occur?"[41] If Begbie's analysis holds and time may be conceived in some sense as consubstantial with music,[42] and the human soul in some sense as consubstantial with both time and music, then we are in desperate need of a change of figure.

---

41. Cited by Begbie, *Theology, Music, and Time*, 55.

42. As far as music is concerned, time is neither a container which music fills, nor is it a river along which music floats. Rather, time is "consubstantial with the tones themselves, with the particular melody they form. Here one thinks not in time but with time; indeed one thinks time itself in the form of the tones." Ibid., 54.

Sir Edward Elgar composed Variations on an Original Theme for Orchestra ("Enigma"), Op. 36, in the winter of 1898–1899. Like Mozart's variations on "Twinkle, Twinkle Little Star," each variation is a beautiful piece in its own right. But unlike Mozart's, Elgar took a mystery with him to his grave. Each variation was composed to delight (or to infuriate!) by capturing in music each of his friends' particular idiosyncrasies (thus each variation is labeled with the friend's initials). As these particularities have become widely known, the identities of the friends are *not* the enigma. Rather, the enigma is that the main theme never has been identified! Each variation is a harmonizable tune meant to be played *on top* of the common theme. If ever identified, the missing theme would complete and unify the entire work. Without the theme each variation (each friend) is beautiful, but beautiful in isolation. Many musical themes have been proposed, but the answer will never be certain since the secret died with Elgar.

Perhaps here we have the beginning of a better conception of the soul. Pascal once said each human soul was materially incomplete, lacking an enormous piece that only an "infinite object," God in Christ, can fill. A hole in the soul? Why not rather understand the soul as a musical variation on a missing theme? What human beings quest for is not a missing "piece," but a missing *tune*, the notes of which continue to sound from a life lived some two thousand years ago.

SECTION III

METAPHYSICS

7

Divine Action in a Dynamic World
Towards an Anabaptist Understanding of Active Matter and a God of Love

—CHRISTIAN E. EARLY

IN THIS ESSAY I wish to address the problems that arise when reflecting on divine action in our world.[1] I hope to solve some of the problems of understanding divine action by *dissolving* them, or to put it in a Wittgensteinian way, I wish to suggest that a picture of matter has held us captive. Specifically, I will claim that the current problems of understanding divine action have the shape that they have because of the way in which we in the Western theological and philosophical tradition have thought that matter is inert.

I say theological *and* philosophical because the inertness of matter did not just create problems for theology, it has also created problems for philosophical ethics. With inertness of matter, initially a distinction between matter and form (Aristotle) and later a dualism between matter and mind (Descartes) is proposed to account for action.[2] Those problems in ethics

---

1. For excellent introductions to the current state of the theological, philosophical, and scientific discussions see Robert John Russell, Nancey Murphy, and Arthur R. Peacocke, eds., *Chaos and Complexity: Scientific Perspectives on Divine Action* (Vatican City: Vatican Observatory, 1995); Robert John Russell, Nancey Murphy, Theo Meyering, and Michael Arbib, eds., *Neuroscience and the Person: Scientific Perspectives on Divine Action* (Vatican City: Vatican Observatory, 2002); Robert John Russell, Nancey Murphy, and William R. Stoeger S.J., eds., *Scientific Perspectives on Divine Action: Twenty Years of Challenge and Progress* (Vatican City: Vatican Observatory, 2009); and Thomas Tracy, ed., *The God Who Acts: Philosophical and Theological Explorations* (University Park, PA: University of Pennsylvania Press, 1994).

2. For Aristotle, matter is the "primary substratum" of each thing and it persists

became acute in the modern period when Immanuel Kant realized that if Hume was right, then one could have science (which required a realist attitude to causation and thus determinism) or ethics (which required a non-realist attitude to causation and thus indeterminism) but not both—hence his deployment of the phenomenal-noumenal distinction. That dualism in turn creates problems of its own, problems that we may need to realize are unsolvable.[3]

In theology, the discussion has centered on two issues. First, how do we reconcile God's pervasive indirect activity and invisible control with suffering and evil? If God is really active in all and through all, then why is there so much suffering and evil? And second, how do we reconcile God's direct activity and visible control, say during a miracle, with the preservation of human and natural freedom? How does God act directly without reducing every other agent to the role of a puppet?[4]

My suggestion, supported by the history of unsuccessful attempts to solve these problems in a persuasive manner, is that if we think of matter as inert—which both Aristotle and Newton did, and following them medieval and modern theologians have as well—then the problems of divine action quite simply *cannot* be solved. Our theories of action (divine or human) will inevitably be trapped by absolute, all-or-nothing dualities since matter can never genuinely respond or creatively contribute on its own in any way. If that freedom to respond and create is not internal to matter itself, then that freedom will have to be superimposed and dualisms will eventually reveal themselves. The language of emergence is helpful, but it does not change the fundamental problem unless matter is capable of significant action on its own, which is to say *autopoiesis*.[5]

---

through the becoming of a thing. Matter, then, is potentially a thing. It becomes actually a thing when it takes on a nature or form. Thus "it would be the shape or form (not separable except in statement) of things which have in themselves a source of motion" (Aristotle, *Physics*, II.1.193b). For Aristotle, then, motion is strictly speaking not a property of matter but a property of the form.

3. See Nancey Murphy and Warren Brown, *Did My Neurons Make Me Do It? Philosophical and Neurological Perspectives on Moral Responsibility and Free Will* (New York: Oxford University Press, 2007).

4. Austin Farrer developed a notion of "double agency" to address this point. See his *Faith and Speculation: An Essay in Philosophical Theology* (New York: New York University Press, 1967). More recently, Kathryn Tanner has advanced this idea in her *God and Creation in Christian Theology* (Oxford, UK: Basil Blackwell, 1988).

5. See Alicia Juarerro, *Dynamics in Action: Intentional Behavior as a Complex System* (Cambridge, MA: MIT Press, 1999) for a physicalist account of *autopoiesis*. A good way to understand this essay is to see it as following and extending the non-reductive physicalist line of reasoning explored by Nancey Murphy—extending it to the conclusion that emergent self-organizations (with its accompanying bottom-up and top-down

I suspect that there are at least two main theological reasons why we have not explored the activity of matter seriously before now. First, it is a way to secure the Creator-creation distinction (God is the primary source of all action and, for Thomas Aquinas, *actus purus*).[6] Second, it is a way to secure God's providential control over the world. If we can limit free will to human beings, then the mystery of providence in human history seems more manageable even if frustratingly slippery (once you grant freedom to matter itself, the nuts are off the cart so to speak).

I also suspect that these two reasons are actually connected theopolitically, or better *theocosmopolitically*. My sense is that what lies underneath certain theologies of divine action and providential control is the political image of God as transcendental Emperor. I speculate that according to this theology, active matter would seem unruly to God's sovereign order of the universe—perhaps even rebellious—but at any rate it is curious why active matter has not been pursued actively.[7] An Anabaptist theology of divine action, which from the outset explicitly rejects a theology of God the transcendental Emperor, might be more open to the doctrine of active matter. For it to be a live option, however, it would need to fit with a robust Anabaptist conception of God. Happily, James Wm. McClendon, Jr. has already provided such a theology in his conception of God as the everywhere and always present Ground of Adventure.[8]

What follows if we begin to think of matter as itself potentially active? I suggest that it becomes possible to think of God's action with and in the world (and our own) as fundamentally an *inter*-action, which is to say that we can understand God's active presence as a sustained conversational encounter. That inter-action takes on the features and dynamics of an unfolding dance, an evolving conversation, an improvisational piece of music

---

causal feedback/feedforward looping) happen and continues to happen because matter is active. See Warren S. Brown, Nancey Murphy, and H. Newton Malony, eds., *Whatever Happened to the Soul? Scientific and Theological Portraits of Human Nature* (Minneapolis: Fortress, 1998) and Nancey Murphy, *Bodies and Souls, or Spirited Bodies?* (Cambridge: Cambridge University Press, 2006).

6. See David Burrell, *Knowing the Unknowable God: Ibn Sina, Maimonides, Aquinas* (Notre Dame: University of Notre Dame Press, 1992).

7. An exception to the rule is Catherine Keller; see her *The Face of the Deep: A Theology of Becoming* (New York: Routledge, 2003); and more recently *Cloud of the Impossible: Negative Theology and Planetary Entanglement* (New York: Columbia University Press, 2014).

8. Note that this is not Tillich's God the Ground of Being; it is rather, to continue with that (more often than not) puzzling terminology, God the Ground of Becoming. For McClendon, God is the God of transformation.

between God and active matter out of which the whole drama of life has emerged.

By conversation, I mean a series of actions and responses to actions that have the feature of call-and-response, lead-and-follow, question-and-answer, distress-and-comfort, and so on. Critical to this view is that a conversation—to be a conversation—cannot be reduced to "mere" mechanisms. This does not mean that mechanisms are not involved, but that the response can genuinely be said to be from the conversation partner and to that extent also indeterminable. What comes next in the conversation is a continuance but also has to be discovered. God acts *with* matter, not *on* matter.

I owe the reader a down home example of how this could work. Imagine a dinner with friends around a table. Someone, let's call him Steve, requests that bread be passed and someone else, let's call her Erin, responds by passing the bread. Now, what caused the bread to be passed? It would be inadequate simply to say that Erin caused the bread to be passed. Surely Steve's request was also the cause of the bread being passed even though Steve did not physically move the bread. And it might also be accurate to say that the one who organized the dinner and invited the guests provided the setting within which bread to be passed and so in some sense also played a role, perhaps the most important role of all. Because matter is active all the way down, it is capable of responding to God's invitation and request just like Erin responded to Steve. So, when someone forgives an enemy at the initiative of Jesus it is a divine act—a miracle—and it is also an act of God when we gather at God's table, or when God's people leave Egypt. Erin does of course need to hear and in some sense be "tuned in" to Steve's voice in much the same way that we ought to be "tuned in" to God's voice by following Jesus's way of life and accepting his invitation.[9] Note that since I am suggesting that this is a genuinely two-way conversation, requests made of God (prayers) are more than merely psychologically helpful.

The distinction between Creator and creation is firmly maintained in such sacred conversational space because what happens in the space of the conversation happens, in a sense, *because* of the conversation (although that *because* can never be turned around and made to yield an argument for the existence of God since matter could have produced the universe on its own).[10] Still, the space between the partners does not collapse even if

---

9. See Pierre Hadot, *Philosophy as a Way of Life: Spiritual Exercises from Socrates to Foucault* (Oxford, UK: Wiley-Blackwell, 1995). I am aware that the language of attunement sounds vaguely Pythagorean, with its *entrainment* and *askesis*, but I get off the Platonic train at the very first stop since for me matter is active.

10. See Eric Chaisson, *Cosmic Evolution: The Rise of Complexity in Nature* (Cambridge, MA: Harvard University Press, 2002).

at times it seems to do so during moments of one-sidedness (it is a one-sidedness that exists as an intimate relation—"where are you?"—and, as the Genesis story has it, we are the first to leave the sacred conversational space with God, and, in so doing we have gotten lost).

While the imagery of an unfolding dance between God and matter requires us to relinquish notions of God the transcendent ruling Emperor, who sees all and controls all from above, it has the advantage of highlighting God's loving invitation for us to follow God's lead in the adventure and thus to experience life as a gift.[11] It is when we say *Yes* to dancing with God that we open ourselves to experiencing not only God's providential, gracious provision "on the way" but also God's caring, comforting presence during moments of disorienting loss and tragedy as they intersect our lives. Following God on God's way does not protect us from the sufferings of life, but it does allow us to know God as Present, as God with us, as Immanuel.

It is my contention that the central unfolding theme of the conversational dance, initiated and steadfastly continued by God, is love. That emergent note of love is not invulnerable; it is intimately and inextricably tied to tragedy: it is because we care and love that suffering and death is truly tragic. To love is to suffer. Parents, partners, and friends realize (often only after the fact) that in welcoming another life and a new love into their worlds they also and at the same time become open and vulnerable to the tragic dimension of life. How much more is that true of God, the parent, partner, and friend of us all, who is love, and who knows intimately the true cost of loving?

It is therefore my claim in this paper that at stake in the doctrine of matter is also the doctrine of God: God the transcendent, controlling ruler over inert matter or God the freedom-loving Parent, Partner, Friend, inviting active matter to dance. Anabaptists, it seems to me, have a horse in that race.

The Current Problem of Divine Action

In order to make clear why our understanding of divine action has been for some time and currently still is problematic, it may be helpful to give a brief historical sketch outlining the central differences between ancient and modern conceptions of cosmology and God's relation to the world in each

---

11. There are good biblical reasons to reject the notion of God the Emperor. See, for example, Walter Brueggemann's critique of the royal consciousness in his *The Prophetic Imagination*, 2nd ed. (Minneapolis: Fortress, [1978] 2001) and Richard Horsley's critique of Empire in his *Jesus and Empire: The Kingdom of God and the New World Disorder* (Minneapolis: Fortress, 2002).

of these conceptions. I hope to show that when our cosmology changes, so does our understanding of divine action—usually around two foci: the creation and sustenance of the universe (indirect action) and miracles (direct action). If that is correct, then it is a clue that we will need a new cosmology before we can re-imagine divine action, and that the key to a new cosmology will be an alternative conception of matter.

In Patristic and Medieval theology, God was understood to act through the processes of the world. God was the first and primal cause of all events, whereas the (natural) processes of the world were secondary causes. This understanding relied on an overall Aristotelian-Ptolemaic cosmology and physics in which objects behave as they do because of their internal, essential natures, or forms. On the Aristotelian hylomorphic view, every object was comprised of matter (primary substratum) and form (essential nature). The principle of action derived from the form, giving it purpose and goal (or ends): an object does as an object is. On the Aristotelian-Ptolemaic view, then, objects have an internal principle of action and behavior that belong to their form.

Being goal oriented and fulfilling a purpose, actions are rational. Theologically, the goal of all things was understood to be God, as God was Alpha and Omega—the One who moves all things and the One towards which all things move by force of attraction. Aristotelians believed that an object in motion would come to a halt when it reached its natural, purposeful resting place towards which it was attracted. Without God, who infused everything with order and purpose, the movement of all things would either grind to a halt or, more likely, descend into disorganized chaos. The fact, then, that the stars are moving in the sky and plants are growing in the soil is evidence of attraction of all things to God. For Thomas Aquinas it was a clear indication of the existence of God, the source of motion.[12] Thus, the orderly goings-on of the universe requires God, or something like God, as a constant source of motion to sustain it. God is the one who keeps it all in motion. This created an important theological puzzle: if God acts constantly through secondary causes to sustain the goings-on of the universe at every moment, and God is good, then why is there so much suffering and evil?

Additionally, God was understood to act directly in the world without using secondary causes when performing miracles. Since miracles were usually healings, those acts of God did not raise the problem of suffering and evil. But direct acts of God are not unproblematic insofar as they create a theological puzzle of their own: how to make sense of acts in which other

---

12. See Thomas Aquinas, *Summa Theologiae*, Part I, Question 2, Article 3. The first argument of the famous *quinque viae* is the argument from motion.

free agents (humans and other creatures) were involved. Could God be said to act with and through humans and other creatures (a double act) or does God act on God's own, overriding every other agent? If God acts with and through others, then how is God alone to be praised for the miracle? Praising humans for a miracle is theologically unacceptable. But if God acts alone, then does God not override the freedom of other agents, making the whole of human life a puppet show?

These two puzzles relating to divine action—suffering and freedom— were never solved to everyone's satisfaction, in part, I suspect, because they are related to each other. If one answers the first puzzle (suffering), with the notion of free will, then it intensifies the second puzzle because it seems that God would then violate that freedom (which was just allowed) by overriding it. But if you answer the second puzzle by asserting that we are never truly free, then it intensifies the first puzzle because if this is all the will of God then why is there so much suffering? It is no surprise that these issues were debated vigorously in medieval theology.

The nature of that discussion changed radically, however, at the beginning of the modern period. In his *Dialogue Concerning The Two Chief World Systems*, Galileo showed, using a simple thought experiment, that forms are not needed to explain the motion of falling objects.[13] Thinking of forms as principles of action, as an Aristotelian would want to do, leads to errors such as supposing that canon balls will drop to earth faster than musket balls due to their different forms. In actuality, of course, they reach the ground at the same time (or close enough to make the point). The inescapable conclusion of the thought experiment is that there are no such things as forms providing objects with their principles of action—at least not in the physical world.

How then did the universe keep going with no forms to move objects? Newton's first law of motion, the principle of inertia, states that an object in motion remains in motion, and an object at rest remains at rest, unless acted upon by an outside force. The universe is much like a marvelous (and, incidentally, newly invented in the seventeenth century) pendulum clock— except that the universe does not require constant rewinding. It is an awe-inspiring infinity machine. It runs perfectly on its own because that is what matter in motion does—it keeps going. By implication, the universe can continue on without God; it does not need God for its moment-to-moment operation. In the resulting Newtonian cosmology, God is no longer needed to act indirectly sustaining the universe.[14]

13. Galileo Galilei, *Dialogue Concerning the Two Chief World Systems*, translated by S. Drake (New York: Modern Library, 2001).

14. Thomas Tracy says that, "Theologians were left to puzzle out the relation between scientific descriptions of the world as a law-governed structure and religious

The conviction that the universe does not require constant rewinding was also important for the way in which God's special acts were understood. It seemed that if God intervened in the causal chain of events, the clear implication was that the clockwork of the universe was in fact not perfect in that it required constant repair. This in turn would imply that God was not an omnipotent, omniscient, omnipresent creator, which was an unacceptable notion because it would amount to claiming that God is not God. Would not God, who is perfect in every conceivable way, have created a perfect universe, one that did not require regular adjustments and repairs, as a magnificent display of creative and artistic skill?

Additionally, it was difficult to see exactly how God *could* intervene in the causal order and move matter. God would have to use forces such as gravitation, but that seemed to create more puzzles. Opinions here differed: some concluded that God did not intervene in human affairs because it would be inconsistent for God to do so; others maintained that God did but they could not specify how.[15] At any rate, by the mid-eighteenth century David Hume had demonstrated that even if a miracle did occur, one could never be rationally justified in believing it.[16] One could always take a miracle on faith, and that option was of course open, but epistemologically speaking and in terms of the way in which miracles function in natural theology it was useless as a rational foundation for religion. Finally, with Darwin's account of natural selection and evolution, the last and most convincing sign of the divine act of creation—the design of life—no longer "unequivocally" pointed to God. It is worth pointing out that if Darwin is right about evolution, and at this point it would be very difficult to argue that he isn't, then there really are no such things as Aristotelian forms or essential natures—not in physics and not in biology.

I wish to make two points from these observations. First, as conceptions of cosmology change, so do the conceptions of divine action. After Newton, God is no longer needed to sustain the workings of the universe; it does that on its own. Moreover, miracles become difficult to understand because they would involve breaking natural law, which is not impossible

---

affirmations about history as the scene of divine action. If the world is understood as a closed causal system . . . then divine action appears to be restricted to ordering that system initially in creation and intervening within it later on in miracle." Tracy, *God Who Acts*, 2. What Tracy does not mention (hardly anyone ever does) is that this is related to the understanding of matter.

15. See Nancey Murphy, *Beyond Liberalism and Fundamentalism: How Modern and Postmodern Philosophy Set the Theological Agenda* (Harrisburg, PA: Trinity, 1996).

16. See David Hume, *An Enquiry Concerning Human Understanding* (Chicago: Open Court, 1921).

for God to do but it seems inconsistent with other characteristics of God: a perfect ruler of the universe would not make exceptions regardless of the particular circumstances of the lives of subjects.

Second, both Aristotle and Newton agree on their doctrine of matter. This often goes unnoticed because they have, of course, very different accounts of motion, of why matter moves. Whereas Aristotle speaks of internal forms and that to which they are attracted, Newton speaks of forces and acceleration. Neither one of them believe that matter is active in and of itself, but of the two of them Aristotle is closer to that idea than Newton.

Interlude: Inert Matter and *Theocosmopolis*

I wish to pause here to pursue a closer look at the story of early modernity in order to pick up more explicitly the political dimension in the conversation between theology and cosmology. Stephen Toulmin, in his fascinating tale of the hidden agenda of modernity, lists a number of beliefs—he calls them principle elements or timbers—belonging to the modern framework of ideas about humanity and nature.[17] The notorious mind-body dichotomy was a central, load-bearing principle element, on which a series of related dichotomies rested:

> To summarize: human actions and experiences were mental or spontaneous outcomes of reasoning; they were performed, willingly and creatively; and they were active and productive. Physical phenomena and natural processes, by contrast, involved brute matter and were material: they were mechanical, repetitive, predictable effects of causes; they merely happened; and matter itself was passive and inert. Thus the contrast between reasons and causes turned into an outright divorce, and other dichotomies—mental vs. material, actions vs. phenomena, performances vs. happenings, thoughts vs. objects, voluntary vs. mechanics, active vs. passive, creative vs. repetitive—followed easily enough.[18]

These principle elements or timbers, then, divide into two groups: a nature side and a humanity side.

One particular belief on the nature side of the framework was central to the new view: the inertness of matter. The idea itself was not new, as I have insisted throughout this paper, but the way in which it functioned—its

---

17. Stephen Toulmin, *Cosmopolis: The Hidden Agenda of Modernity* (New York: Free Press, 1990).

18. Ibid., 108.

socio-political and theological meaning—was new in a way that relates to our topic. Motion was the product of rational agency, which is to say of conscious beings (God and humans), and an example of mind moving matter. Socio-politically, political bodies and rulers were on the active side and thought to be the source of political motion whereas brute masses were thought to be inert and therefore ought simply to obey their higher authorities.

With Toulmin, we might inquire of the reception of the modern framework in the rest of Europe—how much weight did it carry among the rest of the population? In England, there was a sizable literate population excluded from political power on account of class background, distance from London, or religious nonconformity. As the novelist Benjamin Disraeli later saw with clarity, post-restoration England was in actual fact "Two Nations."[19] The modern framework was (predictably perhaps) well received by respectable writers inside the circles of power, but not so enthusiastically outside those circles. Nonconformity was a threat to the newly restored oligarchy and their Anglican preachers in much the same way as Solidarity was a threat to Communist rule and party politicians in Poland.[20]

The doctrine of the inertness of matter provided a ready-made battlefield for the political conflict:

> Commonwealth sectarians read any proposal to deprive physical mass (i.e., Matter) of a spontaneous capacity for action or motion as going hand in hand with proposals to deprive the human mass (i.e., the "lower orders") of the population of an autonomous capacity for action, and so for social independence. What strikes us as a matter of basic physics was, in their eyes, all of a piece with attempts to reimpose the inequitable order of society from which they had escaped in the 1640s.[21]

Toulmin notes that after the restoration of the monarchy in 1660 no English intellectual questioned the inertness of matter in print for fear of being read as a Nonconformist and a Commonwealth reformer.

A little more than a century later, Joseph Priestly argued that Newton's explanations did not actually depend on the doctrine of the inertness of matter, but then again Priestley was an educated (not Oxford or Cambridge) Nonconformist from the province working with the Lunar Society in Birmingham (not Royal Society in London). After giving a banquet celebrating

---

19. Benjamin Disraeli, *Sybil, or, The Two Nations* (London: H. Colburn, 1845).

20. This analogy is from Toulmin. The Solidarity Trade Union was the first independent labor union in a Soviet-bloc country.

21. Toulmin, *Cosmopolis*, 121.

the French Revolution in 1789, he was publicly reviled and later his house was burned down by a mob. As a result, he emigrated to America, settling in Pennsylvania. "Did his case for active matter convince impartial readers in England? It did not."[22]

What stands out from all of this is that we are not dealing here with science as such, but "with a *cosmopolis* that gives a comprehensive account of the world, so as to bind things together in '*politico-theological*', as much as in scientific or explanatory, terms."[23] Nonconformists who questioned the legitimacy of the elements of the modern framework, in particular the doctrine of the inertness of matter, were exposed to public scorn. What was condemned "was never the adequacy of the scientific explanations the Nonconformists gave: rather, what was condemned was their character, their supposed lack of religious piety, or their supposed lack of general respect for established society."[24]

The doctrine of the inertness of matter, then, is an integral element of a *theocosmopolitical* network of doctrines about how the world works, how it is governed, and who governs it. From the perspective of those outside the circles of power, it was easy to see the otherwise hidden theological and political motivations of the doctrine of matter. I suggest that Anabaptists, like the Nonconformists before them, are in the unique position of being able to explore alternatives to the reigning theocosmopolitical network. Since Anabaptist theological resources have already inspired many to critique the notion of God the transcendent Emperor, they also stand to gain by talking about God not as the king of a city but rather, as James McClendon puts it, as the "Ground of Adventure."[25]

Toward a New Physics of Active Matter

In the opening acknowledgments to his *The End of Certainty*, Ilya Prigogine makes this remarkable statement:

> We have come to the end of the road paved by Galileo and Newton, which presented us with an image of a time-reversible, deterministic universe. We now see the erosion of determinism and the emergence of a new formulation of the laws of physics.[26]

22. Ibid., 123.
23. Ibid. 128. My emphasis.
24. Ibid., 129.
25. See James Wm. McClendon, *Doctrine: Systematic Theology, Volume 2* (Abingdon: Nashville, 1994) 319.
26. Ilya Prigogine, *The End of Certainty* (New York: Free Press, 1997) viii.

The new formulation of the laws of physics describes the processes of thermodynamically open, non-equilibrium systems. It has given rise to concepts such as self-organization, dissipative structures, time irreversibility, indeterminism, and (perhaps most importantly) active matter. The indeterminism and time irreversibility of non-equilibrium systems, which we observe in *all* biological systems, are no longer merely epistemological obstacles to be overcome by a more perfect knowledge of initial conditions. They are actual descriptions of the processes of physical systems themselves, and they require a fundamental revision in our doctrine of matter: matter is active. "Figuratively speaking," says Prigogine, "matter at equilibrium, with no arrow of time, is 'blind,' but with the arrow of time, it begins to 'see.'"[27]

As a consequence of the doctrine of active matter, the meaning of the laws of nature changes: instead of expressing certitude, they now express possibilities or probabilities. Those possibilities or probabilities are not the result of imperfect observation or barriers to knowledge of initial states; rather, they are the result of the nature of the systems themselves—matter itself is capable of spontaneous action with the result that the future is not and cannot be determined by the present.

This takes us back to the core dilemma within philosophical ethics mentioned earlier: reconciling science (human understanding of the regularities of the universe) and ethics (human creativity and responsibility). It has seemed, for as long as we have been thinking about this, that we cannot have both. If humans are part of a deterministic universe, then we too are determined and ethics is an illusion; but, if we are free then either science is an illusion or (more likely) we must be fundamentally removed from the natural world.

The new physics of "far from equilibrium thermodynamics" offers a way out of the dilemma.[28] The dilemma dissolves because physical systems take *action*. But here we must be careful not to think of action as an *ex nihilo* event; the action occurs in the dynamic context of inter-actions with a system or systems outside of itself (they are thermodynamically *open*). If matter is active then humans can be understood as realizing matter's potential for action, which is always-already present in the physical universe. It offers a description of the unfolding, evolving universe in which there is room for the patterned regularities of systems close to equilibrium and for

---

27. Ibid., 3.

28. Looking for solutions in quantum mechanics turns out to be a dead end because Schrödinger's equation, which is the basic equation in quantum mechanics, is deterministic and time reversible. This is, in part, *pace* Murphy's early essay "Divine Action in the Natural Order: Buridan's Ass and Schrödinger's Cat," in *Chaos and Complexity*.

the pattern breaking singularities of creative moments of systems far from equilibrium. It is a world in which God can initiate a dance with matter and in which matter can responds genuinely to God's call. It is a world in which God, humans, and nature can be actively present without constantly stepping on each other's toes.

According to wave mechanics, matter vibrates and therefore has fluctuations and resonances. Near equilibrium systems are vibrationally stable, meaning that fluctuations and resonances eventually die out. Far from equilibrium systems are vibrationally unstable, however, and under certain circumstances they "evolve spontaneously to a state of *increased complexity.*"[29] "We therefore begin to perceive," says Prigogine, "the origin of the variety in nature we observe around us. Matter acquires new properties when far from equilibrium in that fluctuations and instabilities are now the norm. Matter becomes more 'active.'"[30] Active matter is the fertile soil out of which emergence grows.

Specifically, far from equilibrium and unstable dynamic systems move towards a bifurcation point. These are points at which a system could self-organize in more than one way, some of which may entail increased complexity. For example, new molecules that cannot be formed near equilibrium can be formed in systems far from equilibrium, and those new molecules in turn set the stage for new organizational evolutions of the system. The process is one-directional and irreversible; the system undergoes an aging process. "Irreversability," says Prigogine, "is inscribed in matter," adding that "[t]his is likely to be the origin of self-replicating bio-molecules."[31]

Far from equilibrium, then, matter begins to respond dynamically to its surroundings using self-organization. Systems at points of bifurcation "choose" from among possible branches available with no mathematical equations justifying preference of one over another.[32] Fluctuations take over and they "decide" which branch will be selected. Now we can speak of *self*-organization, spontaneous innovation, and increased diversification

---

29. Prigogine, *End of Certainty*, 64.

30. Ibid., 65.

31. Ibid., 159. Prigogine is probably correct in this intuition. Jeremy England, a mathematician at MIT, has recently published a paper with the requisite mathematical equations. See his "Statistical Physics of Self-Replication," *The Journal of Chemical Physics* 139, 121923 (2013).

32. Henri Poincaré points out that when an unstable system resonates with another system, you approach "dangerous denominators" (denominators approaching zero) and it is impossible to calculate through thus limiting trajectory calculations. See Henri Poincaré, *Science and Method*, translated by Francis Maitland (New York: T. Nelson and Sons, 1914).

in direct response to an environmental situation. In the words of this essay, dynamic systems are in a conversation with their environment.

When we look at the world from a dynamic systems point of view, we begin to see a story of increased diversity of populations of molecules that adapt and change with time. They go through stages, they adapt, and they age. Those systemic developmental adaptations make up a conversational evolutionary story—an adaptation is understood as a *response* to an environmental situation—that is intelligible to us. It allows us to bring a Darwinian point of view to chemistry and physics and to overcome the divide between biology and physics.[33] We have gone beyond the alienating images of a world of deterministic mechanics or of arbitrary chance. Says Prigogine:

> We are in a world of multiple fluctuations, some of which have evolved, while others have regressed. This is in complete accord with the results of far-from-equilibrium thermodynamics . . . but we can now go farther. These fluctuations are the macroscopic manifestations of fundamental properties of fluctuations arising on the microscopic level of unstable dynamical systems. . . . Irreversibility, and therefore the flow of time, starts at the dynamical level. It is amplified at the macroscopic level, then at the level of life, and finally at the level of human activity. What drove these transitions from one level to the next remains largely unknown, but at least we have achieved a noncontradictory description of nature rooted in dynamical instability. The description of nature as represented by biology and physics now begin to converge.[34]

The question that is before us now, for the purposes of this paper, is how we might imagine divine action in this dynamic world, and how those images might connect with a robust Anabaptist theology?

At Home with God in the Universe—On Freedom from Below and from Above

In order to clarify the connection with an Anabaptist theology of God the Ground of Adventure, I want to explore a philosophical consequence of this cosmology relating to freedom along two dimensions: first, I want to further

---

33. This is the divide that Stuart Kauffmann could never bridge; see his *Reinventing the Sacred: A New Vision of Science, Reason, and Religion* (New York: Basic Books, 2008).

34. Prigogine, *End of Certainty*, 162.

explore our relationship to matter with respect to freedom; and second, I want to explore God's relationship to matter with respect to freedom.

Henri Bergson, a philosophical heir of Darwin and a believer in active matter, thought of the distinction between the determined regularity and the free creativity of the universe as a difference not of kind but of degree. At the determined end, matter is relatively contracted and isolated. Contracted matter is the source of regularity, predictability, and determinism. It is calculable with precision. At the free end, matter is expanded and interconnected. Expanded matter is open to novelty, to unpredictability, and to indeterminism. It can only be calculated using probabilities.

Commenting on Bergson's understanding of matter, Elizabeth Grosz says this:

> At its most contracted, the material universe is regular, reborn at each moment, fully actual and in the present; but at its most expansive, it is part of the flow of pure duration, carrying along the past with the present, the virtual with the actual, and enabling them to give way to a future they do not contain. The universe has this expansive possibility, the possibility of being otherwise not because life recognizes it as such but because life could only exist because of the simultaneity of the past with the present that matter affords it.[35]

For Bergson, expansive possibility and novelty is freedom. Freedom is an event that is not predictable or contained in the present. It emerges, surprises, and cannot be entirely anticipated in advance. This is unusual because freedom has often been understood to be predicated on choice without any constraints, and consequently freedom becomes arbitrary and irrational. On Bergson's view, however, freedom is not linked to the arbitrary but to creativity, to newness, to non-linearity.

Freedom, then, is not a state one is in. Neither active matter nor human beings are "free" as such. Rather, freedom is a capacity, a potentiality, "to act both in accordance with one's past, as well as 'out of character,' in a manner that surprises."[36] That potentiality is present in inorganic physical systems as a consequence of indetermination, but it is even more present in organic physical systems, and especially in human beings.

Indetermination from below liberates mattered life from the mechanical, stimulus-response immediacy and given-ness of objects in the present environment and of the past. Freedom is a struggle, and the struggle of

---

35. Elizabeth A. Grosz, *Becoming Undone: Darwinian Reflections on Life, Politics, and Art* (Durham, NC: Duke University Press, 2011) 71.

36. Ibid., 72.

matter to act in accordance with our past as well as out of character—"a struggle of bodies to become more than they are"—is our struggle too. Life, the struggle of freedom over time, is "the forward thrust of a direction whose path is only clear in retrospect."[37] This capacity of freedom, this indeterminism from below, is characteristic of all of us. We are not alien freaks of free will. We are at home in the universe engaged in the same struggle, groaning for freedom together (Rom 8:21–23).

There is another consequence of active matter relating to freedom. If Prigogine is right that this is a "world of multiple fluctuations," then this is also a world in which there are a multitude of indeterminate systems interacting with each other in unpredictable ways, each infused with the creative capacity to be free and so act out of character and surprise. Such a world is pluralistic and resists being gathered into, as William James would say, an "all-form."[38]

James rejects two visions of the universe: a mechanical materialism, which posits a unified world knowable through fixed laws, and a traditional Christian dualism, which posits an omnipotent, commanding God ruling over both nature and humanity. Both of these invoke a notion of the absolute as over and against, and therefore alienated from, human lived experience, "as if it were a foreign being."[39] The mechanical materialist and the traditional Christian do this by treating either Nature or God as *radically different*, both supposedly having a fundamentally organizing, and therefore deterministic, lock on the human predicament. They are both philosophies of absolutism.

On James's view, by contrast, the universe is messy. It cannot be gathered into a whole. His is a philosophy of pluralism:

> The pluralistic view which I prefer to adopt is willing to believe that there may ultimately never be an all-form at all, that the substance of reality may never get totally connected, that some of it may remain outside of the largest combination of it ever made, and that a distributive form of reality, the each-form, is

---

37. Ibid.

38. See William James, *A Pluralistic Universe* (Cambridge, MA: Harvard University Press, 1977).

39. Ibid., 40. The contrast with David Burrell (arguably the best Catholic account of the Creator-creation distinction) or Karl Barth (arguably the best Protestant account of the same distinction) could not be more vivid. Anabaptists, who find themselves torn between the Catholicism of Thomas Aquinas and the Protestantism of Karl Barth, might consider looking to William James instead.

logically acceptable, and empirically as probable as the all-form acquiesced in as so obviously the self-evident thing."[40]

In the pluralistic optic that James prefers, he can see scientific laws as incomplete summaries and loose approximations rather than as uncovering the deep structure that all events must obey, and he can see God as a participant in the world among other participants rather than as an omnipotent, omniscient God outside or above the world who gathers all things into an intelligible whole. He can see us free from the determinism from above and from below.

James can see us at home in the universe with God and Nature. For James, it is a vision in which he invests hope. Such a God participates as an agent in a world filled with many agents of different types. Such a God is not ultimately responsible for why evil exists because such a God does not govern the world entirely. Such a God can be experienced and can act in the world. It is a God much more like the one witnessed to in Scripture—in the actions of Yahweh, in the person of Jesus, and in the movements of the Holy Spirit.

Anabaptist Theology and Divine Action in a Far-from-Equilibrium World

I have been arguing that with the doctrine of active matter, most problems associated with divine action dissolve. It is now time to acknowledge that while some problems fade into the background, other problems step into the spotlight. To be more precise, the doctrine of active matter shifts the problems of divine action from a problem of physics to a problem of recognition: how do we discern what God does and, perhaps even more importantly, who God is?

In his three-volume systematic theology, James McClendon argues that to get a sense of what God is doing in the world—which is to say, who God is—we need to think *first* of God's coming rule.[41] It is in the light of the

---

40. Ibid., 34.

41. The significance of this move is easily overlooked. By contrast, Keith Ward in his *Divine Action: Examining God's Role in an Open and Emergent Universe* (Philadelphia, PA: Templeton Foundation Press, 2007) has this to say about where we should start: "One indisputable characteristic of the God of Abraham, Isaac and Jacob, the Father of the Lord Jesus Christ, is that he is the creator of all things in heaven and earth ('The Lord is the everlasting God, the creator of the ends of the earth', Isaiah 40:28). If one is exploring the idea of Divine action, this is where one *must* begin, for creation is the first act of God in relation to all other things, without which no further acts would be possible" (4, emphasis added). The problem with this view, and the problem with

end that we can understand the whole of the story; in this light, the qualities of its characters become visible. Viewed from the light of story's end, God's eschatological new creation comes "by way of the politics of the Lamb."[42] History goes on because "God's purpose in Christ is still being achieved, and being achieved by the very method by which Jesus lived and died—not by human conquest, but by the radical politics of the cross."[43] It follows from this that

> [T]he Christian doctrine of last things exists as part and parcel of the doctrine of Christ Jesus; its necessary pictures take doctrinal form exactly within the frame provided by his crucified, risen, ongoing history. To express this in "apocalyptic" form, we may with the Apocalypse (and with my advisor Nancey Murphy) say that the picture of the Lamb standing as one that has been slain—the picture of the crucified and risen one—is the master picture by which we can learn to see all the rest.[44]

McClendon is making the claim here that to understand the coming rule of God, to understand what God is doing in human history, and in fact to understand who God is, we need to focus our attention on one person and one person only: Jesus of Nazareth.

What becomes clear when we do so is that God's action in human history has the recognizable shape of the radical politics of the Lamb. This is a God who does not conquer through the coercion of threats (in this life or the next) and who does not maintain control through the use of force (covert or overt)—those are the politics of Empire and its gods. This God, our God, conquers through the loving, converting power of self-sacrifice. This God, who consistently rejects the use of coercive control, and who instead risks everything in love, is an ever-present God of Adventure.[45]

What kind of adventure? The adventure of liberation, of becoming free: free from dehumanizing slavery of any kind, free from the oppression and obstacles of codes and systems that erect divisions between rich and poor, Jew and Greek, male and female, free in short from sin. "God through

---

all explorations of divine action that begin their reflections with creation, is that it is remarkably susceptible to theocosmopolitical projections—namely that the first thing to know about God is that God is a transcendent ruler. It shouldn't be surprising that that is precisely the God that Ward finds there, and then of course Ward has the usual difficulty of showing that that God is also a God of love who, despite in some mysterious sense wills everything, also cares deeply.

42. McClendon, *Doctrine*, 99.
43. Ibid.
44. Ibid., 101.
45. The function of the biblical story is to identify the true God as God.

the gospel liberates men and women from sin and hindrance, this liberation is . . . into a new polity, that of the rule of God."[46] The adventure of the road of God changes us and as a result we become more than what we were: God joins with us in the struggle of freedom. Thus we make a mistake if we think that this is an adventure only on our end—it is an adventure for God as well. We journey with God together and God too is changed as a result.

Still, it is an adventure in and throughout which something about God remains reliably the same:

> For God to continue to be God, there must be that about God which us utterly reliable. This is God's nature or character, the qualities inherent in God's Godhood. [T]he quality assumed here is God's creative love, the love that sets out on a costly adventure of creation itself. Yet to speak of adventure (and of love) implies reciprocity, God's ability to enter into loving relations with what is outside God and by doing so to bring about changed circumstances in the world, but also for God. Creation is such an act of change, and ongoing creation is a series of such changes. God-who-has-created is other than God-who-only-might-create. Then the changes involved in this world by the human adventure (and who knows what other adventures elsewhere in the cosmos) entail the risk of furthering suffering: to love is to suffer, and to love recalcitrant or rebellious or sinful creatures is costly suffering indeed.[47]

What remains reliably steadfast throughout the adventure is that God never stops loving because the cost of traveling down the road with us is too high. God never stops loving because God *is* love.

God the adventurer who is love leads us into newness—creation and new creation, Israel and new Israel, life and new life, humanity and new humanity. But not all acts of novelty are acts of God. We need discernment if acts of God are to function as data for theology.[48] There is the new to which we ought to say Yes, and there is the new to which we ought to say No because it is not consistent with who God is. In particular, the people of God should have rejected the theocosmopolitical pressure to take a king (cf. 1 Sam 8). One way to read the story of Jesus of Nazareth, then, is that he came to undo the effects of Israel having taken a king for themselves, effects which have had ramifications for the Christian movement as well after Con-

---

46. Ibid., 120.

47. Ibid., 171.

48. Nancey Murphy, *Theology in the Age of Scientific Reasoning* (Ithaca, NY: Cornell University Press, 1990).

stantine.[49] On the view proposed here, however, what is revealed is that God is not a transcendent king, at least not anything like the kind of king known to humankind. Although it is tempting—their temptation is our temptation, and it was Jesus's too—that particular theocosmopolitical vision is false.

Reading the story of Jesus of Nazareth as the story of God, by contrast, we can say this:

> The Christian story in its primal form tells of a God who (unlike gods of human fabrication) is the very Ground of Adventure, the Weaver of Society's Web, the Holy Source of nature in its concreteness—the one and only God, who, when time began, began to be God for a world that in its orderly constitution finally came by his will and choice to include also—ourselves. We human beings, having our natural frame and basis, with our own (it seemed our own) penchant for community, and (it seemed) our own hankerings after adventure, found ourselves, before long, in trouble. Our very adventurousness led us astray; our drive to cohesion fostered monstrous imperial alternatives to the adventure and the sociality of the Way God had intended, while our continuity with nature became an excuse to despise ourselves and whatever was the cause of us. We sin. In his loving concern, God set among us, by every means infinite wisdom could propose, the foundations of a new human society; in his patience he sent messengers to recall the people of his Way to their way; in the first bright glimmers of opportunity he sent—himself, incognito, sans splendor and fanfare, the Maker amid the things made, the fundamental Web as if a single fiber, the Ground of Adventure risking everything in this adventure. His purpose—sheer love; his means—pure faith; his promise—unquenchable hope. In that love he lived a life of hope; by that faith he died a faithful death; from that death he rose to fructify hope for the people of his Way, newly gathered, newly equipped. The rest of the story is still his—yet it can also be ours, yours.[50]

Conclusion

I began by suggesting that a picture has held us captive. That picture is not just cosmological, but a *theocosmopolitical* vision of God, the universe, and

---

49. Just to be clear, these are acts of creative *self*-organization that have had particularly devastating consequences.

50. McClendon, *Doctrine*, 319. I cite McClendon at length here in part because this was also a habit of Nancey's.

human society. It is showing signs of strain, however, because Christianity in particular requires an active God—even, I dare say, an interventionist God—and within the current theocosmopolitical vision it is not clear at all how God is active or even whether God should be active in the world.[51]

At the heart of the matter (my apologies), I have suggested, is the doctrine of the inertness of matter. It is a central, load-bearing, principle element (or timber to use Toulmin's phrase), and without it the whole theocosmopolitical framework threatens to collapse. There are good scientific reasons to reject that particular doctrine, as Ilya Prigogine's work demonstrates. There are, however, theological and philosophical *and* political pressures to resist that rejection and to hold on to the doctrine of the inertness of matter. As any proper Quinian who believes in underdetermination would tell you, here there is much latitude of choice in how to resolve things.

If we do accept the doctrine of the activity of matter, as this essay suggests that we do (extending Nancey Murphy's non-reductive physicalism to a new doctrine of matter), we will need to look for another theology of divine action. I propose that the (Ana)baptist theologian James Wm. McClendon, Jr. has already provided us with one. His theology of God the loving Ground of Adventure who is conversationally present in a dynamic world struggling for freedom is, importantly, not caught on the horns of the dilemma of the problem of evil—and it has the added advantage of being true.

---

51. Interventions, on the view proposed here, have the narrative shape of non-linearity. As such, interventions—non-linear changes in organization and directionality—are actually quite common and evoke no unique problems to divine action in a dynamic universe.

8

Possibility Spaces
Their Nature and Implications for Cosmology and Theology

—George F. R. Ellis

It is a great pleasure to dedicate this paper to Nancey Murphy, who has such a sharp intellect and a great ability to capture philosophical issues and history in a pithy way. My aim in this chapter is to develop the theme of possibility spaces—both their nature and their implications for cosmology and theology. In effect, this furthers arguments Nancey and I developed in our book *On the Moral Nature of the Universe*,[1] published just under twenty years ago. The themes we developed there remain as relevant today as they were then, and here I extend these themes into further areas.

What Things Exist

> We are such stuff / As dreams are made on.
>
> —Shakespeare

When we look at cosmology and the nature of our existence, what are the kinds of entities whose existence we wish to explain? This is the basic question of this essay, which is often discussed in the context of the anthropic

---

1. Nancey Murphy and George F. R. Ellis, *On the Moral Nature of the Universe: Theology, Cosmology, and Ethics* (Minneapolis: Fortress, 1996).

question: namely, *Why is the universe of such a nature that intelligent life can exist?*[2]

People addressing this issue often take it for granted that we want to explain only the existence of material "stuff"; in particular, it is assumed that if we have explained the existence of elements like carbon and oxygen on the one hand and planets orbiting stars on the other, we have covered what is needed to satisfactorily explain the emergence of intelligent life. My thesis here is that we must also consider the existence of other kinds of entities: mental "stuff" such as emotions or thoughts, and perhaps even Platonic entities such as mathematics or logic. So the first issue is, what kinds of things is it reasonable to assume exist? Elsewhere,[3] I have argued that we should recognize the existence of entities of each kind shown in Table 1.

World 1: Matter and Forces

World 2: Consciousness

World 3: Physical and biological possibilities

World 4: Mathematical reality

Table 1: *Different kinds of reality implied by causal relationships, characterized in terms of four Worlds, each representing a different kind of existence.*

The key point is that entities in each world are ontologically real: that is, their existence is just as real as physical entities. My justification for this claim about the nature of existence is that, in order to avoid the existence of uncaused physical entities, we must recognize the existence of any entity that is *either* itself a physical entity (World 1), *or* can be demonstrated to have a causal effect on physical entities (it has demonstrable outcomes in World 1). Entities of Worlds 2, 3, and 4 satisfy this requirement, and can be split up by their different components as follows[4]:

2. Cf. John D. Barrow and Frank J. Tipler, *The Anthropic Cosmological Principle* (New York: Oxford University Press, 1986); Martin Rees, *Just Six Numbers: The Deep Forces that Shape the Universe* (London: Weidenfeld and Nicholson, 1999).

3. George F. R. Ellis, "True Complexity and its Associated Ontology," in *Science and Ultimate Reality: Quantum Theory, Cosmology, and Complexity*, edited by John D. Barrow, Paul C. W. Davies, and Charles L. Harper, Jr. (Cambridge: Cambridge University Press, 2004) 607–36. In that essay I build on the work of Karl Popper and John C. Eccles, *The Self and Its Brain: An Argument for Interactionism* (Berlin: Springer-Verlag, 1977); and Roger Penrose, *The Large, the Small and the Human Mind*, with Abner Shimony, Nancy Cartwright, and Stephen Hawking, edited by Malcolm Longair (Cambridge: Cambridge University Press, 1997).

4. Cf. Ellis, "True Complexity."

SECTION III—METAPHYSICS

The physical world of matter and forces (World 1) is hierarchically structured to form lower and higher levels whose entities are all ontologically real (the hierarchy of structure and causation; see the left side of Table 2, below).[5] That is, a table is just as real as the atoms out of which it is made, which in turn are as real as the electrons and nuclei out of which they are made. At the quantum level the status of existence is complicated because of entanglement and superposition,[6] but at the classical level of reality their existence is quite clear.[7]

Level 8:	*Cosmology*	*Sociology/Economics/Politics*
Level 7:	*Astronomy*	*Psychology*
Level 6:	*Space, solar system science*	*Physiology*
Level 5:	*Geology, Earth Science*	*Cell biology*
Level 4:	*Materials Science*	*Biochemistry*
Level 3:	*Physical Chemistry*	*Organic Chemistry*
Level 2:	*Atomic Physics*	*Atomic Physics*
Level 1:	*Particle Physics*	*Particle physics*

Table 2: *The hierarchy of structure and causation. This figure gives a simplified representation of this hierarchy of levels of reality (as characterized by corresponding academic subjects) for natural systems (left) and human beings (right).*

The world of individual and communal consciousness (World 2) is the arena of consciousness, ideas, emotions, and social constructions (corresponding to Levels 7 and 8 on the right hand side of Table 2). This level is ontologically real and causally effective in World 1. Note that while the *idea* of a fairy is real (it can be written about, talked about, can result in drawings, pictures, and emotions), that fact is independent of whether fairies themselves actually exist or not. Any idea in World 2 may or may not correspond to an entity in World 1. Social constructions (such as language, money, and laws) exist here: They play a key role in shaping social life and its material outcomes, and so are certainly real.

5. Cf. Murphy and Ellis, *Moral Nature*, 86.

6. Chris J. Isham, *Lectures on Quantum Theory: Mathematical and Structural Foundations* (London: Imperial College, 1995).

7. I cannot deal with the issue of reality in relation to quantum existence here, but assume that there is a quantum domain underlying classical reality whose existence I do not doubt.

The world of Aristotelian possibilities (World 3) characterizes the set of all possible physical and biological behaviors from which the specific instances of what happens in World 1 are drawn (you can't act in any specific way unless it is a possible way to act). This is actually a way of characterizing the laws of physics, given that physical entities have to obey these laws; however, this represents the possible solutions of those laws rather than the laws themselves. The point is that while the ontological status of the laws of physics is unknown (specifically, whether they are prescriptive or descriptive), this formulation gets around that problem.

Finally, *Platonic worlds of abstract realities* (World 4) are ontologically real. Key examples include mathematics, logic, and algorithms. These are discovered by humans, whereby they come to be represented in the brain,[8] but exist independently of human existence. Thus, for example, the Pythagorean Theorem, or the fact that the square root of two is irrational, are both true independent of human minds; they are abstract facts true at all times and places independent of culture or belief. They are not physically embodied, but can be instantiated in brain states that represent them, and from there have causal effects in the physical world. We will see below that it is useful to consider these worlds as possible mathematical structures and algorithms—that is, as possibility spaces.

Existence and Possibility Spaces

An adequate explanation of what exists must encompass each of the above kinds of entities. My claim is that these four worlds represent the kinds of entities that might exist in general, as well as specific instantiations of some of these possibilities that have actually occurred in the universe. The first are possibilities, while the second are actualizations of those possibilities. In order to explain the existence of any World 1 entity in adequate depth, we need to discuss their nature, which is characterized by the behaviors they manifest—that is, their regularities of behavior that we describe in terms of effective laws.

A key example is the laws of physics that show how matter behaves, and in some sense govern the existence of material "stuff." Indeed, different kinds of matter are characterized by how they obey such laws: their regularized behavior is how we recognize them over time. (For example, an electron is charged and so responds to an electromagnetic field, whereas a neutrino, which is uncharged, does not.) We can represent these laws in

---

8. Paul M. Churchland, *Plato's Camera: How the Physical Brain Captures a Landscape of Abstract Universals* (Cambridge, MA: MIT Press, 2012).

terms of equations, such as Maxwell's equations, but these equations are just our symbolic representations of the physical laws that control how matter behaves. We must not confuse our representation of the laws (epistemology) with their effective existence (ontology). After all, we can represent the same physical law-like behavior in different ways, mathematically. Thus Maxwell's theory can be expressed in terms of integral or differential equations, or variational principles; in terms of three-dimensional vectors or four-dimensional tensors, or differential forms, or spinors; and so on. These are all different representations of the same abstract laws of physical behavior, none of which explain in what sense these laws actually exist or have a hold on the behavior of matter.

An important point to consider here is that we cannot be certain of whether physical laws *prescribe* how matter must behave, or if they *describe* its behavior in a handy way. This is a fundamental difference. In view of this quandary, it is useful to represent these laws in terms of possibility spaces that show what is and what is not possible for material entities of whatever kind we are discussing.

For instance, consider possibility space Ω_{phy} for physics (World 3), which includes the phase spaces of classical physics showing all possible states of the system; for mechanical systems, these are characterized by position and momentum coordinates.[9] Dynamics in this space (how the system changes over time) is represented by phase space trajectories which characterize the dynamics in operation.[10] These trajectories must satisfy whatever constraints and conservation laws are in operation (e.g., energy and momentum conservation), which indeed may suffice to determine what dynamics is possible.[11] In the case of quantum physics, the state spaces for the system's wave function are Hilbert spaces,[12] and the equations of motion are given by the Schrödinger equation. In each case, the possibility space fully represents the laws, which in turn fully determine the relevant possibility space.

Now the possibility space Ω_{phy} is eternal and unchanging: the same possibilities hold everywhere in the universe independent of time and place, independent of culture and of any representation we may use to try

---

9. These are described well in Lee Smolin, *Time Reborn: From the Crisis in Physics to the Future of the Universe* (New York: Mariner, 2013).

10. An important example is Hamiltonian dynamics; cf. Roger Penrose, *Cycles of Time: An Extraordinary New View of the Universe* (New York: Alfred A. Knopf, 2011).

11. The dynamics are characterized by attractors, repellors, saddle points and so on; cf. V. I. Arnold, *Mathematical Methods of Classical Mechanics*, 2nd ed. (Berlin: Springer, 1978).

12. Cf. Isham, *Lectures*, 34–35, 71.

to capture their nature. No matter what you do, you cannot violate energy or momentum conservation. Thus, underlying the ephemeral events of the physically existing world lie eternal unchanging possibility worlds that are unaffected by the history of the universe—indeed, they govern that history,[13] and may possibly precede the universe's coming into existence.[14] Specific things that actually happen are chosen from these possibilities according to the initial conditions that actually occur. Inter alia, they must conserve energy and momentum as well as any structural constraints imposed by local physical conditions. Specific physical systems S are characterized by extra constraints representing their nature and structure (e.g., mass, shape, and so on) that then determines a subspace $\Omega_{phy}(S)$ of the whole space Ω_{phy} representing the physical possibilities for that particular system.

Similarly, the huge variety of biological life exists on the basis of the possibility space Ω_{bio} that describes what is and is not possible in biological terms at different scales. For example, it is not possible to have an animal that needs no food, or a wingless animal that will fly; and it is probably not possible to have life that is not constituted by some kinds of cells. Because all sorts of physical constraints underlie what is and is not possible in biology, Ω_{phy} underlies Ω_{bio} but is not equivalent to it, because genuinely new biological structure and function emerges from the underlying physics, as allowed by the possibilities characterized by Ω_{bio}. These possibilities underlie the concepts of evolutionary *convergence* and the *fitness landscape* in evolutionary biology,[15] and is central to disputes regarding evidence-based physiology and some dogmatic views on evolutionary biology.[16]

Thus, it is useful to consider possibility spaces in the cases of physics and biology. They can also be used to understand the nature of mental and logical possibilities, as we discuss below, and so provide a useful unified

---

13. Sometimes attempts are made to derive laws of physics that change with time or context (for example, Smolin in *Time Reborn*), but such changes are then phrased in terms of deeper laws that are indeed invariant over time and space—for if that were not so, physics would become arbitrary and unpredictable.

14. The problem with claiming that possibility worlds govern that coming into being is that they are formulated in the context of the properties of the parts of the universe, which is taken to be already in existence.

15. On convergence, cf. George McGhee, *Convergent Evolution: Limited Forms Most Beautiful* (Cambridge, MA: MIT Press, 2011). On fitness landscapes, cf. Sewall Wright, "The Roles of Mutation, Inbreeding, Crossbreeding and Selection in Evolution," *Proceedings of the Sixth International Congress on Genetics* (1932) 355–66; and Hendrik Richter and Andries Engelbrecht, eds., *Recent Advances in the Theory and Application of Fitness Landscapes* (Berlin: Springer-Verlag, 2014).

16. Cf. Denis Noble et al., "Evolution Evolves: Physiology Returns to Centre Stage," *Journal of Physiology* 592 (June 1, 2014) 2237–44.

viewpoint of the underlying causes of what exists. The usefulness of this approach is twofold: One, it helps clarify the relationship between epistemology and ontology (which are often confused); and two, it helps distinguish essentially emergent properties—whose core nature lies in emergence *ex nihilo*—from Platonic properties that we discover, whose essence lies in pre-existing properties.

Epistemology and Ontology for Physical Entities

First, regarding physical systems, possibility spaces enable one to clearly distinguish between epistemology and ontology, which are often confused in these discussions. Consider Table 3 (below), which shows four subsets in an abstract space Ω_{phy} of physical possibilities, characterizing ontological status (including entities that are instantiated and uninstantiated) and epistemological state (including entities both known and unknown).

Physical Possibilities Ω_{phy}		Epistemology	
		Known	Unknown
Ontology	Instantiated	P_{IK}	P_{IU}
	Not Instantiated	P_{NK}	P_{NU}

Table 3: *The ontological and epistemological possibilities for physical entities. They may be instantiated (or not) and known (or not).*

The possibility space consists of a classification of all possible entities of a particular kind, where physical possibilities are understood here to include the physical aspects of life. A first distinction is made between possibilities that have been realized in some context (e.g., earth or our galaxy) and those that have not. Hence some physical entities (e.g., the sun and the moon) have come into existence, whereas some possibilities (e.g., another earth-like planet in the solar system) have not. This is a factual (ontological) issue; the membership is in principle confirmed by observational testing, which is an ongoing process. A second distinction is made between what is known to an intellectual community at some time, and what is not known. The known part will extend over time, becoming more comprehensive as time progresses, and a blurred terrain will exist between what is solidly known and what is unknown—where things are partly understood. Thus the space of possibilities Ω_{phy} is split into:

- subspace $P_{IK}(\Omega_{phy})$,[17] which includes entities or actions that have been instantiated and are known to have been instantiated (e.g., Jupiter, or the Battle of Waterloo);

- subspace $P_{IU}(\Omega_{phy})$, which includes entities or actions that have been instantiated but are not known to have been instantiated (e.g., numerous species on earth, or Napoleon's choice of breakfast each day—possibilities that may or may not have been realized);

- subspace $P_{NK}(\Omega_{phy})$, which includes entities or actions that have not been instantiated but are known to be possible (e.g., another continent on earth, or Amelia Earhart having survived her flight—the space of counterfactuals);

- and subspace $P_{NU}(\Omega_{phy})$, which includes entities or actions that have not been instantiated and are not known as a possibility, either because they have been considered but it is not known if they are possible or not (e.g., controlled nuclear fusion, or useful quantum computing), or because they have not been conceived. By definition, we cannot give examples of the last category[18]; these "unknown unknowns" are the most difficult to deal with, and are the domain of science fiction.

On the one hand, as time proceeds the physically instantiated region will increase as new things happen and new entities emerge; on the other hand, we will also come to understand more of both instantiated and uninstantiated possibilities. Thus P_{IK} and P_{NK} will continually increase, and P_{NU} and P_{IU} will continually decrease. Clearly two quite different dynamics determine these two kinds of change: the dynamics of emergence govern the increase of the instantiated entities, whereas the dynamics of learning and knowledge govern the increase of known entities.

Epistemology and Ontology for Abstract Entities

Is there a similar classification for the possibility spaces of abstract entities such as mathematics? There is indeed, but with a crucial difference: in this case, by the very nature of the entities represented, the ontological status cannot change with time. All that changes is what we know about them: their epistemological status.

17. In the notations that follow, P represents "projection operators"; $I = P_{NK} + P_{NU} + P_{IK} + P_{IU}$.

18. To echo the famous quip from Donald Rumsfeld, "there are known knowns; there are things we know we know. . . . there are also unknown unknowns. There are things we don't know we don't know."

Mathematics and Logic

As an example, consider the possibility space Ω_{mat} for mathematics, the abstract space of all possible mathematical entities (e.g., numbers, groups, Euclidean space, vector spaces, Banach spaces, Riemannian spaces, and so on) and proofs (the proof that the square root of two is irrational, the Pythagorean theorem, Fermat's last theorem, and so on). These are timeless, eternal truths that can be expressed in many different formalisms.[19] At any point in time, we are aware of some of these entities and associated theorems and proofs, but unaware of others, and indeed, over time mathematical discovery extends our understanding of this space.[20] Hence, one must be very aware of the difference between the *subject* of mathematics as developed by intelligent beings (which is the total of what is known about mathematical truths at some time and is a developing human construct) and the mathematical truths themselves, characterized by the timeless unchanging possibility space Ω_{mat}.

Just as the status of the laws of physics is unclear, it is a moot point as to whether the relevant equations themselves are in Ω_{mat} or not: they are the symbolic formalisms we use to represent mathematical truths. Can the latter exist without *some* formalism? The most likely proposal is that the mathematical truth is an equivalence class of equations, using different formalisms, notations, and concepts that convey the same idea, and it is the abstract idea, rather than any representation of it, that is in Ω_{mat}.

In any case we can represent the relation of known to unknown mathematical possibilities in a table (Table 4, below), consisting of:

- subspace $P_{RU}(\Omega_{mat})$, which includes mathematical entities or relations that have been recognized and understood (e.g., integers, functions, integration)[21];

- subspace $P_{RN}(\Omega_{mat})$, which includes mathematical entities or relations that have been recognized but are not understood[22];

---

19. Cf. Jean-Pierre Changeux and Alain Connes, *Conversations on Mind, Matter, and Mathematics*, edited and translated by M. B. DeBevoise (Princeton: Princeton University, 1995); Penrose, *The Large, the Small*; and Edward Frenkel, *Love and Math: The Heart of Hidden Reality* (New York: Basic, 2013).

20. For a fascinating account of this process of discovery for the great mathematician Alexander Grothendieck, see Pierre Cartier, "Alexander Grothendieck: A Country Known Only by Name," *Inference: International Review of Science* 1:1, N.D., http://inference-review.com/article/a-country-known-only-by-name.

21. "Recognized" and "instantiated" are the same in this case.

22. For example, the Langlands program mentioned in Frenkel, *Love and Math*.

- and subspace $P_{NR}(\Omega_{mat})$, which includes mathematical entities or relations whose existence or nature has not yet been recognized, much less understood (the "unknown unknowns").

Abstract Mathematical Possibilities Ω_{mat}		
Recognized		Unrecognized
Understood	Not Understood	
P_{RU}	P_{RN}	P_{NR}

Table 4: *The ontological and epistemological possibilities for abstract entities. Their existence may be recognized (or not), and if recognized, understood (or not).*

The key point here is to distinguish Ω_{mat}, the timeless eternal set of mathematical entities and relations, from its representation $R(\Omega_{mat})$ in human minds. This is the human construction of our understanding of mathematics that represents the relations and entities in Ω_{mat} in some suitable notation, and continually changes with time as we explore mathematical possibilities and learn more about Ω_{mat}. We are able to do this because our brains are neural networks capable of exploring abstract Platonic spaces through their ability to recognize and classify patterns.[23] Clearly $R(\Omega_{mat})$ only represents the subspace P_{RU} of Ω_{mat}. At one time the Pythagorean theorem was unknown; once Pythagoras discovered it, it has been known ever sense. This marked a change in human knowledge which proved useful for surveyors and builders; the way in which the equation $a^2 + b^2 = h^2$ "represents" made no difference whatsoever to the abstract mathematical relation, or to Euclidean geometry. At any particular time, there are some issues in mathematics that are known to exist (e.g., the distribution of primes) and not yet understood; these form the subspace P_{RN} of Ω_{mat}. And there are some aspects we have yet to conceive, which form the subspace P_{NR} of Ω_{mat}; by its very nature we are not in a position to characterize these entities or relations.

The space Ω_{mat} is closely related to the space Ω_{log} containing the rules of logic, because mathematics is by nature based in a purely logical set of operations and statements; both are abstract spaces that do not depend on any physical realization for their existence.

---

23. Cf. Churchland, *Plato's Camera*.

Algorithms

For algorithms, the possibility space Ω_{alg} is rather different: an algorithm, such as a sorting algorithm, is not a logical statement; it is a set of instructions for getting from an initial state to some desired final state.[24] There will only be a finite number of ways of doing this; for example, if the aim is to sort a list, there is a limited set of sorting algorithms one could use to go about this task. Just as mathematicians anywhere in the universe will discover the same set of theorems because they are touching up against eternal, unchanging truths, so will computer scientists anywhere in the universe discover the same set of algorithms because they are the only logically possible way to get from an arbitrary initial state to a desired final state. These algorithms can then be realized in computer programs written in some specific computer language—an abstract instantiation of abstract structure, which can then be run on a digital computer and instantiated in physical form.[25] Neither the algorithm nor the program are the same as any one of the possible physical instantiations, but because they can be realized in multiple ways at the digital level (depending on the hardware and software used), they are each in an equivalence class of lower level realizations. A table like Table 4 will apply in this case too, relating what is known to what is not known.

Epistemology and Ontology for Mental Entities

How does the concept of possibility spaces relate to mental entities such as thoughts and theories, as well as emotions and qualia, which all exist as aspects of consciousness?

Thoughts and Theories

The idea of a possibility space can be extended to the space Ω_{tho}, which consists of all possible thoughts. As with the aforementioned possibility spaces, so here: you can't think a thought unless it is a possible to think it. Any thought you or I may have is preceded by the possibility that it may be

---

24. On the importance of algorithms, see John MacCormick, *Nine Algorithms that Changed the Future: The Ingenious Ideas that Drive Today's Computers* (Princeton: Princeton University Press, 2012).

25. Specifically, this is done in terms of electron flows through gates connected together in such a way as to implement logical structures; see M. Morris Mano and Charles Kime, *Logic and Computer Design Fundamentals*, 4th ed. (Upper Saddle River, NJ: Prentice Hall, 2007).

thought, which is built into the abstract logical structure of the universe in a timeless and eternal way. As in the case of mathematics, thought can be represented in many different ways (this is the function of language, which serve as a set of coordinates in Ω_{tho}). Thus a mapping from Ω_{tho} to a specific representation $R(\Omega_{tho})$ is provided by each language, and may be realized mentally, in spoken words, in writing, print, on computer screens, or in computer memories. What they all represent is the same.

Each representation $R(\Omega_{tho})$ is finite. It is not true, despite what some language theorists claim, that there are an infinite number of sentences possible in any natural language. This is because the function of a sentence is to convey information from one person to another; the brain has a finite short term memory, and you have to remember the beginning of a sentence by the time you reach the end.[26] Thus, any meaningful sentence is necessarily finite (actually, one could not even speak a sentence if it were infinite). The upshot for my purposes here is that what is *possible* to think is timelessly written into the abstract possibility structure Ω_{tho}. Our thoughts individually and collectively over time explores this possibility space.

The space Ω_{tho} contains subspaces related to each specific topic: for example, a possibility space $\Omega_{tho}(Mat)$ for thoughts regarding mathematics. The representation $R(\Omega_{mat})$ mentioned above is a mapping R from the subspace P_{RU} of Ω_{mat} to the space of representations of $\Omega_{tho}(Mat)$; in symbolic form,

$$R: P_{RU}(\Omega_{mat}) \rightarrow R(\Omega_{tho}(Mat)). \quad (1)$$

In a similar way there will be a subspace $\Omega_{tho}(Phy)$ of Ω_{tho} for theories in physics, including theories of electromagnetism, dark energy, dark matter, quantum gravity, and so on. The theories may or may not correspond to reality (that is, they may or may not be good representations of Ω_{phy}) but you can't explore the theory unless it's a theory that is possible to conceptualize. Because theories in physics are expressed in terms of equations, $\Omega_{tho}(Phy)$ is closely related to $\Omega_{tho}(Mat)$: specific entities in $\Omega_{tho}(Phy)$ will have a mathematical representation (and usually a number of different ones). Again there will be a subspace $\Omega_{tho}(Bio)$ of Ω_{tho} for biological theories, including the theories of evolution, physiology, developmental biology, epigenetics, animal behavior, and so on. Each will have multiple representations in specific symbolic form.

---

26. I have explored this topic in an unpublished paper (authored with the late William Stoeger) entitled "Language Infinities."

Ontology and Epistemology for Theories

These definitions, and equation (1), help clarify a crucial distinction: theories exist, and the realities they represent may exist; they are not the same thing. The key point here is that we can separate our theories from the things the theories are about; there are possibility spaces for both. Thus we can distinguish ontology from epistemology not only for material entities, but also for abstract entities such as mathematical theories in physics, which are often confused with the realities they represent. Any fundamental theory of the universe must explain existence of both kinds of possibility space: those for the abstract entities themselves (such as mathematics, Ω_{mat}), and those for theories about those entities, such as $\Omega_{tho}(\text{Mat})$.

Emotions, Qualia, and Consciousness

Possibility spaces can be extended further to a possibility space Ω_{con} for consciousness. Then space Ω_{tho} of all possible thoughts is a subspace of this space, for thoughts are an aspect of consciousness (they are the subspace captured by "cognitive science"). However, it also has subspaces Ω_{qua} for qualia and Ω_{emo} for emotions, that are of a different character, because qualia (the way it feels to have mental states such as pain, seeing red, smelling a rose, etc.) and emotions are very different than thoughts. However the rationale for their inclusion in a possibility space is the same: if these aspects of consciousness occur, then their possibility must precede this occurrence, and so constitute a feature of the universe. The physical existence of brains enables the actualization of their potential existence.

It is at this level of analysis that one may encounter very different kinds of things than one is used to, as Thomas Nagel famously showed.[27] Regarding qualia, different kinds of living beings may experience consciousness very differently due to their different sensory apparatuses; each species can only sample some part of Ω_{con}, and perception plays a key role in what they see or hear. As regards emotions, existence of the primary emotional systems characterized by Jaak Panksepp is a major difference between higher and lower species,[28] but these systems are shared in more or less the same form between humans and all other mammals. This is why humans can empathize with animals: we can recognize their emotional states.

27. Thomas Nagel, "What Is It Like to Be a Bat?" *The Philosophical Review* 83 (October 1974) 435–50.

28. Jaak Panksepp, *Affective Neuroscience: The Foundations of Human and Animal Emotions* (New York: Oxford University Press, 1998). I know that language of "higher and lower" is frowned on, but I regard it as a factual characterization of species' abilities.

In contrast to all other (known) animals, self-consciousness is a key characteristic of intelligent beings such as humans.[29] It allows self-reflection and symbolic behavior, enables symbolic representation of what is not immediately present and also of any quality or occurrence or logical argument, and so allows qualitative and quantitative analysis of hypothetical situations.[30] Symbolism underlies language which allows complex communication with others, and hence enables the emergence of coherent social structures. It also underlies abstract thought and planning, and is basic to mathematics and therefore science, engineering, technology, and commerce—the core elements in the rise of civilization.[31] What is more, self-consciousness combined with language also enables reflection on higher purposes such as ethics, meaning, and aesthetics.

Higher Purposes: Meaning, Aesthetics, and Ethics

Crucial subspaces of Ω_{tho} are $\Omega_{tho}(tel)$, thoughts about meaning ("telos": what is seen as the purpose of things); $\Omega_{tho}(eth)$, thoughts about ethics (what is seen as good or bad); and $\Omega_{tho}(aes)$, thoughts about aesthetics (what is seen as beautiful or ugly). These represent the highest aspects of human nature—tendencies that direct all other aspects of human behavior by setting the highest level goals and purposes that shape what we try to do, guide us as to what is desirable, and set constraints on what we consider acceptable behavior.[32] The relation of $\Omega_{tho}(eth)$ to a space Ω_{mor} (the abstract space of moral values) is key to the argument of this paper. There may be similar spaces for aesthetics and telos, but I will not argue for that here.

To analyze this it is useful to consider the way the mind functions, in particular the interaction between rationality, emotion, and meaning/ethics/aesthetics.

First, rationality is a key aspect of human intelligence enabling us to make choices between alternative goals and courses of action, and this based on our understanding of logic. The crucial point for this paper is that abstract possibility spaces exist and influence the logical operation of the

---

29. To say nothing of other possible intelligent beings in the universe.

30. Cf. Terrence W. Deacon, *The Symbolic Species: The Co-evolution of Language and the Brain* (New York: W. W. Norton, 1997).

31. Cf. Jacob Bronowski, *The Ascent of Man* (New York: Little, Brown and Company, 1973).

32. Cf. George F. R. Ellis, "Faith, Hope, and Doubt In Times of Uncertainty: Combining the Realms of Scientific and Spiritual Inquiry" (James Backhouse Lecture presented to the Australia Yearly Meeting of the Religious Society of Friends in Melbourne, January 2008).

mind: $\Omega_{\log}$ underlies our ability to think logically, Ω_{mat} underlies our mathematical abilities, etc. We understand such realities through the pattern recognition abilities of our minds, realized via the specific nature of neural networks in our brain.[33] So we can indeed access and understand Platonic spaces, as Churchland clearly describes, through the well-known physical processes that enable these neural networks to function.

However, while rationality is a key aspect of human intelligence that enables us to make rational choices between alternative goals and courses of action, in order to live humans also need faith and hope, because we always have inadequate information for making any real decision. When we make important decisions like whom to marry, whether to take a new job, start a business, or move to a new place, we never have enough data to be certain of the situation or the outcome. We gather evidence for as long as we like, but we will never be truly sure as to how many people will buy our product, what the weather will be like, how people will treat us, and so on. In the end, our choices have to be made on the basis of partial information, and are necessarily grounded on a considerable degree of faith in others and trust that what we choose will work out. This is true even in science. When my scientific colleagues set up research projects to look at string theory or particle physics, they do so in the hope that they will be able to obtain useful results when their grant applications have been funded. They do not know for sure that they will succeed in their endeavors. They trust that their colleagues will act honestly. Embedded in the very foundations of science there is a human structure of hope and trust.[34]

Crucial to the making of rational decisions is the role played by intuition and imagination.[35] Intuition acts as a short-cut for rational deliberation, embodying an ability to quickly act by activating learnt patterns of understanding in response to recognized patterns; thus intuition is learnt rather than hard wired. The intuition of a doctor, a mechanic, a football player, or a financial analyst is the deeply embedded result of previous experience and training in their respective fields. It is a fast-track ability to see the heart of the situation before you have had time to figure it out rationally, embodying in rapid-fire form the results of previous experience and rational understanding.[36] Similarly, imagination helps us think of possibilities

---

33. Churchland, *Plato's Camera*.

34. Cf. Robert P. Crease, "The Paradox of Trust in Science," *Physics World* (March 2004) 18.

35. On intuition, see David G. Myers, *Intuition: Its Powers and Perils* (New Haven: Yale University, 2002); on imagination, see Arnold G. Modell, *Imagination and the Meaningful Brain* (Cambridge, MA: MIT Press, 2003).

36. Cf. Daniel Kahneman, *Thinking, Fast and Slow* (New York: Farrar, Straus and

to be taken into account in making future rational choices and to envisage what might occur, setting the stage for our analysis of options and choices.

Secondly, emotions are a major factor in real decision making—both the hard-wired primary emotions that are our genetic inheritance from our animal forebears, and the socially determined secondary emotions that are our cultural inheritance from society. As explained so well by Antonio Damasio,[37] no decisions are made purely as a result of rational (i.e., "unemotional") choice; the first factor affecting what we do is the emotional tag attached to each experience, memory, and future plan; rationality kicks in later and supervises how we respond to our emotions. For example, the hoped-for joy and satisfaction of successful achievement underlies most scientific work; without it, science would not exist. The importance of emotions derives from the fact that our primary emotions have evolved over millions of years to give us immediate guidance as to what is good for our survival in a hostile environment,[38] which then guide the development of intellect,[39] as well as secondary emotions (telling us what aids our fitting into society).

Thirdly, we need values to guide our decisions, and so ethics, aesthetics and meaning are crucial to deciding what kind of life we will live. They are the highest level in our hierarchy of goals, shaping all the other goal decisions by setting the direction and purpose that underlies them—they define the "telos" (purpose) of our lives.[40] These values do not *directly* determine what lower level decisions will be made, but set the framework guiding the kinds of decisions that will be made and constrain what are considered acceptable choices.

Rational reflection and self-searching is a key element of well-developed ethics as one searches for values and meaning. Indeed, this is done in the context of overall meaning and purpose ("telos"), for the mind is constantly searching for meaning, both in metaphysical terms and in terms of the social life we share. These highest level understandings, and the

---

Giroux, 2011).

37. See Antonio R. Damasio, *Descartes' Error: Emotion, Reason, and the Human Brain* (New York: G. P. Putnam's Sons, 1994); and Antonio Damasio, *The Feeling of What Happens: Body and Emotion in the Making of Consciousness* (Orlando: Harcourt, 1999).

38. Panksepp, *Affective Neuroscience*.

39. Cf. George F. R. Ellis and Judith A. Toronchuk, "Neural Development: Affective and Immune System Influences," in *Consciousness and Emotion: Agency, Conscious Choice, and Selective Perception*, edited by Ralph D. Ellis and Natika Newton (Amsterdam: John Benjamins, 2005) 81–119.

40. We argued for this in Murphy and Ellis, *Moral Nature*.

associated emotions they evoke, drive everything else.[41] This is the guiding light for what we do—whether we realize it through art, sport, religion, science, commerce, friendship, or whatever—and so shapes our lives. Our appreciations of meaning are based in the possibility that we can indeed have a concept and experience of meaning; that is, they depend on the existence of the possibility space $\Omega_{tho}(tel)$ for thoughts about meaning.

For some, meaning may be based in aesthetics—an understanding and love of beauty. For those people, they will suggest that the realm of beauty is a deeper, timeless order of absolutes behind the surface, confuting the randomness of the temporal world.[42] Whether true or not, the ability to appreciate beauty is a reality, a major driving force in many people's lives. This ability exists because of possibilities for thoughts about aesthetics $\Omega_{tho}(aes)$. This is based on the fact that beauty can exist in a way that can be perceived.

The Nature and Emergence of Ethics and Morality

However, because interpretations of what is beautiful and what is not tend to be culturally dependent, I will not pursue this further here, but will concentrate on the third of the trio: the possibility space for ethical stances and understandings. Whether one makes it explicit or not, ethics plays a key role in all our actions. Crucially, we choose our actions on the basis of what we believe to be right and wrong, which is the purview of ethics and morality. In what follows, I will distinguish ethical emotions (what feels right), ethics itself (what communities or individuals deem to be right), and morality (what is right, as a matter of fact). Many discussions of ethics confuse these concepts, sometimes even denying these distinctions exist, but in my view this is incorrect: emotions influence our understanding of morality, but the two are not synonymous. Road rage is a helpful example: I may feel like killing a driver who cuts me off in traffic, but that is not the right thing to do. Such feelings often can give us an indication of what is right or wrong, but as they do not involve rational reflection, they may also be deeply misleading. Determining what is actually right is the perennial task of moral philosophy, inspired by the highest thoughts on these topics that society can provide, whatever their source; it involves thinking at the level of *telos* (purpose) rather than in terms of emotional feeling only. What is more, our views on what is right and wrong can err spectacularly. For example,

---

41. The importance of humanity's search for meaning is strongly emphasized in Viktor Frankl, *Man's Search for Meaning* (Boston: Beacon, [1946] 2006).

42. Cf. John Lane, *Timeless Beauty in the Arts and Everyday Life* (Cambridge: UIT Cambridge, 2003) 63.

the fundamentalist wings of the great religions are in each case travesties of what these religions actually stand for, and can lead to morally wrong acts such as the Inquisition and suicide bombings. In my view, such actions do not merely *seem* wrong, but are *in actuality* wrong, in an absolute sense.

Thus on this view, which I will develop below, there exists not just the Platonic possibility space $\Omega_{tho}(eth)$ for ethical thoughts and Ω_{eth} for ethics, but a Platonic space Ω_{mor} for morality, which underlies the possibility of ethical thought.

Possibility Space for Ethics

The existence of ethical discourse demonstrates the existence of $\Omega_{tho}(eth)$—the possibility space that underlies the ability to engage in such discourse, and which includes the possible existence of the categories of right and wrong as mental categories. Ethical possibilities are realized through ideas about ethics which are developed by one's interaction with other individuals and one's community (which will have its own ethical standards), as well as through writings, experiences, and cogitation on each of these, partly guided by ethical emotions. Rational thought about ethical issues helps separate these emotions from ethics itself.

The possibility space $\Omega_{tho}(eth)$ is the source of the very possibility of thinking some action is right or wrong. It relates classes of actions that may be claimed to be ethically relevant to possible judgments as to which of these actions might be considered right or wrong. Thus, the very possibility of the existence of the categories of right or wrong is due to the existence of this abstract space. It is also a space of possible human judgments, relating to how our minds may deem things to be right or wrong, and does not represent an absolute classification of what is indeed right and wrong (such an absolute classification is the function of Ω_{mor}, discussed below).

Any particular understanding of ethics is a normative projection drawn from the space of ethical thoughts to an evaluation function, with values in the real line R:

$$P: \Omega_{tho}(eth) \to R. \quad (2)$$

Thus P will label some possibilities in $\Omega_{tho}(eth)$ as good and others in bad. This judgment may depend on biology to some extent, but it will also depend on personality and cultural context that shifts over time. Its origins can be explained in psychological, social, and evolutionary terms, and there are major battles as to which is more important and how these influences interact. However, the key issue is whether there are universals that can be perceived through these processes (whatever they are, in whatever combination) that everyone can agree on. Can there be more than a culturally dependent understanding of right and wrong?

Moral Realism

Just as a valid understanding of mathematics is based on correctly perceiving the nature of the abstract possibility space Ω_{mat}, one can claim the same applies as regards ethics: ethical understanding is underpinned by the existence of a Platonic space Ω_{mor} for morality, also capable of being recognized by the mind, and that can indeed be universally recognized by morally sensitive individuals and cultures.

The existence of morality—valid judgments as to what is in fact right or wrong—depends not merely on the existence of a space of ethical possibilities: it depends on the existence of an abstract characterization of what is *in fact* good and bad, as well as an ability to discern this characterization. This only makes sense if there exists an abstract space Ω_{mor} of moral possibilities (possible actions related to good or bad) along with a metric that can give a classification that identifies what is in fact good or bad. This is the proposal of moral realism: in the same way that there is a physical and a mathematical Platonic reality underlying existence, there is also a Platonic moral reality.

I have argued the case for such a moral reality elsewhere.[43] I will not repeat those arguments here, but will simply state that if you want to avoid both moral relativism (which implies we cannot classify any deed as actually evil, only that we think it is evil, because such judgments are socially determined and are simply reflected in what people do) and moral vacuity (the stance that there is no such thing as good or evil), some version of moral realism is implied. Whether such a moral reality is well-represented by any specific community's concepts of good and bad is a separate issue.

The concept of a moral reality is described well by none other than Sam Harris, who writes, "The whole point of *The Moral Landscape* was to argue for the existence of moral truths . . . every bit as real as the truths of physics."[44] That is my position in this paper, as well. In my view, it is the only ethical view that takes morality seriously, and is implicit in much

---

43. Murphy and Ellis, *Moral Nature*; Ellis, "Faith, Hope, and Doubt."

44. Quoted in Dwayne Holmes, "Clarifying Sam Harris' Clarifications," *Scientia Salon*, July 24, 2014, http://scientiasalon.wordpress.com/2014/07/24/clarifying-sam-harriss-clarification/. Cf. Sam Harris, *The Moral Landscape: How Science Can Determine Human Values* (New York: Free Press, 2011).

other writing, even when it is not explicitly stated or recognized. Indeed, the existence of a moral reality is implied by the characterization of anything as *in fact* evil, as this assumes ultimate moral standards exist. Thus, it is implicit in the writings even of Richard Dawkins and Viktor Stenger when they characterize all religion as evil: they assume meaningful moral standards exist (that are not just social constructs) by which to judge religion. That is, they believe not just in the existence of the possibility space $\Omega_{tho}(eth)$ for ethical thought, but in a characterization of what is in fact good or bad; they believe in the possibility space Ω_{mor} of genuinely meaningful moral judgements.

In functional terms, the space Ω_{mor} provides a set of preferred possible behaviors that are equivalent to norms n in the space $\Omega_{tho}(eth)$ of ethical possibilities; that is, it defines a mapping M:

$$N: \Omega_{mor} \to n[\Omega_{tho}(eth)]. \quad (3)$$

Human minds may then map these into moral thoughts accurately or inaccurately, depending on the ethical maturity of the society or individual in question (see "The Origin of Ethical Values," below).

Nature of Morality: Kinds of Logic

Given my claim that a moral reality exists, one has a duty to be explicit about what kind of reality this is. My proposal, unpacked elsewhere,[45] is that the true nature of morality is *kenotic*. Kenosis is understood as a joyous attitude that is willing to give up selfish desires and to make sacrifices on behalf of others for the common good, doing this voluntarily in a generous and creative way, avoiding the pitfall of pride—and guided and inspired by love. This is a generous rather than punitive morality, based in the attitude of "letting go" of one's own interests on behalf of others; this attitude is transformational in nature, carrying the possibility of changing the quality and meaning of any situation one faces. It is a form of virtue ethics and contrasts strongly with the kind of morality implied by the rational logic of benefit maximization that is usually assumed as the basis of economic behavior. Indeed, kenotic morality is profoundly paradoxical by nature, explained

---

45. Murphy and Ellis, *Moral Nature*; Ellis, "Faith, Hope, and Doubt"; George F. R. Ellis, "The Theology of the Anthropic Principle," in *Quantum Cosmology and the Laws of Nature: Scientific Perspectives on Divine Action*, edited by Robert John Russell, Nancey Murphy, and C. J. Isham (Vatican City: Vatican Observatory, 1993) 367–406.

beautifully by Parker Palmer, among others.⁴⁶ It confounds the rational logic of economic calucation.

Kenosis is the way to fight evil at the most fundamental level, as it has as its purpose the transformation of evil intentions to good. Such a deep transformation cannot be achieved by military force or bribery, nor even through intellectual argument or persuasion: it is achieved by touching them at their deepest, human level. Each of the major world religions has a spiritual tradition that believes seriously and deeply in a kenotic ethic. It is exemplified in the life and work of Martin Luther King Jr., Mahatma Gandhi, and Desmond Tutu. It also is a profoundly important principle in family and community life, art, and learning.⁴⁷

The Origin of Ethical Values

In making this argument for moral realism, I am clearly pushing against the variety of attempts at deriving ethical values from science alone. In particular, some have claimed that science can explain ethical value through evolutionary psychology or by neuro-psychological study, but these attempts will fail, as such phenomena are by their very nature beyond the scope of science.

Firstly, if the origin of ethics is solely a matter of kin or group survival, then clearly any number of violent actions are morally permissible. It's fine to massacre one's enemies, war is by nature justified. There is no place for a deeper conception of ethics—the ethics of self-sacrifice—in such a worldview. But there are two larger problems with this view: the evolutionary explanation fallacy, and the "ought" from "is" fallacy.

In the evolutionary origins fallacy,⁴⁸ it is proposed that once you have an evolutionary explanation of something, the work of explanation is complete, and the thing in question (e.g., ethics) has been fully understood. This is simply not the case. In actuality, an evolutionary psychology explanation for any human activity, theory, or belief is always partial and incomplete, and its existence is irrelevant to the truth claims of the theory involved.

---

46. Parker J. Palmer, *The Promise of Paradox: A Celebration of Contradictions in the Christian Life* (San Francisco: Jossey-Bass, [1980] 2008). See also G. K. Chesterton, *Orthodoxy* (Chicago: Moody, [1908] 2009) ch. 6.

47. Cf. Ellis, "Faith, Hope, and Doubt."

48. Cf. George F. R. Ellis, "Why Are the Laws of Nature as They Are? What Underlies Their Existence?" in *The Astronomy Revolution: 400 Years of Exploring the Cosmos*, edited by Donald G. York, Owen Gingerich, and Shuang-Nan Zhang (Boca Raton, FL: Taylor and Francis, 2012) 387.

The flaw in this thesis becomes clear when we realize that it applies to every human activity, including all scientific theories and indeed evolutionary psychology itself. The influence of evolutionary psychology is just one strand in the causal web influencing each of these topics. The claim there has to be an evolutionary psychology explanation for the existence of special relativity theory does not prove that any specific aspects of that theory are either correct or incorrect! In the case of ethics, identifying an evolutionary origin to a particular ethical conviction does not by itself prove anything about its worth or truth. It just proves that there can be mechanisms whereby we come to believe certain acts are good or bad. The fact that people behaved in a particular way in the past (or do so today) does not necessarily mean it is good. It just means it is how humans have behaved.

Other popular attempts to explain morality away hinge on neuroscience in combination with genetics, proposing for example that as there are neurotransmitters that make us happy, so we can reduce morality to the neuroscientific investigation of molecules related to happiness, and thus leads some to refer to oxytocin as the "moral molecule."[49] Like a series of other recent books trying to derive morality from science, this ignores two thousand years of debate in moral philosophy about the nature of good and evil, and the nature of the good life.

Relatedly, the "ought" from "is" fallacy attempts to derive morality (ought) from what exists physically, or else how people behave (is); it rests on a category mistake. Evidence of a person's ethical understanding and behavior—how they understand morality in theory and how this is made manifest—does not say anything about the moral rightness (or lack thereof) of any such behavior. Such judgments require essentially moral criteria that help categorize what is good and bad.

Every such reductive explanation smuggles in a view of the nature of the good life through the back door (for example, that happiness or group survival is the same as morality, or that how people behave towards one another is what ought to be), which is the trick whereby what *is* becomes what *ought* to be. But against such a simplified view, morality encompasses many emergent dimensions of life, and cannot be reduced to neural laws alone, as claimed by Samir Zeki.[50] That's the reductionist dream—which ironically rests on misunderstandings about the way the mind works, which is not reducible to neural laws in the way normally assumed by such theories.[51]

49. Paul J. Zak, *The Moral Molecule: How Trust Works* (New York: Penguin, 2012).

50. See Phillip Ball, "Neuroaesthetics is Killing Your Soul," *Nature*, March 22, 2013, http://www.nature.com/news/neuroaesthetics-is-killing-your-soul-1.12640.

51. Nancey has worked to dismantle this reductionist tendency in Nancey Murphy and Warren S. Brown, *Did My Neurons Make Me Do It? Philosophical and*

In conclusion, that people tend to behave in a certain way does not make that behavior ethically or morally right. The occurrence or evolutionary origin of a behavior does not entail its normativity. These arguments amount to arbitrary assumptions about the mapping of n in (2), above; you can't get "ought" from "is" (or from what tends to happen or what people do). This is a category mistake. Darwinian logic suggests ethics is based in survival, but this speaks to what people do (or did), not to what they ought to do.[52]

Ethical Discovery of Moral Truths

So where do ethics come from? My proposal is that ethics is a human endeavor that develops as we explore the nature of morality over time; one can call this the "Moral Discovery Thesis." The nature of the space Ω_{mor} of morals is discovered by humanity over time, just as in the case of mathematics, and at any particular time, a particular society's or individual's understanding of morality may or may not be a good reflection of the true nature of Ω_{mor}, which is the source of moral values.

Thus, my proposal is that there is a moral reality (alongside a physical and mathematical reality) underlying the universe, just waiting to be discovered, and which is valid in all times and places. Human moral life is the search to understand and implement that moral reality. Thus morality characterized by Ω_{mor} selects moral behavior in the space of thoughts about possible ethical actions $\Omega_{tho}(eth)$, as per (3), rather than $\Omega_{tho}(eth)$ reflecting human constructions of what is right and wrong on the basis of evolutionary or social pressures. This distinguishes essentially emergent properties from pre-existing Platonic properties that we discover, the essence of whose nature lies in eternal truths about abstract entities depicting the possibilities they encompass or represent.

Is this pure philosophy without any connection to observable data? Certainly not: there is massive data about right and wrong in our personal experiences and communal lives stretching throughout history. We face morally weighted situations everyday, and observe how what is done works out. We get good and bad advice on how to interpret these situations from friends and leaders and moral philosophers. And we make our own choices which shape how our moral lives develop and how our own character takes

---

Neurobiological Perspectives on Moral Responsibility and Free Will (New York: Oxford University Press, 2007).

52. Besides, where does the assumed moral imperative that human survival is good come from?

shape. Some have even suggested that our global moral understanding is slowly improving (but of course with major throwbacks in particular local areas of conflict).[53] In any case, ethically sensitive individuals—the spiritual leaders of their time—have understood this moral reality for thousands of years, which is variously reflected in each of the great world religions.

Implications for Philosophy and Theology

Given all this analysis, the final question that arises is, What is the origin of all these possibility spaces, but particularly those for meaning, ethics, and morality? If one is to explore the nature of existence, these too will need explanation, and not merely the possibility spaces that relate to the purely physical aspects of existence. Where do the possibility spaces come from? Why do they have the nature they do?

Science cannot answer this question: it is a philosophical question. What kind of origin can there be? Chance, necessity, and purpose are all at work in the universe and we want to understand how they interact with each other. But then, we want to understand where the very concepts of chance, necessity, purpose, good, and evil all come from. What underlies the existence of the possibilities of thinking in these categories? Answering that question depends not merely on the space of possible thoughts, which is the space of representation of these concepts, but on the space of logical possibilities which is the origin of why we are able to think about them in the first place. You can only think about them if it is possible to think about them, which means they must exist as abstract categories that can be contemplated.

The implication is that if we want to understand the nature of the universe in its fullness and depth, we need to consider not just physical existence and its underlying laws—why anything exists at all—but also the existence of the possibility spaces of thoughts and meaning, and in particular those pertaining to meaning, ethics, and morality. Their existence is the evidence that the universe is not merely materialistic. Did these come about my chance, necessity, happenstance, or purpose? I have suggested that purpose is the best contender,[54] as it seems unlikely that they could arise *ex nihilo*. The obvious conclusion is that morality expresses the deep nature of purpose underlying existence—a conclusion that would seem to have obvious theological implications.

53. Steven Pinker, *The Better Angels of Our Nature: Why Violence Has Declined* (New York: Viking Penguin, 2011).

54. Ellis, "Faith, Hope, and Doubt."

Thomas Nagel's recent work explores these same issues and comes to broadly the same conclusions I have reached here, except for the last.[55] Nagel contends that the mental side of existence must somehow have been present in creation from the very start; morality, too, according to Nagel, pre-existed the universe as a kind of Platonic form, into which we gradually grow as we discover morality in the same way we discovered the Pythagorean theorem. Nagel believes that certain deeds would be wrong whether humans thought so or not, and this structure of morality must have existed independently, before conscious minds started contemplating such matters. That is the argument I have made here; I suggest that distinguishing the various possibility spaces and the relations between them can make Nagel's argument more rigorous.

My conclusion, however, is different than Nagel's. The obvious outcome is that *telos* (meaning) is at the foundations of existence and closely related to morality: the two are intimately intertwined. Essentially emergent properties—the essence of whose nature lies in the interrelation between bottom up and top down causation—allow us to discern this *telos*, as the emergent nature of our brains enables our discovery of these abstract Platonic realms. Any analysis of the nature of the universe that ignores such realms' existence is incomplete. Their existence suggests that at its foundations, the universe is not meaningless.

---

55. Thomas Nagel, *Mind and Cosmos: Why the Materialist Neo-Darwinian Conception of Nature is Almost Certainly False* (New York: Oxford University Press, 2012).

9

God: Discovering Yet Another Empiricist Dogma?

—J. B. Phillips

"What is philosophy?" This is a rather embarrassing question for some philosophers, not least because it is a question without obvious answers. The sort of embarrassment at issue here is not of the more frequent, mundane variety that some specialists feel when trying to explain something taken to be abstruse. Neither is this the sophistical, simplistic, nor impudently dilettantish question that it might appear to be at first blush. Rather, taken in the proper spirit, this question is one way of expressing what has been called meta-philosophy or the philosophy of philosophy. Allied questions in this area concern things like: "What counts as philosophy?"; "Is there an audience for philosophy?" (Stanley Cavell); "What counts as a philosophical problem and its solution?"; "Is philosophy primarily a theoretical investigation or a way of life?" (Pierre Hadot); "How does one distinguish philosophy from science, literature, logic, or theology?"; "Is philosophy simply as W. V. O. Quine claimed, 'a chapter in science'?"; "Are the literary forms used in philosophy irrelevant to philosophy itself?"(Cavell); "What is philosophy's relationship to its past?"(Alasdair MacIntyre); and "How does one write or teach philosophy, and what is the relationship of one's answer to those questions to what one takes philosophy to be?" There are no self-evident answers to these questions. Indeed, the various ways of doing philosophy (which are more or less recognized) are themselves constituted by answers to questions such as these. More accurately still, answers to these questions make clear what is at stake for disputants in understanding something to be a philosophical text, for example, or apprehending what conception of philosophy is revealed by arguments mounted that a particular text is not a "philosophical" text.

There indeed may not be any self-evident rational answers in the case of philosophy generally, but surely in the case of philosophy of religion, things are much more clear cut and regular. Surely the genitival relation between religion and philosophy implies the possibility of a more satisfactory reply than is likely to be given in answer to the more generic question "What is philosophy?" Though some practitioners of philosophy of religion may feel settled about what constitutes their discipline, coziness is not the same as cogent self-awareness and self-critical justification. To be fair, until very recently it was widely held that many of the above meta-philosophical questions not only had self-evident answers, but that those answers were taken to be isomorphic with "Reason" itself. Thus, on this view, the answers to meta-philosophical questions can and should be grasped by those rightly orientated to an objective "Reason" which always holds, come what may, in all times and places. This is one way, among others, to apprehend the socio-intellectual hope of modern reason. Criticisms of modern rationality are *de rigeur*, and risk becoming hackneyed and passé. However, the needed shift in philosophical discussions to a greater level of sophistication by moving to criticism of the meta-philosophical, or to what one might call the metaphysics of inquiry, has not yet taken place, at least not amongst most philosophers of religion.

In this essay, I hope to show that it is frequently the case that the metaphysical or meta-philosophical assumptions embedded in many approaches to epistemology entail a rather peculiar view of God as a kind of object, or God as a deficient thesis of physics. I will use the philosophy of W. V. O. Quine to help illustrate the problem with this view, and to map a tentative suggestion for avoiding an error that seems to continue to bedevil much of the work done at the boundary of philosophy and theology.

Quine, Epistemology, and the Metaphysics of Inquiry

What could possibly be meant by "metaphysics of inquiry"? Or better, what might it mean to pay attention to the metaphysical assumptions that often frame inquiry? Let us consider the case of epistemology as a possible way of answering this question. Epistemology has long been a dominant critical discourse in philosophy of religion. Indeed, the standard view of modern philosophy is that it is demarcated by the rise of epistemology, a technique for testing claims and arriving at veridical knowledge. Unquestionably this tradition most determinatively shapes philosophy of religion, especially in the Anglophone world. Further, epistemology in this tradition is profoundly influenced by the empiricist inheritance and its strong connection to scientific inquiry. As we shall see, there are good reasons to rethink this alliance between analytic philosophy the epistemological tradition from within the terms of analytic philosophy itself. The implications of broader philosophical criticism of the epistemological tradition play out in philosophy of religion, not least because of its distinct subject matter and intellectual past. Philosophy of religion as an academic guild constitutes a culture of inquiry and is also a manifestation of a culture. It is, in historical terms, a manifestation of cultural struggle with the place of "the religious" against a backdrop of vast changes that seemed to render religious belief problematic and dubious. While this fact in itself is not remarkable, what is problematic is that the account of reason that typically governs philosophy of religion takes it as unproblematic that its account of reason sufficiently transcends the particularities of this past as well as the particularities of the religious views it seeks to criticize. To put the matter more succinctly, there is no argument or justification for how this form of inquiry achieves its aim nor for how its procedures and methods are up to the task apart from the apparent persuasiveness of its criticisms of religion (taking criticism in the generic Cavellian sense) which may already be welcomed by an anti-religious (or religious) culture. The absence of this sort of argument is part of the meta-philosophical limitation of much analytic philosophy of religion. It is vulnerable to mistaking ideology for rationality because of its lack of resources for critically addressing its meta-philosophical commitments. Philosophical procedures are part of what philosophy takes itself to be and one must be prepared to embrace the implications of the fact that those procedures have a history of relative success or failure in satisfying criteria of investigations. Moreover, it is not an insignificant recognition that these procedures have a history which can (and must be) rationally criticized and justified as being adequate to the object at which one aims in rational inquiry.

In order to judge whether the epistemological tradition is adequate to the object of its inquiry in philosophy of religion, we would do well to consider the case of philosopher W. V. O. Quine. There is perhaps no more revolutionary exponent of the epistemological tradition in Anglophone philosophy than Willard Quine, nor a greater critic of this tradition from within. Quine is an important case to consider because he is one of two figures whose work many analytic philosophers take to be determinative of the present and future course of analytic philosophy.[1] He occupies this

---

1. See Avrum Stroll, *Twentieth-Century Analytic Philosophy* (New York: Columbia University Press, 2000); and Robert L. Arrington and Hans-Johann Glock, eds., *Wittgenstein and Quine* (London: Routledge, 1996).

space not least because he determinatively and sophisticatedly overturned the positivist assumptions of analytic philosophy from within the disciplinary parameters of analytic philosophy itself. In spite of this corrective, his work is clearly the apotheosis of the positivist hope in the all-determining explanatory power of science. Quine's quarrel with the positivist tradition could be interpreted in terms of his elimination of the residual Cartesianism that he believed bedeviled this tradition. His work in this area was twofold. On the one hand, both foundationalisms and fact/value distinctions had to be abandoned in favor of something like epistemological holism, or his notion of "webs of belief." On the other hand, this holism rested its metaphysical head on the pillow of science and the deliverances of scientific investigation. Simply put, for Quine science gives philosophy all of the metaphysics it needs to do its work, and philosophy thus becomes a "chapter in science." This project, what Quine comes to call "naturalized epistemology," is a complete rejection of the "Cartesian dream of a foundation of scientific certainty firmer than scientific method itself."[2] But if this project is to be realized, then how does one account for traditional epistemology in terms of scientific method alone?

On the one hand, Quine wishes to assert, like any good empiricist, that he remains "occupied ... with what has been central to traditional epistemology, namely the relation of science to sensory data." However, he wishes to maintain that this connection is not found in Cartesian consciousness but is instead a "relation open to inquiry as a chapter in science," of an "antecedently acknowledged external world."[3] If one does not have Cartesian mental states to sort out this connection between data and science, then what is to take its place? This is precisely the point of Quine's advocacy for a "naturalized epistemology." Rather than hold a place for metaphysically dubious mental entities, the "pursuit of naturalized epistemology" is simply "operationalized" by the study of "neural receptors and their stimulation rather than of sense or sensibilia."[4] Thus, Quine writes, "[T]heoretical epistemology gets naturalized into a chapter of theoretical science, so normative epistemology gets naturalized into a chapter of engineering: the technology of anticipating sensory stimulation."[5] Against his critics, Quine wishes to stress that natu-

---

2. W. V. Quine, *Pursuit of Truth*, rev. ed. (Cambridge, MA: Harvard University Press, 1992) 19.

3. Ibid.

4. Ibid. In connection with Quine's account of holism, see "Two Dogmas of Empiricism," reprinted in W. V. Quine, *From a Logical Point of View: Nine Logico-Philosophical Essays* (Cambridge, MA: Harvard University Press, 1953) 20–46; W. V. Quine and J. S. Ullian, *The Web of Belief*, 2nd ed. (New York: McGraw Hill, 1978).

5. Quine, *Pursuit of Truth*, 19.

ralized epistemology remains normative, and it still retains what he claims is a central norm of epistemology, namely the empiricist conviction that *"nihil in mente quod non prius in sensu"*: "Nothing is in the intellect that was not first in the senses." This norm of traditional epistemology exactly coincides with his view of naturalized epistemology; it is simply that now this notion is "a finding of natural science itself . . . that our information about the world comes only through impacts of our sensory receptors. And still the point is normative, warning us against telepaths and soothsayers."[6]

Interestingly, Quine claims that science (and by extension one may say philosophy) is not constitutionally committed to the physical, because science itself has shown that "[b]odies have long since diffused into swarms of particles, and the Bose-Einstein statistic has challenged the particularity of the particle. Even telepathy and clairvoyance are scientific options, however moribund."[7] Quine takes telepathy and clairvoyance to be defunct theories of prediction for the "primitive science" of bygone eras. Not only have such "theories" been left behind, but the aim of science has shifted to focus on knowledge and understanding. For Quine, one cannot rationally rule out in advance the possibility of "telepathy," "revelation," or "divine input." This is so, Quine claims, because science is "fallible and corrigible." However, he claims that it would take some sort of extraordinary occurrences to breathe new life into these outmoded perspectives. If such evidence were to emerge, "empiricism itself—the crowning norm, we saw, of naturalized epistemology—would go by the board. For remember that that norm, and naturalized epistemology itself are integral to science."[8] Clearly, Quine considers the possibility that empiricism could be overturned by any sort of revelation or telepathy to be extremely remote. Yet, he claims, even in the highly unlikely event that empiricism was overturned, the test of "the resulting science" that admits revelation "would still be predicted sensation."[9]

What is interesting about Quine's case, regardless of whether one accepts his argument for naturalized epistemology, is the isomorphism of empirical explanation and metaphysics. The sufficiency of epistemology, whether on the traditional or naturalized account, depends on a metaphysics of inquiry which is indebted to a view of material causes and their impact on the senses. Moreover, this sort of inquiry relies not only on views of sufficient causal explanation, but shows epistemology to be based in the exclusion of any other causal explanation or potency. It is this procedure

---

6. Ibid.
7. Ibid., 20–21.
8. Ibid., 21.
9. Ibid.

of reduction in the epistemological tradition, as Quine has characterized it, which in turn warrants verdicts about the existence or non-existence of certain entities or phenomena. In one sense this procedure is unproblematic and is part and parcel of much scientific investigation, a fact which motivates Quine's philosophy and gives it is innovative edge. Quine has not been the first to resort to a kind of clearing away of "unnecessary entities" by virtue of epistemological argument. One could say that Quine simply stands within, reformulates, and extends this practice of doing ontology via the "first philosophy" of epistemology with its concomitant metaphysical commitments to a version empiricism and empirical enquiry.

If one understands Quine's work (as many do) as the apotheosis and transformation of the empiricist tradition, or at least a definitive representative of it, then there are two observations that follow from this for the purposes of this essay. First, the metaphysical consequences of Quine's account are increasingly contested within analytic philosophy itself. This contest has emerged most clearly in the area of the nature of human agency and the sort of "neurophilosophy" resident in Quine's view (and those who have carried this work further), giving a more fully-fledged view of the marriage of philosophy and neuroscience.[10] Quine's disciples are taken to offer a reductionist view of human agency, preferring instead to talk about beliefs and intentions at the level of neural activation. One of the central issues in this debate concerns the legacy of reductionism, and this inheritance has provoked examination and criticism of the adequacy of the kind of metaphysical judgments written into this form of philosophical inquiry. Allied to this is criticism of Quine's more general faith in science as offering totalizing explanations for all reality, a position sometimes referred to scientism, or the fusing of philosophy with science. Perhaps more accurately, scientism is the view that a certain version of the scientific method of investigation is adequate to unveil *all* knowledge worthy of the name. This particular view of the metaphysics of inquiry informs Quine's view that philosophy can be taken as a chapter in science. And this view is something for which he has been both celebrated and reviled. Whatever one makes of Quine's work, he does show a critical awareness of, and a willingness to own up to, his metaphysical debts to scientistic empiricism. Quine shows how deeply embedded a particular view of the material is in the philosophical tradition and, as we shall see, how deeply problematic it is.

---

10. One can think here of Paul Churchland and Daniel Dennett, among others, but Patricia Churchland offers a particularly robust philosophical account of just how Quine's work is being carried on by reductionist and eliminativist accounts of philosophy of mind. See especially her *Neurophilosophy: Toward a Unified Science of the Mind-Brain* (Cambridge, MA: MIT Press, 1986).

The second observation generated by Quine's perspective actually comes in the form of critical questions for practice in analytic philosophy of religion and its close alliance with the epistemological tradition. This line of questioning concerns whether the epistemological tradition could in principle ever grasp the concept of transcendence vis-à-vis the material, beyond the Cartesian conception thereof. Is this tradition of critical inquiry conceptually closed to such a notion by virtue of the metaphysical assumptions that are written into its practice? How would one come up with a notion of reason within this tradition that is open to (or at least not determined against) the divine, as opposed to being oriented exclusively toward the material (as God's opposite, the evacuator of God, God's causal competitor) as a matter of metaphysical necessity and explanatory success? How does one overcome or account for the way in which this tradition pits the material and its transcendence in a zero-sum fashion? Can the epistemological frame, so conceived, ever be constitutionally, conceptually adequate to, or open to the divine?

Quine's naturalized epistemology illustrates simultaneously the criticism and renovation of epistemology with its materialist empiricist assumptions. Yet, it is clear from Quine's account that God in principle cannot reveal God's self. God is by definition a threat to explanation, not least because God is not "metaphysically" (read constitutionally, causally) adequate to get a grip on the senses, and by definition cannot meet the criteria of the epistemological tradition. This view also informs not just epistemologists in philosophy of religion but fuels the hopes of many cognitive scientists of religion. Many hope that an account of religion in terms of brain science will either explain religion away or situate it within the matrix of certain brain processes.

The difficulty here for those who wish to engage in epistemology, in philosophy of religion, or in cognitive science of religion is the antecedent metaphysical assumptions that frame such an inquiry. One must tread carefully, because when expressing scruples about the modern project of proving God's existence one may well find oneself open to the charge of "fideism," i.e. persisting in belief in God without the sort of rational justification taken as credible within the epistemological frame. However, the charge of fideism cannot cover over a certain metaphysics of inquiry which is privileged and remains uninterrogated within the epistemological tradition. Be that as it may, is it fideistic to ask how Quine's account of reason could ever meet the "religious" on its own terms? I don't propose to answer this meta-philosophical question in a fully-fledged way, but to point to the need to interrogate the status of antecedent, often metaphysical assumptions that give rational inquiry its form, and point to a new terrain for inquiry.

Philosophy of Religion and Rational Inquiry about "God"

The relationship of metaphysics to inquiry has become hidden from view because some version or other of empiricist materialism has been the self-evident standard of rationality to which all parties in Anglophone philosophy generally, and analytic philosophy of religion in particular, have assented. Indeed, this inheritance is arguably what has given this style of philosophy its distinctiveness. This manner of inquiry comes to grief, however, not just with the form of inquiry, but the problematic nature of how it relates the material to God. The adequacy of one's conceptions of God and the material are often hidden deep from view, especially when it comes to the question of how these concepts might impact the form of one's inquiry itself. What *could* it mean to "prove" God's existence against the backdrop of this metaphysics of inquiry?

Rarely do philosophers of religion consider the role of philosophy in their deliberations; it is more or less assumed that religion provides the subject matter and "philosophy" the means of critical exploration, disputation, analysis, and clarification of issues raised by religion. Like analytic philosophy in general, philosophy of religion so conceived is problem focused, and in fact is conceived as a collection of problems raised by religion. Rarely do such philosophers pay attention to the role philosophy plays in the construction of these problems. Rarely do they ask themselves where it is that philosophy and religion touch and how that interface is understood. In other words, rarely do they ask themselves meta-philosophical questions. Even those analytic philosophers of religion who criticize the epistemological tradition appear to focus on the metaphysics of possible worlds and the implications of logical possibility, and thus hew to antecedent metaphysical convictions which are perhaps over-determined by a reaction against the dominance of naturalism. This has led in some instances to a kind of epistemological rationalism which risks reifying the logic of language to support its anti-naturalism. There is a version of philosophy of religion that is happy to see religion criticized and even some philosophers of religion see that religion is a force that needs to be tamed by a certain sort of critique. There are those who see this as the remit of analytic philosophy of religion in particular to ensure that religion is criticized from within antecedent commitments to political liberalism. Religion should be trimmed via critiques from philosophers of religion because internal processes of critique are not sufficient. This project is formed by prior commitments to a specific sort of polity which makes it possible to position religious traditions in such a fashion that their various claims can be more or less assessed via certain analytic tools. These various tools and procedures are presumed to be sufficient for rational criticism and the winnowing process of assessing the validity or otherwise of religious claims. However, rarely does this sort of account of epistemological rationality understand itself and its own antecedent commitments, its own location, its own meta-philosophy. Is it possible to recognize this as a failure in philosophical inquiry, a failure to understand, rather than as one party failing to be rational *tout court*? To the extent that epistemology is practiced by Quinian lights or in its traditional form, it rests on a set of metaphysical assumptions that pit God against the material order in a way that makes it inherently impossible to "think transcendence."

It is not a minor datum for philosophy of religion that the rational frame on which it has relied to criticize religion is conceptually inadequate for thinking transcendence or thinking of the divine. This situation has persisted not least in analytic philosophy of religion because of its troubled past in relation to metaphysical criticism and metaphysics generally. Effectively, science has taken over the job of metaphysics full stop, and this circumstance leaves the issue of God as one of the subjects in an oft-repeated story in the present culture: because science is true, there is no God. Or at the least, there is no intelligible way to talk about God's action in the world without threatening the causal closure presumed to be demanded by science. Might not there be a role for critical inquiry into the metaphysics of inquiry in philosophy of religion which highlights the problematic tendency of rationally pitting God and the material against one another? Exploring the metaphysics of inquiry in this case reveals that the form of rationality in epistemological inquiry, in its traditional or naturalized form, as Quine makes clear, is *predicated* on being *metaphysically* closed to the divine. Furthermore, one can question, as Nancey Murphy has done, the metaphysical adequacy of modeling rationality on the functioning of the natural sciences which tends to privilege bottom-up reductionist accounts of causation that put God and the material into a zero-sum relationship.[11] This fact alone should signal that the form of inquiry in philosophical thinking about religion has been bedeviled by, if not constitutionally closed to, the *ratio Dei*. Therefore, it is not simply the case that philosophy of religion needs to turn to religious practice while still retaining the epistemological frame, or to simply "epistemologize" practices. It must settle its constitutional meta-philosophical accounts and enrich its notion of what counts as philosophy. Philosophy of religion must live with the question of whether or not its account of philosophy is constitutionally, conceptually unable to think transcendence. To raise this issue might constitute a more fruitful level of engagement than

---

11. See Nancey Murphy and George F. R. Ellis, *On the Moral Nature of the Universe: Theology, Cosmology and Ethics* (Minneapolis: Fortress, 1996).

rehashing old proofs and trading epithets. This move does not cease to take rational disagreements with or criticisms of religion seriously; rather it attempts to render the nature of those disagreements rational by gaining a clearer understanding of the nature of reasoning about transcendence and the intellectual demands of the *ratio Dei*.

The *Ratio Dei* and Knowing the Unknowable God: A New Ground for Rational Engagement?

In order to get some clarity about these matters, perhaps it would be helpful to return to the case of Quine's philosophy. However much one may wish applaud the anti-Cartesian bits of his philosophy, it does appear to be the case that having got rid of one side of Descartes's dualism one is left with the *res extensa* side of his dualism. On this view, the physical-material is inert, closed, deterministic, and mechanistic, which of course is why, in Descartes's view, a non-material entity, the soul, is required to act upon matter. In this way it is not surprising that Quine anticipates, and his followers deliver up, an evacuation of the concept of human agency as somehow an offense against science: because, against a certain backdrop, it appears to be an "occult" cause. Of course, Nancey Murphy is renowned for arguing that the conclusions of Quine's disciples are dubious and that reductionism is not entailed in a commitment to physicalism. Murphy and others have been at pains to display that physicalism not only does not imply reductionism nor eliminativism in philosophy of mind, but also that nonreductive physicalism has much to recommend it in the realm of theological anthropology and theology generally.[12]

What I intend to do here is not to offer further reflections on the issue of agency and nonreductive physicalism, but to explore how one might challenge the reductionist legacy of Quine with respect to thinking about the existence of God. My intention is not so much to offer a definitive solution to this problem, but to follow up on some of the observations about suggesting a way forward for thinking about God that resists and problematizes the reductionist frame. The reflections offered here occupy the borderlands of theology and philosophy proper. As noted above, it is frequently assumed that philosophy controls the terms of the debate. However, as we have seen,

---

12. For the philosophical side of this argument, see Nancey Murphy and Warren S. Brown, *Did My Neurons Make Me Do It? Philosophical and Neurobiological Perspectives on Moral Responsibility and Free Will* (New York: Oxford University Press, 2007). In regard to Murphy's theological anthropology, see Nancey Murphy, *Bodies and Souls, or Spirited Bodies?* (Cambridge: Cambridge University Press, 2006).

even accounts of philosophy like Quine's trade on making certain claims about the nature of God in order to determine that such a "god" does not exist. Or perhaps the better way to put Quine's view is that "god" is not a causal potency and therefore has no explanatory power in the light of the elegant sufficiency of natural, law-governed, physical causes. Therefore, as noted above, while belief in God cannot be ruled out entirely, it is nonetheless on par with belief in "telepaths and soothsayers" and threatens trust in physics and the causal closure of universe. Clearly this account assumes that whatever else the nature of God's existence may entail, to believe in God is equivalent to adhering to a moribund account of physics.

As noted above, this view is deeply problematic, as it assumes that to believe in God is to believe in an extra object in the world or a causal force that is somehow in competition with physics. This picture obtains for Quine, not least because it is "a finding of natural science itself . . . that our information about the world comes only through impacts of our sensory receptors."[13] God must be a readily detectable part of the furniture of the world or else suffer the fate of non-existence. What is less often realized is that this is not simply a philosophical claim; it is a claim about the nature of God's existence, and moreover a claim about the conditions under which God's existence can and can't be known. Here we see how the metaphysical and epistemological are mutually implicate. However, it is at precisely this point that the theologian would wish to intervene and note that this frame of inquiry models God on the grammar of knowing physical objects. This is precisely the point at which philosophical inquiry encounters a subject (namely God) in which its metaphysical limitations are displayed. Yet it is also precisely at this point where theology can rely on philosophy for the possibility of making the nature of theology's claims intelligible and perspicuous. At first blush this appears to be an outlandishly gratuitous claim; however, philosophy must reckon with the reality that if its inquiry pertains to claims about the existence of God, it is not a given that its tools are able to avoid category confusions, namely in the confounding of physical existence with divine existence. Of course philosophers such as Quine may not wish to grant that there is such a thing as divine existence, and therefore such talk is simply about distinctions in cloud cuckoo land. However, this ignores that the very grammar of the concept of God that arises out of the Christian theological tradition via the doctrine of creation *ex nihilo* entails that the articulation of the *sui genris* nature of God's existence is bound up in the distinction of God and the created world. In other words, it is part and parcel of the Christian theological tradition that the concept of God entails getting

---

13. See above, note 2.

clear that created reality depends on God for its existence. And the created world, while sufficient to analogously point to the creator, is not sufficient to disclose the inexhaustible divine being. Thus, the nature of God's being is not grounded in, nor can it be categorically assimilated to, the spatio-temporal created order, without obliterating the creator-creature distinction.[14]

Again, don't these sort of stipulations simply leave each party to simply gainsay one another? Not exactly. It would certainly be progress in inquiry to reckon with the fact that Quinian philosophy entails a kind of ersatz theological commitment. Quine's account takes it as a given that "God" must impact the sensory receptors in a certain way as well as be the sort of cause that in principle would replace or supplement physics. Yet many theologians, for solidly theological reasons, would think this madness, and a basic theological error. Does that matter? It may not be the case that gaining clarity here will yield an argument for the existence of God. However, attending to the reality that Quine's scientism and traditional epistemology have unwittingly depended on theological claims opens philosophy up to theological critique and enrichment. This new vista for inquiry means that one could in principle address an issue that has vexed and disfigured not just engagements between philosophy and theology in philosophy of religion, but also theology and science.[15] Gaining clarity about the nature of the *ratio Dei* and the grammar of God may in fact dissolve some of the problems that have bedeviled work in the borderlands of theology and philosophy, as well as offer more fruitful approaches to debates that have become stuck. The promise of gaining of such clarity is that theological inquiry becomes more adequate to its object, in this case God. In this way it becomes possible to detect how philosophy's running up against its limits in its attempts to speak of the divine existence becomes the precise terrain on which theology can display its rational intelligibility.

---

14. For further explication of the implications of *creatio ex nihilo* for the theology and philosophy as well as theology and science see the following: David Burrell, *Freedom and Creation* (Oxford, UK: Blackwell, 2004); David B. Burrell, Carlo Cogliati, Janet M. Soskice, and William R. Stoeger, eds., *Creation and the God of Abraham* (Cambridge: Cambridge University Press, 2010); and Robert Sokolowski, *God of Faith and Reason: Foundations of Christian Theology* (Washington, DC: Catholic University of America Press, 1995).

15. In David Bentley Hart's recent book *The Experience of God* (New Haven, CT: Yale University Press, 2013), Hart has attempted to demonstrate how philosophical critique of God (especially the New Atheism) continually misfires because of philosophy's continual modelling of God on the grammar of objects and physical causes.

SECTION IV

Politics and Ethics

10

Radical Kenosis as Radical Politics
Murphy's Political Vision With and Beyond Radical Democracy

—ANDREW C. WRIGHT

NANCEY MURPHY HAS NOT traditionally been read as a radical political philosopher. Certainly she has been received as a radical in other ways, particularly in her description of a shift from modern to postmodern forms of thought—what she terms "Anglo-American postmodernity."[1] As a philosophical theologian, Murphy has significantly reshaped questions of epistemology, philosophy of language, and more recently has been able to stake her claim at the borderline between philosophy of mind, ethics, and the neurosciences. In each of these contexts, Murphy's work has had a revolutionary character, one that has been able to "go on" from the epistemological crises of modern philosophy and theology.

But Murphy as a political radical? This understanding of her work is at least underdeveloped, and more commonly has gone unperceived. In this essay, I will make the case for a latent political radicalism that is *internal* to Murphy's work in developing an Anglo-American postmodernity, and that when read in this way, she provides a precipice from which to envision a renewed Anabaptist political theology that makes a devastating critique of the modes of power that form contemporary political discourse.

This is not to say that this is the language Murphy herself uses in her contribution to an Anabaptist political theology; rather, her most direct

---

1. See Nancey Murphy, *Anglo-American Postmodernity: Scientific Perspectives on Science, Religion, and Ethics* (Boulder, CO: Westview, 1997).

work of radical political theology comes from an unlikely place: from the resources born of her involvement in theology and science discussions put into conversation with Anabaptist theology and ethics, a vision most directly articulated in her work with South African cosmologist George F. R. Ellis in *On the Moral Nature of the Universe*.[2] In this text, Murphy and Ellis seek to answer the question of how (if at all) resources from the natural sciences, and cosmology in particular, make a difference for understanding the struggles for power and justice in their respective contexts—for Ellis, the anti-apartheid movement in South Africa, and for Murphy, the build-up to the 1991 Gulf War.[3] Together, they argue that *kenosis* (self-limitation in service to the other) is not only confirmed in Anabaptist theology and ethics, but is also confirmed in the cosmological "fine-tuning" argument from the natural sciences, resulting in a coherent view of the nature of reality structured by kenosis. Murphy and Ellis suggest this work requires "new research programs ... exploring the possibilities for human sociality in the light of a vision modeled on God's own self-sacrificing love," while also recognizing the need for a paradigm shift in human understanding across the hierarchy of the sciences.[4]

Along these lines, this essay seeks to extend Murphy's radical political vision by putting her work into conversation with Romand Coles and Sheldon Wolin, proponents of the "radical democracy" movement who provide a set of resources that confirm Murphy's *kenotic* ethic in a specific kind of politics. While radical democratic practice confirms Murphy's political radicalism, it also highlights how Murphy provides a framework for nonviolent social transformation that grounds *kenotic* political practices in a teleology that extends beyond the resources of radical democracy alone. The tension of this dialogue will reveal a deeper sense of Murphy's contribution to Anabaptist political theology in the context of a wider discourse with cosmology, political theory, and radical-democratic practices.

Murphy's Radical Political Vision

Murphy's work in Anglo-American postmodernity traces a *gestalt* shift in Western philosophy and theology that constitutes a change in the basic thought forms of the last half-century. Murphy argues that language used

---

2. Nancey Murphy and George F. R. Ellis, *On the Moral Nature of the Universe: Theology, Cosmology, and Ethics* (Minneapolis: Fortress, 1996).

3. Nancey Murphy, "Wind and Spirit: A Theological Autobiography," in *Dialogue: A Journal of Theology* 46:3 (Fall 2007) 307.

4. Murphy and Ellis, *Moral Nature*, xv.

to describe these shifts has "taken on new uses . . . [that entail] radical consequences for all areas of academia and presumably the living of life as well."[5] In this section, I will argue that one of "the living of life" consequences internal to this shift from modern to postmodern is a revision of certain conceptual assumptions that structure political theory in the modern period—namely, anthropological and causal reductionism—that has significant implications for politics and Christian political witness in the postmodern period. While perhaps underdeveloped in the reception of Murphy's work as a whole, careful attention to the contours of her work will demonstrate the depth and scope of Murphy's radicalism not only in epistemology or philosophy of language, but also in reframing the central questions of Christian ethics, political theology, and the political witness of contemporary Christian communities.

The Political Radicalism of Murphy's Anglo-American Postmodernity

One year before the publication of her award-winning *Theology in the Age of Scientific Reasoning*,[6] Murphy co-authored an article with James Wm. McClendon Jr. entitled "Distinguishing Modern and Postmodern Theologies" that would become a "vista" for understanding recent shifts happening in contemporary theology and philosophy, and would set the course for her early work.[7] In that article, Murphy and McClendon sought to articulate what they saw as an emerging Anglo-American postmodernity that was distinct from other "postmodernisms" exemplified in Continental thinkers, and that was characterized by specific shifts away from "modern" forms of thought along three distinct axes: epistemological foundationalism, referential theories of language, and metaphysical reductionism—specifically, an atomistic reductionism applied to people and communities (which Murphy later described as *generic modern individualism*).[8] Modern thinkers, Murphy and McClendon suggested, could be located by means of "Cartesian coordinates" in a "three-dimensional conceptual space," while postmodern

---

5. Murphy, *Anglo-American*, 1.

6. Nancey Murphy, *Theology in the Age of Scientific Reasoning* (Ithaca, NY: Cornell University Press, 1990). This won the American Academy of Religion award for the best book in the Study of Religions in 1992.

7. See Murphy's foreword in volume 2 of *The Collected Works of James Wm. McClendon, Jr.*, edited by Ryan Andrew Newson and Andrew C. Wright (Waco, TX: Baylor University Press, 2014) xiv. "Distinguishing Modern and Postmodern Theologies" also appears in that volume, 38–65.

8. Murphy, *Anglo-American*, ch. 1.

thinkers "succeed in breaking free from this space altogether" by rejecting foundationalist, referentialist, and atomistic reductionist assumptions. Together, such thinkers constitute what Murphy and McClendon call an "an emerging unity" and are among those who advocate for "holist" epistemologies (e.g., W. V. O. Quine), "ordinary language" philosophies (e.g., J. L. Austin, the later Ludwig Wittgenstein), and more complex social theories of community (e.g., Alasdair MacIntyre).[9] The upshot of this shift, for Murphy and McClendon, is the recognition of the irreducible link between knowledge and the social character of human nature, such that (following MacIntyre) the Cartesian "space" is dissolved by the recognition of the role of real, embodied, practicing human communities.

For the purposes of this essay, I will focus on Murphy's dissolution of atomistic reductionism as a beginning point for understanding the radical political vision internal to her work. On Murphy's view, atomistic reductionism "provided inspiration for modern approaches to knowledge and language" and indeed structured modern political theory by assuming a conception of human nature framed by generic modern individualism, with the implication for political theory that "all human beings were the same for the purposes of ethics and politics."[10] In this modern frame, all political communities are *nothing but* collections of individuals; when paired with the modern attempt to sever moral facts from moral values, this created a form of political theory that rested on an ethics that could do nothing but express an individual's moral preference.[11] In this moral space, there is no sense of political boundedness between human beings beyond complementary interaction mediated by social contract; absent is the ability to debate about a "common good" for human social life, which would require—at least in a limited sense—some shared conception of a *telos*. As such, modern political space functions to maintain a moral vacuum that is ripe for the manipulation of power.

Arguing that MacIntyre's ethical theory dissolves the atomistic reductionism that so dominates modern conceptions of human nature and political theory (the third "axis" of postmodernity), Murphy suggests that MacIntyre represents a shift from modern to postmodern forms of thought by (1) his recognition of the role of embodied *traditions* in human life that precede the thought and behavior of individuals, and (2) his understanding that "individual goods are unintelligible apart from the goods inherent

9. Ibid., 2.

10. Ibid., 16.

11. Ibid., 28. Here, Murphy is drawing on MacIntyre's description of emotivism as structuring the moral relativism of the modern period.

in *practices*, which are essentially communal."¹² In this perspective, the communal shapes human knowledge of the good (embodied in communal traditions), and in this way suggests a reshaped conception of politics as constituted by embodied social *practices*.

The implications of this shift for our understanding of Murphy's radical political vision can be brought into focus by following MacIntyre's insistence that *every* moral philosophy "characteristically presupposes a sociology."¹³ In this light, Murphy's recognition of the *philosophical* mistakes of modernity, and her description of a "shift" to postmodern forms of thought, carries a political and sociological implication: if human beings are not actually autonomous individuals but are creatures that are unavoidably dependent on one another for the achievement of human flourishing, then postmodern conceptions of human nature imply a radically different form of political organization than the atomistic assumptions of modern political theory.¹⁴

Murphy's Radical Political Vision in *On the Moral Nature of the Universe*

If atomistic reductionism is the methodological assumption that is characteristic of the modern period, then Murphy's articulation of Anglo-American postmodernity recognizes the need for a more complex political theory in relation to a more complex conception of human nature, and both in relationship to the ultimate purposes of human life (and indeed, the nature of reality). Murphy moves beyond reductionism in many places, most directly in relation to radical political vision in *On the Moral Nature of the Universe*, in which she takes on a second form of reductionism related to causation and the hierarchy of the sciences. Developing a "research program" from this vantage point, Murphy and Ellis argue for an ethics of kenosis as a coherent theory that accounts for the "way things are," linking the purposes of human beings and the purposes of the natural world in a single teleological orientation. A close reading of their argument reveals how an ethics of kenosis is indeed an outworking of Anglo-American postmodernity, and offers an important set of resources for Anabaptist political theology.

---

12. Ibid., 29.

13. Alasdair MacIntyre, *After Virtue*, 2nd ed. (Notre Dame: University of Notre Dame Press, [1981] 1984) 23.

14. Cf. Alasdair MacIntyre, *Dependent Rational Animals: Why Human Beings Needs the Virtues* (Chicago: Open Court, 1999).

Causation and The Hierarchy of the Sciences

Murphy and Ellis structure their argument around the hierarchy of the sciences.[15] At its most basic level, the hierarchy develops an organizing description of the natural and human sciences in relation to levels of complexity, relating all of the sciences not as separate modes of inquiry but as related and dependent.[16] Ordering the sciences in this way highlights two things: (1) *constraint* of higher (more complex) sciences by the laws and properties of the lower sciences (the properties of biology do not contradict the properties of physics), and (2) *emergence*, suggesting that the higher sciences do indeed have *some* properties that are unique in their own right. Together, the hierarchy suggests a "systems" approach to understanding the sciences, including social systems; the more complex a system is, the more complex are its emergent properties. The upshot is that higher-level descriptions are necessary to explain the higher level sciences.[17]

Murphy and Ellis argue that in the modern period, the dominant form of causation was "bottom-up," in which the lower-level sciences were seen as *determinative* of the higher-level sciences (as in the biological reductionism that characterizes some contemporary uses of neuroscience).[18] Conversely, from a postmodern perspective one recognizes the reality of "top-down" causation; lower-level laws alone cannot explain all of the genuinely emergent properties of the higher-level sciences.[19] Indeed, Murphy and Ellis see in each discipline a set of "boundary questions" that call for higher-level explanation: in some cases, only resources from a discipline "higher" in the hierarchy will enable one to make sense out of the phenomena at a lower level, suggesting that "top-down" causation (along with "bottom-up" causation) are crucial non-reductive resources for describing the natural and human sciences.[20]

From this perspective, if the hierarchy of the sciences is organized by increasing levels of complexity, then the higher levels within the hierarchy point to a need for a "top-layer" that offers a comprehensive description of

---

15. Murphy and Ellis, *Moral Nature*, 19-20. For a discussion of their understanding of the hierarchy of the sciences, including how the human sciences operate as complex "higher-level" sciences, see ibid., 19-38 and 64-87.

16. Ibid., 22.

17. Ibid., 23.

18. For a critique of this tendency, see Nancey Murphy and Warren S. Brown, *Did My Neurons Make Me Do It?* (New York: Oxford University Press, 2007).

19. Murphy and Ellis, *Moral Nature*, 24.

20. Ibid., 27.

the lower level sciences.[21] By separated the upper level sciences into two columns (the human, social sciences forming one branch, and the natural sciences forming the other), Murphy and Ellis are able to show how cosmology and ethics function as top-level disciplines for the natural and social sciences, respectively. For the natural sciences, this is done by offering explanations of origins beyond what is available at the lower-levels alone[22]; for the social sciences, this occurs despite their "lawlike" descriptions of human society, and which require explanation beyond the social sciences themselves in order to understand how *every* form of collective human activity—political, economic, or social—works with *some* sense of goal-oriented direction.[23] For Murphy and Ellis, this top-layer of the "human science" branch is best identified as the "science" of ethics, which evaluates the explicit and implicit assumptions of the lower sciences and evaluates differing conceptions of the good.

Beyond even cosmology and ethics, Murphy and Ellis recognize that for both branches of the hierarchy, an even higher science—theology—is required to explain the boundary questions that emerge from cosmology (specifically relating to the "fine-tuning" question) and ethics (specifically in answering questions of the ultimate purposes and goals for human beings and social systems). Theology, in Murphy and Ellis's perspective, provides a description of ultimate reality that offers explanations extending from the boundary questions about the ultimate purposes of human life in relation to the wider purposes and goals (*teloi*) of the universe as a whole (drawn from both ethics *and* cosmology), repairing the modern split between fact and value by answering questions of human flourishing in relation to the purposes of the natural world.[24] Of course, the content and character of that theological "top-layer" is certainly contestable, and in describing the role of

---

21. Ibid., 64–65.

22. Ibid., 59–60, 64. Murphy and Ellis argue that the anthropic (or "fine-tuning") principle answers such boundary questions as: Can the uniqueness of human life be explained by lower-level sciences, or even cosmology itself? Or does understanding the nature of things—particularly human life—point to a need for an even higher level of explanation, an even higher science, that can offer explanations beyond even the resources of cosmology?

23. Ibid., 76–77. A crucial part of Murphy and Ellis's argument, that I do not have space to emphasize here, is the goal-oriented nature of *all* hierarchical control systems (e.g., an economy or political structure, an automated aircraft pilot system, an ant colony, photosynthesis); see ibid., 79–87.

24. Murphy and Ellis are drawing heavily on MacIntyrean concepts here. For the political implications of MacIntyre's reckoning with the fact-value distinction, see Ryan Andrew Newson, "Alasdair MacIntyre and Radically Dialogical Politics," *Political Theology* (in press, 2016).

theology and ethics at the top of the hierarchy, Murphy and Ellis are making a *philosophical* rather than theological point. Even so, their work is meant to provide a framework for their primary contribution: defending a *kenotic* theological ethic as the content and character of ultimate reality.

Modern Social Science, Manipulation, and the Powers

Put within the context of modern causal reductionism, Murphy and Ellis recognize that the traditional absence of ethics and theology from the hierarchy of the sciences allows the social sciences to provide an "ethically loaded" vision of reality—despite their purportedly neutral stance towards the goals and purposes of what they describe—that is assumed in the functioning and orientation of human systems, not least in modern conceptions of political theory.[25]

Assuming the same generic individualism that is characteristic of the modern period, key figures in modern political theory pictured human society as a collection of individuals who are in a war of "each against all," and thus by nature require a "social contract" to avoid devolving into unchecked violence. The effectiveness of this contract is protected by the right of the nation-state to use violent coercion in order to guarantee that individuals not break their agreement with one another.[26] From this standpoint, arguments for *kenosis* (self-limitation) as a means of positive social transformation become significantly more difficult to rationally sustain, from the perspective of the social sciences, as coercive political practices frame the discourse of modern politics.[27] The ostensible "neutrality" of this process is part of what Murphy sees as modern social sciences's most pernicious aspect: "to the extent that social sciences maintain a neutral stance towards the social powers they describe, they inevitably *mislead* us about the true nature of social reality,"[28] particularly by normalizing and legitimating the conceptions of human nature and sociality that support coercive machinations of manipulative power, while also rendering competing forms of hu-

---

25. Nancey Murphy, "Social Science, Ethics, and the Powers," in *Transforming the Powers: Peace, Justice, and the Domination System*, edited by Ray Gingerich and Ted Grimsrud (Minneapolis: Fortress, 2006) 33; Murphy and Ellis, *Moral Nature*, 97–98.

26. Murphy, *Anglo-American*, 14–18. Here, Murphy refers to the "catachretical extension" of reductionism in the modern political theory of Hobbes and Locke.

27. Murphy and Ellis, *Moral Nature*, 98–99.

28. Murphy, "Social Science," 33. Here one can see the impact of MacIntyre's radical critique of modern society on Murphy. See his "Social Science Methodology as the Ideology of Bureaucratic Authority," in *The MacIntyre Reader*, edited by Kelvin Knight (Notre Dame: University of Notre Dame Press, 1998) 53–68.

man sociality based on another conception of philosophical anthropology and ultimate purpose unreasonable. The upshot of Murphy's analysis (with and beyond her work with Ellis) is that she recognizes how causal reductionism in the hierarchy of the sciences and anthropological reductionism in certain conceptions of human nature are not politically insignificant; rather, modern reductionism preserves a space for the distorting influence of the "will to power" to shape human systems towards particular and self-serving ends. From this view, the reductionist tendencies of the modern period are perhaps better described as reductionist *ideologies*, existing as resources for sustaining the manipulative power that shapes contemporary political discourse.

One additional resource can be gleaned, specifically from the resonance between Murphy's work on the hierarchy of the sciences and insights from MacIntyre's critical engagement with the genealogical philosophical tradition. While offering a broad commitment to kenosis on the basis of the cross and resurrection of Christ (cf. Phil 2:1–11), Murphy draws on the Anabaptist concept of the "powers and principalities" to describe how the social sciences function as a tool for the deeper and collective nature of evil embedded in institutions and contemporary political practices.[29] Murphy's appropriation of this concept provides the beginnings of a novel political theology that enables a way of seeing and critiquing modern forms of manipulative power, and offers three unique responses to this problem. First, Murphy insists (following MacIntyre) that it is inherently within *practices* that human beings gain a deeper understanding of the goods that contribute to a life of flourishing. As such, she suggests that true political practices are only political when they entail engagement not only with questions of technique, but with the higher-level questions of the goods and ends of human life and assumptions about ultimate reality—the questions of ethics. Second, through her Anabaptist tradition, Murphy has the resources to recognize and name the ways that modern reductionism functions to structurally sustain the distorting influence of the "will to power" (the "powers and principalities"). And third, Murphy's Anabaptist tradition enables her to sustain a radical political vision that both extends beyond the nihilistic tendencies of the genealogical tradition through the hopeful resources of embodied *powerful practices* to tame the "will to power," while recognizing that social practices themselves are not immune to the powerful manipulation of the "powers and principalities."[30] From these resources, Murphy's

---

29. Murphy, "Social Science," 32–33.

30. Here, Murphy is drawing on McClendon's concept of *powerful practices*. See James Wm. McClendon, Jr., *Ethics: Systematic Theology, Volume 1*, rev. ed. (Nashville: Abingdon, [1986] 2002) 178–79.

radical political vision consists of a revision of the hierarchy of the sciences in light of an Anabaptist theological and ethical "top-layer" that, following the anti-reductionism of her Anglo-American postmodernity, suggests a downward causation of kenosis through the hierarchy of the lower sciences, made possible by the *powerful practices* that offer an alternative to the practices of contemporary political discourse.

Self-Renunciation and Radical Political Vision

The convergence of these resources for Murphy and Ellis's research program leads them to argue for an ethical "hardcore" of kenosis that provides a very different vision of human sociality than what is typical in the modern social sciences, with its assumptions about the inevitability of violence. Indeed, kenosis necessitates a radical revision of the hierarchy of the sciences. Murphy and Ellis suggest that kenosis provides "top-down" causal effects that shape the whole of the human sciences towards the ultimate purposes of God, which are also embedded in the contours of the natural world. What is also important to recognize, particularly in deciphering Murphy's radical political vision, is that while self-renunciation functions as a *telos* for all of reality, and while kenosis can and does have a downward causal effect on the lower natural and human sciences, the character of kenosis as *telos* means that there cannot be *coercive* downward causal effects on the lower sciences. This means that the autonomy and "will to power" embedded in the practices of some of the lower (particularly human) sciences remains persistent even in the recognition from the higher sciences of a *kenotic* structure to the entire universe. Kenosis, then, effects the humans sciences, but also respects the laws and practices of those sciences as they are practiced by not "doing violence" to those lower sciences through coercive causation. Kenosis works within the structures of the human sciences in a way that respects the laws and practices that constitute the sciences, while also pulling these sciences towards their ultimate purposes in the context of a self-renunciatory universe.

In this light, radical *kenotic* political vision lacks the character of violent revolution, opting instead for a slower, more dialogical, step-by-step process of social change. To be political in a way that is in tune with a *kenotic* universe entails a set of political practices that are significantly different from the modes of modern politics, particular in that they will refuse violence, accept suffering, and submit to the needs and perspectives of others (including those who are considered adversaries) as central to one's own well-being.[31] However odd this may seem in the theater of sociological and political theories that assume the necessary role of violence in the preservation of social order, Murphy and Ellis argue that if their analysis of the *kenotic* structure of the universe is coherent, then *kenotic* action will be able to be embodied as a feasible and even effective means of lasting social transformation.[32]

Murphy and Ellis ground their argument for the transformative power of kenosis in both the human (social) and natural sciences. From a sociological perspective, they demonstrate (in dialogue with Gene Sharp, among others) that kenosis aims not merely to achieve the goals of a social campaign, but also aim at the *change of character* on both sides of a social struggle, offering a "shock treatment" to the patterns of the "will to power." This shock treatment is administered through the self-sacrificial action of nonviolent social change. This change is meant not only to resist the spirals of violence and coercion that inevitably lead to more violence, but also to sharpen the perception, understanding, worldview, attitudes, feelings, and indeed, the very aspects with which a human being or community understands the world. In this light, the causal effect of *kenotic* action in the form of radical politics is effective because of its direct relationship to the non-coercive form of ultimate reality. In a world structured by kenosis, the more coercion that is used to support social transformation, the less effective that social transformation will be.[33] Additionally, drawing on the work of neuroscientist Richard Gregg, Murphy and Ellis argue that this sort of *kenotic* response to threat creates an involuntarily sympathetic response in the nervous system of the beholder, demonstrating how even small actions that create empathy in an adversary offers tremendous potential for change.[34]

In this section, I have offered a limited consideration of the implications of Murphy and Ellis's research program in some of the "lower" human sciences, in particular their "hardcore" commitment to kenosis as the purpose of the universe. However, as Murphy and Ellis recognize, such a limited engagement provides insufficient confirmation of their research program. They recognize that, if their hypothesis about the *kenotic* nature of reality is to be sustained as a coherent vision, it will require widespread

---

31. Murphy and Ellis, *Moral Nature*, 120.

32. Ibid., 165.

33. Ibid., 157.

34. Ibid., 149–59. Since the time of Murphy and Ellis's book, evidence for this kind of experience has only been strengthened with neurological research into the existence of mirror neurons and other neural responses to social stimuli. For example, see James A. Van Slyke, et al., eds., *Theology and Science of Moral Action: Virtue Ethics, Exemplarity, and Cognitive Neuroscience* (New York: Routledge, 2013).

confirmation throughout the hierarchy, in both the natural and human sciences. Drawing on this concern, the following section seeks one avenue of confirmation in dialogue with radical-democratic political theory that may confirm kenosis as a crucial aspect of democratic political theory. As such, this section extends Murphy's work towards a radical political vision by bringing into focus the way that kenosis and radical politics are critical resources for resisting modern modes of manipulative power and for advancing the flourishing of human beings.

Extending Murphy's Radical Politics: Radical Democracy the Politics of Kenosis

In their coauthored book *Convictions*, McClendon and James Smith create and unpack the Austinian concept of *loci*, which I will use to structure this section.[35] Recognizing that different sets of convictions stem from differing narratives and conceptions of the good, loci designate particular words, phrases, or concepts by which common ground is found on an ad hoc basis, around which persons and communities of differing conviction sets might engage in dialogue. In this way, an opportunity is formed for strengthening and adjusting one's convictions in light of the critique and cross-pollination offered by another. Following McClendon and Smith's concept, this section will draw out four loci for a conversation between Murphy's radical political vision and two proponents of radical democracy theory (Romand Coles and Sheldon Wolin) in order to demonstrate a family resemblance between the two, as well as deepen an understanding between their shared conceptual resources. While there are certainly significant differences between Murphy's project and radical democracy, the resources of the latter provide confirmation of Murphy's *kenotic* ethic by demonstrating how self-renunciation and openness to the other through receptive political practices are crucial aspects of achieving and cultivating human flourishing in contemporary society. On this view, the resources of radical democracy extend Murphy's argument towards a radical political vision and in particular, an Anabaptist political theology.

---

35. James Wm. McClendon, Jr. and James M. Smith, *Convictions: Defusing Religious Relativism*, rev. ed. (Valley Forge, PA: Trinity, [1975] 1994) chs. 4 and 6.

Locus One: Local Politics and Receptive Body Practices

A first locus for a conversation between Murphy and radical democracy centers on the development of *slow, local, and receptive practices as constitutive of radical politics*. These practices of "small politics" are well-represented by figures like Ella Baker and Bob Moses of the Student Nonviolent Coordinating Committee (SNCC), Ernesto Cortés of the Industrial Areas Foundation (IAF), and Jean Vanier of L'Arche communities. Each characteristically strives for a set of political achievements through slow, local, and receptive political practices that radical democrats see as the core of democratic political organizing.[36]

The insistence of "small politics" among radical democrats demonstrates a characteristic and persistent concern about modes of power in liberal political discourse that betray an *anti*-democratic bent. These modes of power combine the force of the bureaucratic nation-state, the megacorporation, and the military-industrial complex in a way that preserves the influence of "super-elites" while maintaining a "deafness" to questions of the common good.[37] Examples of this combination can be found in just about every sphere of liberal "democracies": government contracts given to multi-billion dollar corporations, indirect (and direct) profiteering among decision-makers in government, extended or limited voting practices sustained by the courts (for instance, corporate spending and the "Citizens United" decision, or the repealing of certain aspects of the Voting Rights Act), and the drive to excess consumerism as a basic "form of life."[38] For radical democrats, each of these examples betray what Sheldon Wolin calls a "methodism" in contemporary democratic society, in which political practices function as *techniques* for managing and pointing society towards an already agreed upon set of arrangements in as effective a way as possible.[39] Here, a particular form of liberal-democratic politics—rather than a set of discourses for reflective decision-making and human experience—functions as an "emotional-affective-perceptual" stance towards the world (as Coles, following Wolin, puts it) that is "suited for a technological society,"

---

36. These examples are drawn from a volume that I will utilize heavily in this section: Romand Coles and Stanley Hauerwas, *Christianity, Democracy, and the Radical Ordinary: Conversations Between a Radical Democrat and a Christian* (Eugene, OR: Cascade, 2008).

37. Romand Coles, "Democracy and the Radical Ordinary: Wolin and the Epical Emergence of Democratic Theory," in *Christianity*, 120.

38. Ibid.

39. Ibid., 122. See also Wolin's description of "inverted totalitarianism" in *Democracy Incorporated: Managed Democracy and the Specter of Inverted Totalitarianism* (Princeton: Princeton University Press, 2008) 51.

and that rests on an alleged "neutrality" of the social sciences as a crucial resource for sustaining this technological vision.[40] Even a basic analysis of our contemporary political context reveals the resonance between radical democracy and Murphy's own understanding of the manipulative role of the social sciences in *implementing* an already agreed upon social arrangement. For proponents of radical democracy, if political practices are to move beyond the dominant and dominating anti-democratic forms of liberalism, then contemporary politics must recover a core democratic vision marked by political practices of ordinary, localized, and particular communities seeking to radically transform the powerful modes of mega-state and corporate interests through concrete practices of political renewal.[41]

For Wolin, this is best described as a set of embodied political practices of reception that tend to the "manifold character of the world," recognizing the "perspectives of difference" and "emergent irregularities" that extend from those communities held outside the dominant modes of power in contemporary political liberalism.[42] These social practices entail a sense of bodily presence and skills of dialogical problem solving, each of which directly correlate, or at least deeply resonate, with Murphy's own conception of politics in postmodern context. In particular, radical democratic political practices recognize that it is difficult to destroy one's enemy when you are committed to understanding them through *kenotic* and receptive political practices of tending, listening, and learning from them as a means of one's own flourishing.[43] These political practices of receptivity, of course, demonstrate a very different conception of human sociality that neither sustains a technological society through ongoing "methodism," nor seeks coercive revolutionary political change through having the right "handles on history," but postures political discourse as tending to differences and possibilities of dynamic emergences that may slowly rework modes of power, within and beyond the manipulated realities of contemporary liberal democratic society.[44] Here again radical democrats confirm Murphy's conception of *kenotic* political practices as the means for lasting social transformation,

---

40. Ibid.,123. See also Sheldon Wolin, "Political Theory as a Vocation," *The American Political Science Review* 63:4 (December 1969) 1064.

41. Hauerwas and Coles, *Christianity*, "Introduction," 8.

42. Coles, "Democracy," 129–31.

43. Coles sees this kind of tending exemplified in the political practices of Ella Baker. See Romand Coles, "'To Make this Tradition Articulate': Practiced Receptivity Matters, Or Heading West of West with Cornel West and Ella Baker," in *Christianity*, 67.

44. Coles, "Democracy," 135, 153.

exemplifying her claim that the least coercive practices lead to the most effective long-term change.[45]

What is unique about Wolin and Coles's concern, however, is that the receptive practices of radical democracy have a characteristically episodic, "fugitive" quality, which is stressed in order to demonstrate their persistent concern about the danger of "methodism" in political and ethical theory, particularly in traditions that draw on a strong teleological framework.[46] While both Coles and Wolin emphasize the role of teleological traditions for understanding the political convictions embedded in inherited histories of moral inquiry (something that liberalism strongly works to *forget*), they maintain a concern with these teleological traditions, as they may hold on to particular conceptions of goals and purposes for human life, and thus deny the ateleological sentiment that they think is required to listen to and learn from the other.[47] This concern about teleology thus marks a key difference between Murphy and radical democracy; however, it may be that Murphy's reworking of a teleology of kenosis (in light of the Anabaptist tradition) reveals her shared concern about the ease with which teleologies are subsumed into the "will to power."[48] Despite this difference, radical-democratic theorists confirm the *kenotic* possibility of practices in overcoming the dominant forms of power in contemporary politics.

Locus Two: Wild Patience

A second and related locus for a conversation between Murphy's radical political vision and radical democracy is a shared commitment to *patience* as a necessary virtue for long-term social transformation. For radical democrats, one of the characteristics of managed democracy and the *antidemocratic* patterns of liberalism is a kind of speed that erases differences among human beings (recall Murphy's concern with *generic* individualism), and cultivates an artificial unity that is initiated through the formation of political, legal, and economic arrangements. This "unity" sustains a kind of power that places diverse and complex social, cultural, and political realities

---

45. See Murphy and Ellis, *Moral Nature*, 149–65.

46. Coles, "Democracy," 147.

47. Romand Coles, *Beyond Gated Politics: Reflections for the Possibility of Democracy* (Minneapolis: University of Minnesota Press, 2005) xv–xvi.

48. See Nancey Murphy, "Traditions, Practices, and the Powers," in *Transforming the Powers*, 89–93. See also the concluding section of this essay.

into a single managed form of human life, over against the complex realities of human life.[49]

For radical democrats, the very concept of slow, receptive, and vulnerable political practices requires a sense of *time* that allows one to "apply oneself to looking after another," a political stance that Wolin likens to tending to a garden, or tending to the sick, and thus is far from typical managerial practice.[50] To cultivate a politics of tending is to cultivate a politics of *patience*, one that starts from the recognition of conflict and difference among the basic convictions of how human beings construe and experience the world. It begins the difficult work of tending to these differences through the formation of relationships—even friendship—in a way that does the difficult work of engaging the genuine differences that divide human beings rather than paving over them with a veneer of liberalized democracy.[51] For Coles, this kind of politics is captured well in the Anabaptist practice of footwashing, which requires patience in order to become a foot *washed* people, capable of *receiving* from others.[52] For Wolin, this politics consists of a labyrinth of political engagements that work within particular places, problems, and practices by way of the "slow politics" of political refashioning.[53] The politics of tending opens communities to the "density" of human complexity, dismantling both the simplicity of a unitary political vision and the temptation of the "will to power."[54] As such, the waiting required in this kind of "slow politics" is in fact a *condition* of lasting social transformation. Paradoxically, the "slow-time" required for radical dialogical politics *actually helps social transformation move more quickly*, as Coles notes with reference to SNCC. This move is counterintuitive, however, in a political atmosphere that is "increasingly frenetic, and thus stuck."[55]

The patience advocated by proponents of radical democracy confirms and extends Murphy's work on the patience required by a *kenotic* ethic.

49. Sheldon Wolin, *The Presence of the Past: Essays on the State and the Constitution* (Baltimore: Johns Hopkins University Press, 1989) 91.

50. Ibid., 89.

51. The picture that radical democrats offer here is strikingly similar to McClendon's recognition of the *convictional* character of divisions that divide human beings. Thus does McClendon write that "the answer to relativism is not to deny the divisions that rend the world, but instead to mend it as we can by changing its enmities and misunderstandings into understandings and friendships—the hard work that undermines relativism." James Wm. McClendon, Jr., "'Convictions' After Twenty Years," in *Collected Works, Volume 2*, 149.

52. Coles, "Gentled into Being," in *Christianity*, 213.

53. Cf. Murphy and Ellis, *Moral Nature*, 159–61.

54. Ibid.

55. Coles, "To Make this Tradition Articulate," 69.

Recall that Murphy and Ellis argue from a "hardcore" in which the very structure of the universe is *kenotic*, suggesting that the *most effective* means of long-term social transformation is strategic *kenotic* action, and that the effectiveness of a movement extends from its relationship with various levels of non-coercion.[56] In dialogue with radical democracy, Murphy's political radicalism comes into even better focus: if tending to the needs and perspectives of those who are different from me are crucial to a democratic and *kenotic* form of politics—and if I cannot, through disciplinary modes of power, force those who are different from me to see the world as I do—then the difficult work of persuasion and dialogical engagement that is internal to *kenotic* and radical-democratic politics *requires* the virtue of patience that is absent from the present character of managed democracy.

What the radical democrats offer Murphy is a set of resources within the lower-level sciences of political theory that confirm her ethical hardcore. And while Coles and Wolin would certainly not want to say that receptivity is a *teleological* statement about the nature and purpose of the world in general, they nonetheless point to a social embodiment of Murphy's *telos*.

Locus Three: Trickster Politics

The third locus for a conversation between Murphy and radical democracy is the notion of "trickster politics." In the context of managed democracy, both Coles and Wolin advocate for a kind of politics that has a "trickster" quality to it. Both characterize radical democratic organizing as working "around relatively minor issues precisely in order to generate the activities, relationships, changes, and acquisitions that are integral to cultivating radical-democratic modes of culture and power."[57] Trickster politics work in partnership (on a limited, *ad hoc* basis) with those who have no interest other than the "will to power," seeking small changes towards, and cultivation of, a "radical-democratic maturity" in which those in the "liberal interest group game" may develop a radical-democratic sensibility towards reciprocal practices of listening and vulnerability. This trickster mentality may even enable unlikely people to collaborate with radical democrats—even if one only sees that this has happened retrospectively.[58] Coles describes this latter purpose as the primary motivation "trickster" politics, in which the ultimate aim is not to *win* the game as much as it is to *change* the game, despite how easily even the most radical of democrats can be tricked into the "liberal

56. Murphy and Ellis, *Moral Nature*, 154.
57. Ibid., 143.
58. Ibid., 143–44.

interest group" pressures.[59] In this sense, "trickster" politics is a means of resisting that does not demonize others in the way "that kills democracy from within as surely it destroys it from without."[60]

This locus of trickster politics deeply resonates with the kind of politics Murphy explicitly advocates. Whereas radical democrats such as Coles and Wolin suggest that the effect of "trickster" politics is the slow possibility of tilting the game towards more democratic forms of political practice, Murphy argues that the point of *kenotic* actions in the social and political sphere is to offer a "shock treatment" to the patterns of violence and power that characterize modern politics. This work provides alternative (*kenotic*) practices that are "aimed at a radical change in the moral character of the participants" in a way that changes perception and worldview, and that offer a different picture of the means and timeframe of political effectiveness.[61] Like Coles, Murphy seeks to include even political adversaries in changing the "game" of politics. Hence, revolutionaries that steamroll political adversaries, or the manipulative politics that tilt the "game" in one's own favor, undermine the purposes of both Murphy and Coles. Rather, a politics of kenosis (as is seen in radical democratic theory) supports slow, step-by-step movements that include one's adversaries in the process.

From this perspective, one may wonder if *kenotic* forms of politics can truly be sustained in a world of manipulative power. For Murphy and Ellis, the answer is yes, but not without a significant struggle against the dominant practices of the power-infused methodologies of the social sciences that function as methodologies for social control. If downward causation is truly justified, then it must be able to be socially embodied in *some* kind of on-the-ground political practices. While maintaining some differences between the two, the embodiment of radical democracy in theory (as represented by Wolin and Coles) and in practice (represented by SNCC, IAF, and L'Arche) provide a confirmation of Murphy's kenotic vision.

Locus Four: Sustained Political Imagination

A fourth and final locus for this conversation might be described as the crucial role of *imagination* in initiating and sustaining kenotic political activity

---

59. Romand Coles, "Of Tensions and Tricksters: Grassroots Democracy Between Theory and Practice," in *Christianity*, 291. In this essay, Coles sees "trickster" politics embodied in the work of organizations like IAF, which plays a kind of "political jujitsu" in relation to power and its insidious temptation.

60. Coles, "Democracy," 143 n71.

61. Murphy and Ellis, *Moral Nature*, 158–59.

in a context of a managed democracy. For Wolin, imagination is an important political category because it has the unique ability to join power with conceptions of possibility and reality.[62] Indeed, the *anti*-democratic modes of contemporary political "methodism" gain their energy and affective influence through the resources of a political imaginary that has a habitual effect on political actors and contemporary Western culture, preserving the space for a systematized democracy that serves the needs of contemporary mega-corporation and nation-state.[63] This political imagination both limits and extends conceptions of reality in a systematized frame that is justified *outside* of the discourse of democratic practice, rendering discourse about and even perception of the frame as itself unreasonable.

As such, Wolin's hopes for the prospect of radical democracy in the contemporary political scene are tempered. If there is *any* hope for radical democracy in the face of managed democracy, it is only through the formation of local, receptive political practices that operate on a different kind of time—practices that "tend" to the manifold differences between and among human beings. It is from such differences that the energy for creative possibilities will emerge. Whether such receptive practices can be initiated and sustained in the shadow of managed democracy, Wolin is pessimistic; but he begins by emphasizing the crucial role of memory in shaping radical-democratic vision, in particular by remembering the radical-democratic struggles in the past (e.g., SNCC) in which an impossible vision and impossible world became so.[64]

Murphy argues for a conception of *kenotic* political action in the context of a managed democracy that also necessitates the formation of imagination as integral to the practice of politics. By recognizing how modern forms of manipulative social science limit imagination to violent means of social transformation, Murphy suggests that *kenotic* activity works to widen the imagination of political contexts by offering small scale, step-by-step examples that "stock the storehouse" of possibilities for a wider political alternative.[65] However, Murphy also recognizes how this kind of imaginative politics is difficult to sustain without the ongoing and continuous "stocking" of one's own repertoire of creative resources for sustaining *kenotic* action.

---

62. Wolin, *Democracy Incorporated*, 18.

63. Ibid., 19.

64. I am drawing on Coles for my reading of Wolin on this point. See Coles, "To Make This Tradition Articulate," 76–86.

65. Murphy and Ellis, *Moral Nature*, 151, 165–71. See also John Howard Yoder, "The Hermeneutics of Peoplehood: A Protestant Perspective," in *The Priestly Kingdom: Social Ethics as Gospel* (Notre Dame: University of Notre Dame Press, 1984) 30.

There is an allure to the dynamic and manipulative forms of violence; we are "as if by gravitational force" drawn to the will to power.[66]

While Murphy and Ellis advocate for a kind of spiritual life that cultivates an alternative theological "top-layer" that is necessary to sustain *kenotic* action, Murphy makes the case beyond her work with Ellis that long-term *kenotic* social transformation requires something like an Anabaptist ecclesial context, consisting of social practices aimed at discerning *kenotic* alternatives amidst the "distorting influences of the will to power."[67] For the Anabaptist tradition, a theological imagination of kenosis provides the resources for sustaining the willingness to suffer, recognizes the vulnerability of one's own motives, and values the other as central to one's own flourishing. In Murphy's perspective, imagination is not only memory of past radical-democratic achievements, but also a wider memory of the death and resurrection of Christ, the life of the saints (both ancient and contemporary), and the cultivation of hope in the resurrection that is to come.[68] As such, Murphy shares Wolin's concern about the crucial role of imagination in vulnerable and receptive political practices, while structuring *what* a *kenotic* imagination entails in different ways.

Together, this conversation between Murphy and proponents of radical democracy extends Murphy's radical political vision. Following MacIntyre's argument that *all* moral and ethical theories must be socially embodied—that is, that they all assume *some* kind of sociology—the proponents of radical democracy advocate for a political theory that confirms Murphy's *kenotic* hardcore through one possible social embodiment of her moral conviction. While this does not function as "proof" of Murphy's work, it does demonstrate that it is by no means *impossible* to live out a *kenotic* ethic that also offers transformative possibilities to the wider society.

Conclusion and Prospect:
Of Teleological Tension and Hope

It is time to take stock of the ground covered in this essay. I have developed a wider understanding of the significance of Murphy's work in articulating

---

66. "Gravitational force" is drawn from Omri Elisha's work on progressive evangelicals and the persistence of individualist conceptions of social problems; see *Moral Ambition: Mobilization and Social Outreach in Evangelical Megachurches* (Berkeley: University of California Press, 2011) 109.

67. Murphy, "Traditions, Practices, and the Powers," 92.

68. McClendon offers a helpful perspective on the role of saints in shaping Christian imagination. See James Wm. McClendon Jr., "Story, Sainthood, and Truth" and "Do We Need Saints Today?," in *Collected Works*, 2:207–18, 285–94.

the shift from modern to postmodern modes of thinking in Anglo-American postmodernity. My thesis has been that while Murphy is widely understood to articulate revolutionary changes in epistemology and philosophy of language, her work also entails a shift away from the anthropological and causal reductionism of the modern period, and that this shift suggests a radical political vision that is structured by kenosis as the structure of the goals and purpose human life and the universe. This vision, embedded in Murphy's work, offers crucial resources for an Anabaptist political theology. However underdeveloped the implications of this vision are, radical democracy's emphasis on receptive and vulnerable practices of tending confirms Murphy's work, and extends her philosophical and ethical arguments in an embodied sociology of kenosis through an analysis of radical democratic political practices. Radical democracy offers a picture of how Murphy's work might be pertinent for our contemporary political context—marked as it is by the manipulative power-weave of mega-corporation and nation-state—by showing how Murphy's resources unmask the will to power in contemporary political practices.

However, while the radical-democratic theory of Coles and Wolin confirm and extend her radical vision, Murphy may provide an explanation for their lingering pessimism about the future of radical democratic practice in the context of managed democracy. Whereas Coles and Wolin assume an ateleology as a crucial condition for receptive political practice, this ateleology leads them to make no guarantee that things will work out for the better. This presents a sobering view of the future of receptive democracy, and along with it, human flourishing.

Murphy offers such pessimism an important gift: it is not *teleology-in-general* that ought to be the object of our concern. If, as for Murphy, it is a teleological vision of kenosis that sustains vulnerability and receptive openness as crucial to human flourishing, then not only does this provide grounds for the ongoing receptivity that Coles and Wolin seek in radical-democratic practice, but it also offers a broader vision of hope that grounds, energizes, and sustains *kenotic* action as the means and direction of human flourishing. As such, this may not only provide a stronger warrant for ongoing radical democratic practice, but it may also allay the lingering pessimism that threatens the project of radical democracy from within by offering a deeper and stronger sense of politics that are embedded in the structure of the universe. In the meantime, however, Murphy's resonance with proponents of radical democracy betrays the radical character of her own work.[69]

---

69. I am indebted to Brad Kallenberg, Ryan Newson, and Eric Schnitger for criticisms of this essay.

11

Preaching on Rough Ground
MacIntyre, Yoder, and Murphy's Embodied Philosophy

—Gregory D. Walgenbach

A JULY 1, 2014 *Los Angeles Times* story included a minor correction: "An earlier version of this post included a photo gallery that referred to 'residents opposed to immigration.' The reference should have been to 'residents opposed to illegal immigration.'"[1] This "correction" purports to smooth out a rough story: a mob of protesters in Murrieta, California, wave American flags, angrily shout and block the path of a bus carrying unaccompanied migrant child detainees and single women with kids. The enraged, possessed visages of "patriots" stare down the confused, frightened faces of migrants headed for a detention facility where they will be processed by Immigration and Customs Enforcement (ICE). The correction quoted at the outset tries to blunt the hateful attacks levied by anti-immigration voices not only against "illegal aliens" but those who support, harbor, respect, or even look like them. Bodily rage meeting bodily fear is glossed over as opposition to immigration law. Rage in Murrieta bursts forth during the same summer as the brutality in Ferguson, Missouri. A marriage of spiritual crisis and religion of the state buries the solidarity of love called for in the gospel. If preachers or parishes, especially *white* preachers and parishes, tackle the issue of the treatment of migrants at all, not to mention white supremacy, it is more in the mode of the *LA Times*' correction than honest description. That is, calls to welcome the stranger are carefully couched in explanations

1. Matt Hansen and Mark Boster, "Protesters in Murrieta Block Detainees' Buses in Tense Standoff," *Los Angeles Times*, July 1, 2014, http://www.latimes.com/local/lanow/la-me-ln-immigrants-murrieta-20140701-story.html#page=1.

of how America has always been an immigrant nation, that we need to keep our borders secure, and that legality is paramount. Moreoever, calls for justice for particular lives are seen causing division rather than healing it. Preaching that all lives matter is acceptable; preaching that immigrant lives or black lives matter brings an edge perceived as a threat. With rough edges removed, preachers are unable to preach and disciples unable to walk. Yoder (with Murphy's MacIntyre) addresses precisely this paralysis of faithfulness, which is a failure of truthfulness.

Nancey Murphy tells the story of a time at the cemetery as a little girl when her mother sought to comfort her with a hopeful "We know he's in a better place." Nancey recalls thinking to herself, directing her gaze downward into the earth: "I know exactly where he is." This anecdote reflects Nancey's preoccupation that philosophy should touch the ground. Indeed, one of Nancey's favorite texts is Stephen Toulmin's *Cosmopolis*, which describes the modern detour into the quest for abstract Cartesian certainty from which Westerners are recovering, and suggests a recovery of a politics of persuasive influence more than force. Murphy herself was drawn to the philosophical (epistemological) problems of embodiment, and her research program developed alongside her engagement with the practical life, prayer, and speech of Christian communities—the sort of rough ground to which Wittgenstein called philosophers to return.[2] Following in this vein, in this essay I will extend Murphy's exposition of Alasdair MacIntyre's epistemology, suggesting that the theology of John Howard Yoder can be read as a concrete example of tradition-constituted rationality that also extends the concept and the Christian tradition itself in key ways. I conclude with a brief reflection on how Yoder's Jesus read through Murphy's MacIntyre produces a space of resistance to the death-dealing principalities and powers. The production of this space is one of the primary goals of preaching and one which cannot be achieved without the socially embodied response of the people of God.

Embodied Philosophy: Radical Tradition in Yoder's Jesus and Murphy's MacIntyre

One way to understand Nancey Murphy's philosophical-theological research program is as a Wittgensteinian, Quinean untangling of the methodological and epistemological knots of embodiment, particularly at the intersection of theology and science. Three prominent components of her

---

2. Ludwig Wittgenstein, *Philosophical Investigations* (Malden, MA: Blackwell, [1953] 2001) §§107–8.

research project include: (1) the elucidation of a scientific theology through Lakatosian (later MacIntyrean) research programs[3]; (2) the narration of modern/postmodern habits of thought, arguing for epistemological, linguistic, and metaphysical holism[4]; and (3) the search for a nonreductive physicalist anthropology.[5] My interest lies in the relationship of Murphy's recommendation of Alasdair MacIntyre's tradition-constituted rationality to her appreciation for Yoder's theology.

The work of MacIntyre, who Murphy sees as the heir apparent to Imre Lakatos, increasingly served as an epistemological north star for Murphy. "MacIntyre," Murphy writes, "is the only philosopher who adequately grasps the complexity of the current epistemological predicament and also provides hope for avoiding relativism."[6] Murphy came to agree with MacIntyre's project at the same time as she moved into the Anabaptist tradition. Recalling a seminar at GTU led by James McClendon on radical reformation history and theology, Murphy remembers: "Reading about the widespread torture and killing of Anabaptists had a profound impact; I felt a claim on my life to join a church in which nonviolence was not an optional extra."[7] It was through McClendon that Nancey learned about Yoder, and the work of both profoundly influenced her theology.[8] Bringing these two strands together and extending Murphy's insights, I argue that reading Yoder through MacIntyre both confirms MacIntyre's account of moral enquiry by revealing its broad applicability *and* recommends Yoder's theology as a concrete instantiation of MacIntyre's theory of tradition-constituted enquiry. In each subsection below, I will begin with a quote from MacIntyre,

3. Nancey Murphy, *Theology in the Age of Scientific Reasoning* (Ithaca, NY: Cornell University Press, 1990) xi.

4. Nancey Murphy, *Beyond Liberalism and Fundamentalism: How Modern and Postmodern Philosophy Set the Theological Agenda* (Harrisburg, PA: Trinity, 1996) Part II. Cf. "Nature's God: An Interview with Nancey Murphy," *The Christian Century* (December 27, 2005) 20–26.

5. Warren S. Brown, Nancey Murphy, and H. Newton Maloney, eds., *Whatever Happened to the Soul? Scientific and Theological Portraits of Human Nature* (Minneapolis: Fortress, 1998); Nancey Murphy and Warren S. Brown, *Did My Neurons Make Me Do It? Philosophical and Neurobiological Perspectives on Moral Responsibility and Free Will* (New York: Oxford University Press, 2007).

6. Nancey Murphy, "Wind and Spirit: A Theological Autobiography," *Dialog: A Journal of Theology* 46 (2007) 306.

7. Nancey Murphy and Charles H. Hackney, "Interview with Nancey Murphy: Constructing an Anabaptist Vision of Ideal Psychological Functioning," *Edification: The Transdisciplinary Journal of Christian Psychology* 4:2 (2011) 73–78.

8. Her fullest treatment of Yoder is in Nancey Murphy and George F. R. Ellis, *On the Moral Nature of the Universe: Theology, Cosmology, and Ethics* (Minneapolis: Fortress, 1996) 178–201.

and then show how Yoder can be read as exemplifying and extending the insight. The space that Yoder's work creates, I will show, moves far beyond a "project of retrieval" and opens up new avenues for resistance.

History

> So rationality itself, whether theoretical or practical, is a concept with a history: indeed, since there are a diversity of traditions of enquiry, with histories, there are, so it will turn out, rationalities rather than rationality, just as it will turn out that there are justices rather than justice.[9]

After World War II Yoder was doing relief work in a Europe that was in the process of owning up to an embarrassing failure in discipleship.[10] "The small *Freikirchen* within Germany (Mennonites, Baptists, Open Brethren, Methodists) were no more critical of the Nazi vision than were the big churches."[11] "In fact," Yoder writes, "there were some petty ways in which the free churches were better off than before. The Mennonites were granted by Heinrich Himmler himself the privilege of not needing to use the form of an oath to affirm their loyalty as citizens."[12] How did a Christian community that held to the peaceful witness of Jesus, and emphatically rejected collusion with the state's violence that characterized the "Magisterial Reformers," so utterly fail in the face of Nazism? In his dissertation, Yoder turned for answers to the period of history in which the Anabaptists themselves were birthed[13]

This kind of historical turn would continue to mark Yoder's work throughout his life. For example, in *Christian Attitudes to War, Peace, and Revolution: A Companion to Bainton*,[14] Yoder crafts a broad historical

---

9. Alasdair MacIntyre, *Whose Justice? Which Rationality?* (Notre Dame: University of Notre Dame Press, 1988) 9.

10. Cf. Mark Thiessen Nation, *John Howard Yoder: Mennonite Patience, Evangelical Witness, Catholic Convictions* (Grand Rapids: Eerdmans, 2006) 16ff.

11. John Howard Yoder, "Karl Barth, Post-Christendom Theologian," in *Karl Barth and the Problem of War & Other Essays on Barth* (Eugene, OR: Cascade, 2003) 178.

12. Ibid., 178n11.

13. John Howard Yoder, *Anabaptism and Reformation in Switzerland: An Historical and Theological Analysis of the Dialogues Between Anabaptists and Reformers* (Kitchener, Ontario: Pandora, 2004) xiii.

14. Elkhart, IN: Co-op Bookstore, 1983 (Unpublished); citations are to the unpublished version. An edited version was published as John Howard Yoder, *Christian Attitudes to War, Peace, and Revolution*, edited by Theodore J. Koontz and Andy Alexis-Baker (Grand Rapids: Brazos, 2009).

narrative in order to reshape the story of Christian theological ethics and resituate Christian memory and identity: "to confess clearly the considered commitment of the theological ethics of the historic peace church position and then to build into the telling of the story the correctives which flow from that critical self awareness."[15] Like MacIntyre retells the narrative of Western Liberalism's moral philosophy from the standpoint of the Aristotelian-Thomistic tradition in order to explain why Western morality is in such a fragmented state, Yoder not only makes audible another voice, but *in* this other voice explains the quandaries faced by the Catholic Church and the Protestant ("Magisterial") Reformers.

Yoder claims that "[t]here are a limited number of possible ways to take history seriously."[16] He agrees with MacIntyre that a tradition can incorporate history in ways that inevitably lead to crisis. If a tradition cannot generally wrestle with particular aspects of the historical record, theological ideas, significant events, etc., that contradict its interpretation of history, in such a way that it is able to either incorporate them into the narrative as it stands or transform the narrative by incorporating the alien elements while maintaining continuity, that tradition will continue to slide into obscurantism. Absent a deeper historicism, Yoder claims, a (sub)tradition will struggle in vain to go against the grain when necessary—unable to even identify the challenge—and will fail to reject a long-received part of the tradition which may have been corrupted and in need of recovery.

He cites several examples of deeper historicism among early Anabaptists.[17] "Official" churches are able to accuse the radical reformers of ahistoricism because the former are blinded by power structures that assume the particular way that things turned out is the way that things had to be. Any other view is against history. Anabaptists' attentiveness to embodied discipleship in historical context was learned in the debates with Magisterial Protestants (e.g., Zwingli) over baptism and collusion with the state's violence. "The nonresistance that remained typical for Anabaptists and Mennonites in the later decades and centuries," writes Yoder, "was not the fruit of some development. It arose neither from exhaustion nor embarrassment. From the moment of its birth on, the essence and reason for the existence of Swiss Anabaptism was its rejection of state resources."[18] Both Protestants and Roman Catholics, it would seem, had accepted what had taken place in history, particularly the radically different understanding of

---

15. Yoder, *Christian Attitudes*, 12.
16. Yoder, *Anabaptism and Reformation*, 127.
17. Ibid., 128–29.
18. Ibid., 132.

history engendered by the "Constantinian" shift, broadly construed. "It was otherwise for the Anabaptists, whose right to exist stood or fell on whether their understanding of the historical development of the church was correct or not. The true church that Jesus founded and that the apostles built up had become unfaithful."[19]

Tradition

> A living tradition then is an historically extended, socially embodied argument, and an argument precisely in part about the goods which constitute that tradition.[20]

> Such a tradition . . . has to be embodied in a set of texts which function as the authoritative point of departure for tradition-constituted enquiry and which remain as essential points of reference for enquiry and activity, for argument, debate, and conflict within that tradition. Those texts to which this canonical status is assigned are treated both as having a fixed meaning embodied in them and also as always open to rereading, so that every tradition becomes to some degree a tradition of critical reinterpretation in which one and the same body of texts, with of course some addition and subtraction, is put to the question, and to successively different sets of questions, as a tradition unfolds.[21]

Yoder's understanding of historical rationality both fits MacIntyre's frame and presses forward with its own Anabaptist apocalyptic and pacifist lens. Yoder refuses, as does MacIntyre, to let people get away with thinking about themselves as free from traditioning. Although he does not provide a technical definition of tradition, Yoder's practical understanding fits MacIntyre's theory. The Christian (sub)traditions he hints at above are socially embodied arguments over what particular goods are central to the life of the church, particularly arguments over the interpretation of Scripture and of those other texts formative to the tradition. Yoder distinguishes between a more pedantic use of the term "tradition" and a more robust version that approaches MacIntyre's use. Yoder's concern, like MacIntyre's, is to be able to discern which "traditioning" is faithful, and which constitutes betrayal.[22]

---

19. Ibid., 193–94.

20. Alasdair MacIntyre, *After Virtue*, 2nd ed. (Notre Dame: University of Notre Dame Press, [1981] 1984) 222.

21. MacIntyre, *Whose Justice?* 383.

22. John Howard Yoder, *The Priestly Kingdom* (Notre Dame: University of Notre Dame Press, 1984) 67.

Anabaptists did not merely return to the Bible. They paid attention to Scripture in light of the witness of early church tradition. Conrad Grebel wrote to Thomas Müntzer, "[We believe] that infant baptism is a senseless, blasphemous abomination contrary to all Scripture and even *contrary to the papacy*, for we learn through Cyprian and Augustine that for many years after the time of the apostles, for six hundred years, believers and unbelievers were baptized together, et cetera."[23] Anabaptists identified sources in tradition other than, but in line with Scripture and used them to argue that the record on baptism was confused for many centuries after Christ. They were able to recognize the development of a doctrine of infant baptism, for the purpose of arguing that it was not consistent with the early tradition, let alone Scripture. My point here is not to promote one argument or another but merely to recognize Anabaptists' use of "tradition" in theological argument.

Similarly to MacIntyre, Yoder demonstrates the integration of tradition, formative text(s), and the "historical baseline" with which that tradition must wrestle honestly in order to remain rational. Whereas MacIntyre arrives at this insight via Aristotle, Yoder arrives at it via Israel and the Incarnation.[24] Yoder's claim to rationality is wrapped up in the logic of the Christian tradition, in a manner not dissimilar to MacIntyre's recognition that "on Aristotle's view being virtuous is a prerequisite for . . . rationality."[25] Yet precisely because Jesus is the universal Lord, and the powers are being "reenlisted" in the service of humanity, we will not be surprised to discover rationality in other places besides the Christian tradition. In fact, we are freed to acknowledge other rationali*ties* in the world as God's gifts to humankind, preparations for the gospel, and even potential correctives to the people of God. "The point is not that all the truth is in Jesus or in the Bible. It is that the truth which is in Jesus is the truth which matters the most, which must therefore regulate our reception and recognition of other kinds and levels of truth rather than being set in parallel or subordinated thereto."[26]

Parallel to MacIntyre's detailed historical narratives is Yoder's (biblical) metaphor for tradition as a vine, a "looping back" wherein the past is rediscovered "because only a new question or challenge enables us to see it speaking to us."[27] Like MacIntyre, Yoder understands that traditions grow

23. Quoted in Yoder, *Anabaptism and Reformation*, 194.
24. Yoder, *Priestly*, 60–62.
25. MacIntyre, *Whose Justice?*, 109.
26. John Howard Yoder, "The Use of the Bible in Theology," in Robert K. Johnston, ed., *The Use of the Bible in Theology: Evangelical Options* (Atlanta: John Knox, 1985) 117.
27. Yoder, *Priestly*, 69–70. In light of Murphy's interest in George Tyrrell, it is

because they are able to incorporate "dissonance," created by the tradition itself, in ways that are fruitful. This process is sought out by the healthy tradition, rather than taking place only in reaction to outside threats. A theology of repentance is inherent to a traditioning process that seeks to live in the "new creation" (2 Cor 5:17). Far from a "settled reality," tradition depends upon ongoing "[tests] by its fidelity to that origin."[28] Just as a vine wants to constantly loop around to flourish and remain strong, tradition wants to weave back and forth to incorporate "dissonance" and repair struggling aspects. The vine image recognizes the complexity of traditioning in a way that makes maximal space for competing voices while also maintaining a concern for faithfulness that permits it to remain true to itself.

Texts

> Every such form of enquiry begins in and from some condition of pure historical contingency, from the beliefs, institutions, and practices of some particular community which constitute a given. Within such a community authority will have been conferred upon certain texts and certain voices. Bards, priests, prophets, kings, and, on occasion, fools and jesters will all be heard.[29]

> To ask how the Bible functions in theology is like asking how the ground floor functions in a house: there are several possible right answers, and any one of them looks a little silly when spelled out.[30]

Yoder is neither a biblicist, nor a foundationalist.[31] For Yoder, the biblical text functions as part of a dynamic process of Christian tradition*ing* by Christian communities. In describing the development of the canon, for instance, Yoder echoes MacIntyre's characterization that the initial development of a tradition involves three stages, wherein a tradition is unquestioned, then

---

interesting to note his use of a similar metaphor for the "growth" of Catholicism, used as an indicator of both its strength and need of pruning, in "Reflections on Catholicism," *Through Scylla and Charybdis or The Old Theology and the New* (London: Longmans, Green, and Co., 1907) 25.

28. Yoder, *Priestly*, 77–78.
29. MacIntyre, *Whose Justice?*, 354.
30. Yoder, "Use of the Bible," 103.
31. Cf. John Howard Yoder, "Walk and Word: The Alternatives to Methodologism," in Stanley Hauerwas, Nancey Murphy, and Mark Nation, eds., *Theology Without Foundations: Religious Practice and the Future of Theological Truth* (Nashville: Abingdon, 1994).

tested, then confirmed.³² Scripture serves as the historical baseline in this process, and the center of catechetical teaching and correction.³³ Just as MacIntyre admits that any tradition-constituted enquiry "begins in and from some condition of pure historical contingency,"³⁴ Yoder writes that "[t]here is no need to theorize about *why* the Bible has authority when one finds oneself living in a community in which that authority is presupposed and which is constantly being renewed through the simple experience of its operation." The theologian's task is "to defend the text against a wrong claim to its authority,"³⁵ to retain "some fundamental continuity"³⁶ with the tradition's source even as that tradition develops.

In the community of discipleship, Scripture provides essential memory that not only constitutes our identity but through which we are led to proper vision.³⁷ Narrative, MacIntyre claims, "turns out to be the basic and essential genre for the characterization of human actions."³⁸ When the Swiss Anabaptists, for example, asked, "How are we to be faithful followers of Jesus in the chaos of sixteenth-century Europe?" they found answers in the stories of believer's baptism and the cross in Scripture, inadvertently embodying MacIntyre's maxim: "I can only answer the question 'What am I to do?' if I can answer the prior question 'Of what story or stories do I find myself a part?'"³⁹ Yoder reminded Mennonites that they were not Protestants and did not need to be seduced by that particular style of interpretation which "transformed a living narrative into a collection of timeless norms and made it difficult . . . for a non-Fundamentalist use of the Bible to be listened to."⁴⁰

Crises

> [There are] three stages in the initial development of a tradition: a first in which the relevant beliefs, texts, and authorities have not yet been put into question; a second in which inadequacies of various types have been identified, but not yet remedied; and a third in which response to those inadequacies has resulted in a

---

32. MacIntyre, *Whose Justice?* 354.
33. Yoder, "Use of the Bible," 104–8.
34. MacIntyre, *Whose Justice?* 354.
35. Yoder, "Use of the Bible," 110–11.
36. MacIntyre, *Whose Justice?* 362.
37. Yoder, "Use of the Bible," 113.
38. MacIntyre, *After Virtue*, 208.
39. Ibid., 216.
40. Yoder, "Walk and Word," 88.

set of reformulations, reevaluations, and new formulations and evaluations, designed to remedy inadequacies and overcome limitations.[41]

According to Yoder, correction is a gift that reminds us that our life is sustained by the One who brought us into being: "We should feel guilty not when we need to be corrected but when we claim to bypass that need, as if our link to our origins were already in our own hands."[42] Crises are opportunities: "One way the same old data yields new information is that we bring to it another set of questions, just as the natural sciences find more facts in the same plant or animal than before their present instruments were developed. A new question permits the old event to respond in ways that earlier patterns of questioning had not made self-evident or perhaps had hidden."[43] In his work, Yoder points to several key crises in a way that has analogies to MacIntyre's work on crises. Most poignantly in *The Politics of Jesus*, Yoder asked: What if Jesus and his cross actually have something to do with Christian ethics? Of course, this sounds ridiculous; but what is *more* ridiculous, Yoder points out, is that most of what often passes for Christian ethics in mid-twentieth-century Protestant liberalism has little or nothing to do with Jesus and his cross.

In Yoder's narrative, the early church's confession of and discipleship to Jesus as Lord determined its corporate life and witness to the world. Jesus had not merely begun a new progressive social movement, but had conquered the principalities and powers through his cross and resurrection. As the crucified and risen Lamb, Jesus now rules the world. The church is called to be the people who, knowing that Jesus rules the world, lives under his reign and in the cruciform shape of his life. The church of the first couple centuries was pacifist for precisely this reason: its king was Jesus, the one who died *for* his *enemies*, at the hands of the powers. Things went fairly well—that is, the church struggled to follow Jesus faithfully, with frequent periods of bitter persecution—until the Caesar, Constantine, became a Christian. Constantine is more significant for what he represents than the specifics of what he actually did; the Constantinian shift took place over several generations. For the church, this turn of events seemed to mean

41. MacIntyre, *Whose Justice?* 355.

42. Yoder, *Priestly*, 70. I must mention here that in contrast to his commendations of correction and nonviolence, Yoder was himself corrected for acts of sexual violence against women. While these actions by Yoder are inexcusable, I believe his theological contributions remain important; in fact, resources from his own project indict him on this moral failure, containing resources for resistance to such evil, and for repentance and forgiveness.

43. Ibid.

that now the bearer of history was no longer the church but the world: Before Constantine, one knew there was a church but had to trust that God governed history; after Constantine one knew God controlled history (for the Christian emperor was on the throne) but finding the church was an exercise in faith![44] The outsider (or enemy) is no longer privileged as the ultimate test of one's commitment to love as God loves but is now the enemy of the state and, therefore, the enemy of the faith. Faithfulness to the tradition was subsequently defined in the context of *destroying* one's enemy rather than dying *for* one's enemy. Centuries pass until, at long last, radical reformers such as the Swiss Anabaptists, among others, recognized the discrepancy here between the voice of Scripture and the voice of the ruling powers and its church—and chose the voice of Scripture, even though this meant that they, like the early church, would be persecuted. They recovered those virtues which had atrophied in the midst of Christian empires.

If in *After Virtue* MacIntyre describes a Western moral landscape bereft of shared narratives or practices with which to make sense of inherited philosophical language, Yoder faces a Christian theological tradition that lost the ability to make sense of theological language like "Jesus is Lord" and "take up your cross." Yoder keys on two issues central to the early dialogues between the Anabaptists and Zwingli: the question of justice and the question of baptism. Both have to do with what Yoder calls Zwingli's "dualistic anthropology, according to which human nature is so burdened by its 'original failure' that it is never capable of good, not even among Christians. The outer world is precisely the location for this inability, whereas the inner person can be brought closer to God."[45] On the matter of *justice*, Zwingli had convinced his followers that "divine justice did not belong to a special inner area of the personal or the religious. It is ethical above all, even in terms of social ethics, and it exists in the concrete calls of God that lay claim to the entire life of humanity within the social order." The emphasis is on world and not church and depends upon the enforcement of an ethical regime rather than an ecclesial witness in a way that fits Yoder's description of the major shift in Christendom. However, as Zwingli's followers, the early Anabaptists agree that God's justice is a social ethical call *to the church*. For Zwingli himself divine justice "is valid only if a person is not a sinner; therefore, it is attached to an unreal condition." Zwingli repeats the Constantinian line, except that now he has more "realistic" expectations for the state. So divine justice is for heaven and a separate standard for human justice is geared toward the sinful civic order. There is justice for heaven

---

44. Yoder, "Constantinian Sources," 137.
45. Yoder, *Anabaptism and Reformation*, 155.

and approximate justice for the world. But for Zwingli there is no church as a space of resistance. While it is tempting to suggest that this vision lacks social embodiment, in reality its embodiment is to be found in that order imposed by the state and enforced by the magistrates.

On the matter of *baptism*, Zwingli's dualism creates what Yoder calls a theory of "non-correspondence." In the same way that divine justice does not directly "correspond" to earthly justice, and in some areas is completely different, so with baptism, Zwingli (at least in 1524) claimed that it "need not be bound temporally to faith." He brings out examples of unbaptized believers and baptized unbelievers in Scripture in order to demonstrate "non-correspondence." Therefore, says Zwingli, there is a spiritual baptism of faith and a water baptism of the flesh, and the two may not correspond. So for Zwingli, although outer baptism can point to inner baptism, there is no necessary connection between the two. Therefore, there is no reason to halt the practice of infant baptism just because the theology of justification by faith has shifted. He is intentionally "breaking with the entire baptismal theology of the past." Once again, outward baptism is for the world; spiritual baptism is on another plane entirely, "grounded solely in election." This leads to an unfortunate conclusion: There is no church. At least, there is no visible church, participating bodily in God's salvation through visible sacraments. In contrast, because they refuse to allow a disjunction between the sacrament and the reality, the Anabaptists arguably retain a more Catholic view of baptism, albeit limited to (adult) "believers." In critiquing Zwingli from the Anabaptist perspective Yoder makes a sort of sacramental argument. He notes that the "simple biblicism" of the Anabaptists allowed them "to preserve a healthy sense of the unity of the Gospel, which simply allowed no room for a fundamental dualism."[46] Therefore, the Anabaptists did perhaps the only thing they could do in the context: they held onto the traditional Catholic teaching on baptism but, in keeping with Reformation teaching, affirmed that it applied to believers. Contrary to Zwingli, baptism corresponded to faith; analogously, divine justice corresponded to the church. The Christian community, distinct from the state, is to live according to divine standards and bear witness to the reign of God.

To summarize the argument thus far: history, tradition, texts, and crises in Anabaptist life fit the forms laid out by MacIntyre and reveal serious problems in the Christian tradition caused by the decoupling of social embodiment from Christian witness, whether through driving a wedge between

---

46. Ibid., 151–57.

divine and earthly justice or between faith and sacrament. Instead of a disembodied theology, what is left is a social ethics determined by the state.[47]

Practices

> By a "practice" I am going to mean any coherent and complex form of socially established cooperative human activity through which goods internal to that form of activity are realized in the course of trying to achieve those standards of excellence which are appropriate to, and partially definitive of, that form of activity, with the result that human powers to achieve excellence, and human conceptions of the ends and goods involved, are systematically extended.... In the ancient and medieval worlds the creation and sustaining of human communities—of households, cities, nations—is generally taken to be a practice in the sense in which I have defined it.[48]

Yoder, in "Sacrament as Social Process," explains that he often avoids the use of the word "practice" because he does not want those who disagree with MacIntyre's or others' technical use of the term to ignore what he has to say.[49] Even so, in his *Body Politics*,[50] Yoder delineates the importance of five practices of the Christian community before the watching world. For Yoder, these are "specific human activit[ies]," mandated by Jesus, in which "God would at the same time be acting 'in, with, and under' that human activity."[51] These practices are specifically of the type MacIntyre describes, the very performance of which realizes goods internal to them, with the result that the ends of the Christian community are extended. Moreover, the church, described as a household, a city, a nation, is exactly the sort of community that MacIntyre articulates: an embodied argument over time the

---

47. This is also clear in Yoder's work on Just War theory and histories of war, peace, and revolution, a series of crises I will not address here.

48. MacIntyre, *After Virtue*, 187–88.

49. John Howard Yoder, *The Royal Priesthood: Essays Ecclesiastical and Ecumenical*, edited by Michael Cartwright (Scottdale, PA: Herald, 1998) 363 n7.

50. John Howard Yoder, *Body Politics: Five Practices of the Christian Community Before the Watching World* (Scottdale, PA: Herald Press, [1992] 2001). See Nancey Murphy's own interaction with this text in chapter two and the introduction to chapter six in *Virtues and Practices in the Christian Tradition: Christian Ethics after MacIntyre*, edited by Nancey Murphy, Brad J. Kallenberg, and Mark Thiessen Nation (Harrisburg, PA: Trinity, 1997).

51. Ibid., 1.

participation in which is necessary for identifying individual and common goods that lead to human flourishing.

The practices constitutive of Anabaptism, although intended for the whole church, include the following: (1) *Binding and Loosing*: Also known as the Rule of Christ, this process, delineated in Matt 18:15–20, is the way the church is "authorized . . . to deal with moral and legal matters," particularly how the church is to call out sin, encourage repentance, reconcile, discipline, and forgive. (2) *Disciples Break Bread Together*: the Lord's Supper is *both* economic sharing and religious ritual. The Supper is easily transformed into an inner subjective, or an outer, worldly ritual with the effect that the church disappears. As the church is the people of God that shares their bread with one another, they learn to live out of God's economy of abundance rather than the world's economy of scarcity. (3) *Baptism and the New Humanity*: a MacIntyrean practice, "the primary meaning of baptism is the new society it creates, by inducting all kinds of people into the same people. The church is. . . that new society; it is therefore also the model for the world's moving in the same direction."[52] The very act of baptism extends the community and expands the breadth of the body of Christ, incorporating difference into the unity of the body of Christ. (4) *The Fullness of Christ*: a new politics in which members are empowered by the Holy Spirit and encouraged by one another to exercise their gifts for the good of the body. (5) *The Rule of Paul*: According to Paul (1 Corinthians 14), the church should hold meetings such that anyone can speak, and God's Spirit is known through the open conversation of the community. This model of meeting exemplifies the epistemological humility required in order to grow faithfully by being open to challenge from outsiders—the very dialogical approach to truth that MacIntyre claims is necessary.

Such practices serve as a bulwark against the very co-option of history, traditions, texts, and crises by the powers that seek to undermine them. Practices are worship-constituted and worship-constitutive: "Worship is the communal cultivation of an alternative construction of society and history."[53] It is faithful practices that ultimately give shape to and extend the ends and goods that are extended. Early Anabaptists believed that in order to *be* the church, that is, to *be* the alternative to the world, the entire community needed to take on practices that built up society and history. The goods of individuals and particularly the good of the community are extended as the whole community is shaped by divine practices. Not the least of these goods was the witness of peace: "[W]hereas the Reformation could

---

52. Ibid., 32.
53. Yoder, *Priestly*, 43.

only survive *with* the state, the Anabaptists had created something that could survive *against* the state, and that could look enemies both within and without directly in the eye, as could no other church of the Reformation."[54]

Virtues

> A virtue is an acquired human quality the possession and exercise of which tends to enable us to achieve those goods which are integral to practices and the lack of which effectively prevents us from achieving any such goods.[55]

Yoder does not make much explicit use of "virtue" language in his description of Christian moral formation, finding it unhelpful when used exclusively, but he does expand MacIntyre's list of virtues. Reasons for his reticence to commit to virtue theory include his resistance to systematization and his refusal to favor one of the many moral language games—a practical concern for the incorporation of those outside a particular systematic fold. In what is for Yoder a paradigmatic case, "The equal dignity of both kinds of people, those with and those without the heritage of Torah, was affirmed not on the grounds of the possession by both of certain virtues, but on the grounds of the cross."[56] With respect to Jews and Gentiles, it is not a common ground built through participation in some sort of virtue theory but the power of the cross that had brought the two together. Nonetheless, when writing about the Catholic tradition of moral reason as the "cultivation of virtue" Yoder writes quite favorably of this venerable tradition of formation, citing Francis of Assisi, Dorothy Day, and Mother Teresa as favorable examples.[57]

In any case, Yoder recommends certain virtues in a way that is quite compatible with MacIntyre's Aristotelian understanding thereof. To St. Thomas's Aristotelian virtues—prudence, justice, temperance, and courage—MacIntyre adds patience, humility, and truthfulness, as well as "the virtue of having an adequate sense of the traditions to which one belongs or which confront one."[58] A sort of catalogue of virtues in Yoder's work would include still others: community-formation,[59] concrete obedience,

---

54. Yoder, *Anabaptism and Reformation*, 295.

55. MacIntyre, *After Virtue*, 191.

56. John Howard Yoder, *For the Nations: Essays Public and Evangelical* (Grand Rapids: Eerdmans, 1997) 29–30.

57. Yoder, *Christian Attitudes* (2009) 395.

58. MacIntyre, *After Virtue*, 177, 223.

59. Nancey names "community formation" as the essential, over-arching practice that constitutes the church; see Murphy, *Virtues and Practices*, 37.

non-conformity to the world, autochthonous [indigenous] leadership, simplicity, transparency, meekness, hunger for righteousness, peacemaking, and charity, with Yoder's specific gloss as enemy-love.

Unpredictability and Teleology

> But it is crucial that at any given point in an enacted dramatic narrative we do not know what will happen next.[60]

> There is no present which is not informed by some image of some future and an image of the future which always presents itself in the form of a telos—or of a variety of ends or goals—towards which we are either moving or failing to move in the present.[61]

Finally, Yoder's theology has MacIntyrean analogies in its attention to unpredictability and (indirectly) teleology. Central to both MacIntyre's and Yoder's respective projects is the recognition of the contingency of our traditions and the insight that we can predict neither what future challenges will occur nor what the response to those challenges will look like. "The stories can be told of how [questions] have been answered before. The trust is not unreasonable that they can be answered again; yet this is not true a priori. It is true only in the actual encounter between a believing community and the next challenge. *The only way to see how this will work will be to see how it will work.*"[62]

Yoder agrees with MacIntyre in rejecting the "predictability" inherent to Cartesian and Hegelian accounts of rationality. MacIntyre's epistemology is anti-Cartesian in that first "principles will have had to vindicate themselves in the historical process of dialectical justification," and anti-Hegelian in that "[n]o one at any stage can ever rule out the future possibility of their present beliefs and judgments being shown to be inadequate in a variety of ways."[63] In working neither from an unattainable foundational certainty nor an arrogant "teleology," any natural theology that would follow Yoder's theology and MacIntyre's philosophy has to tell the story of nature humbly, highlighting human vulnerabilities, contingencies, and solidarities. Rather than await fate, Christianity calls for prayerful action in response to that

---

60. MacIntyre, *After Virtue*, 215.
61. Ibid., 215–16.
62. Yoder, *Priestly*, 45. Emphasis added.
63. MacIntyre, *Whose Justice?* 360–61.

which is coming into the world.[64] Because enemy-love is paramount, predictability is off the table. For nothing is more predictable than the "vicious cycle" of violence,[65] and nothing is more exhilarating and surprising than peace.

The unpredictability of tradition-constituted rationality does *not* mean that "all we shall be confronted with in the end is a set of independent rival histories." Instead, MacIntyre emphasizes that, contrary to both Cartesian and Hegelian alternatives, the nature of tradition-constituted rationality is such that the positions of relativism and perspectivism make no sense. The relativist has to make her claim from outside all traditions and therefore is incapable of making any rational claim. Similarly, the perspectivist "fails to recognize how integral the conception of truth is to tradition-constituted forms of enquiry."[66] Far from being relativistic or perspectivist, both MacIntyre and Yoder operate within particular traditions that have particular understandings of *ends*. That MacIntyre, working in the tradition of moral philosophy, looks to "a social, moral and intellectual context ordered teleologically towards the end of a perfected science,"[67] and that Yoder, working as a theological ethicist, has his eyes set on the apocalyptic vision of a coming kingdom to which the church is called to be faithful, suggests eschatological visions which are not so much incompatible as they are reflective of their respective disciplines, philosophy and theology.

For Yoder, biblical apocalyptic is nothing if not related—by way of the incarnation, life, death, and resurrection of Jesus Christ—to a Christian account of teleological ends of tradition-constituted enquiry.[68] On teleology, there are few portions of Yoder's work more to the point than the concluding passage of his *Politics of Jesus*:

> Then to follow Jesus does not mean renouncing effectiveness. . . . It means that in Jesus we have a clue to which kinds of causation, which kind of community-building, which kinds of management, go with the grain of the cosmos, of which we know, as

---

64. See Nancey Murphy, "Does Prayer Make a Difference?" in *Cosmos as Creation: Theology and Science in Consonance*, edited by Ted Peters (Nashville: Abingdon, 1989) 235–46.

65. See Glen H. Stassen and David P. Gushee, *Kingdom Ethics: Following Jesus in Contemporary Context* (Downers Grove, IL: InterVarsity, 2003) 125–45.

66. MacIntyre, *Whose Justice?* 361, 367.

67. Alasdair MacIntyre, *First Principles, Final Ends and Contemporary Philosophical Issues* (Milwaukee: Marquette University Press, 1990) 43.

68. Cf. Yoder's 1988 address to the Society of Christian Ethics, "To Serve Our God and Rule the World," in *Royal Priesthood*, 127–40.

Caesar does not, that Jesus is both the Word (the inner logic of things) and the Lord ("sitting at the right hand").[69]

This "difference" is not only about teleology and unpredictability but about how the nature of things, which obviously includes the body, is "enclosed within, smaller than, the sovereignty of the God of the Resurrection and Ascension."[70] Yoder's resistance to systematization is, perhaps counterintuitively, due to his openness to the greater participation of all things in the reconciling work of God and the particular peaceable kingdom.

Preaching and Other Powerful Practices of Resistance

This reading of Yoder through MacIntyre—putting Yoderian lenses in MacIntyrean frames—is exactly what Murphy has taught us to do, and it affects her reading of Yoder and MacIntyre both. She's interested in MacIntyre because, without succumbing to relativism, he takes the embodied, historical arguments of communities seriously as essential for accounts of common good and human flourishing; she's interested in Yoder because for him Jesus and the communities constituted by and constitutive of his Body uniquely reveal the shape of the universe and the concrete way of life that goes with its grain. Both offer a way forward in nonviolently adjudicating between competing developments within the tradition. MacIntyre is the form; Yoder, the content. If we read Yoder through MacIntyre (and not MacIntyre through Yoder), as Murphy has taught us to do, what does this get us? There are many things one could say here, but I want to focus on how this reading of Yoder through MacIntyre leads to a theological approach that necessarily takes account of questions of how it will be *socially embodied*. Such a reading disallows, just as Yoder does, a gospel that floats above the fray, ignoring the questions of the everyday.

In contrast to Zwingli's theological abstractions which turned out to concretely legitimize the magistrates as arbiters of the moral life of Christians, early Anabaptists insisted against giving the magistrates that role (despite historical and scriptural reasons available for doing so). They followed a strand in Christian theology that posited an embodied community of witness that challenged political regimes and their violence rather than adjusting to them. This strand is not foreign to other Christian sub-traditions, but it is often downplayed and overshadowed. What MacIntyre and Yoder

---

69. John Howard Yoder, *The Politics of Jesus: Vicit Agnus Noster*, 2nd ed. (Grand Rapids: Eerdmans, [1972] 1994) 246.

70. Ibid.

help us to see is just how this move is a particular theological recovery of Christian history, tradition, and practices, and not simply a biblicist restorationism, reiterating "New Testament Christianity." Anabaptist theology is a particular tradition-constituted rationality that makes alternative sense of the sixteenth century by constituting an alternative way of living.

Let me return to the contemporary examples from the beginning of this essay. There is a type of preaching that remains above the fray of current events, communicating "timeless truths." Other modes of preaching use current events as glorified "illustrations" of gospel themes. The kind of preaching called for in Murphy's vision of embodied philosophy is a practice of resistance. The proclamation of the Good News should liberate captives to not capitulate to law and order as a cover for a refusal to instantiate the gospel's radical inclusivity. In the debates over immigration and immigrant rights, the church too often reiterates state concerns around border security and enforcement. Furthermore, the state expects the church to reinforce its moral adjudications of who constitutes a "good immigrant," who will be given preferred status or excluded from relief (not unlike how the crowd in the Gospel accounts were asked to condemn Jesus to crucifixion). The kind of embodied theology to which Murphy constantly returns us is essential to Christian witness because the principalities and powers constantly seek the production of bodies for the state even as they offer generous "spiritual" benefits. By all means show Christian compassion to immigrants but their bodies are primarily determined by the laws of the land! This in effect translates: go ahead and care for *legal* bodies; and care for *illegal* bodies by compliance with the law. There is an echo here of the Protestant (Zwinglian) logic which Anabaptists resisted. Not only is there no correlation between divine and earthly justice, they may by necessity be at odds. Spiritual welcome and charity—divine; exclusion and "tough love"—earthly. Simultaneously and problematically, contradictory visions of common good and human flourishing are promoted within the Christian community.

Debates about racial justice in the United States exhibit this tension perhaps to an even greater degree. The cultural and epistemological force of white supremacy, ever-present in American life, hides in plain sight, becoming visible in the resistance to the powers as seen, for example, in Ferguson, Missouri. Solidarity with black bodies requires an alternative, embodied narrative that is able not only to make sense of contemporary disparities in the criminal justice system but to create an alternative space of witness. The "Zwinglian" theological regime in this case is not only arbiter of earthly justice but also "polices" church response for two reasons. First, the state has sovereignty over earthly justice, so the church defers to it. Second, within that deferral, faith is a disembodied intention that is individualized and ultimately unknowable. This line of enquiry is made possible by MacIntyre and Yoder. A Christianity of resistance takes seriously the principalities and powers and the way in which they simultaneously demand loyalty of bodies even as they constantly catechize the human person away from the bodily towards dualistic, spiritualized anthropologies. If Yoder's apocalyptic vision calls into question what McClendon calls "the generally optimistic and progressive ring of MacIntyre's overall account of practices," Murphy points to a "Radical Reformation" epistemological alternative (informed by McClendon's account) that she presents as a fourth option to MacIntyre's *Three Rival Versions of Moral Enquiry*.[71] I hope to have shown here how Yoder's account does not *necessarily* overturn but can be read as actually *extending* MacIntyre's account toward a more peaceable, embodied epistemology.

J. Kameron Carter and Willie James Jennings have opened up genealogical analysis of theological constructions of racism and point forward to the creation of spaces wherein Christian bodies are freed from the principalities and powers.[72] Honest Christian preaching (and other practices) will not shy away from addressing the rocky ground of xenophobia and racism in contemporary American culture and honest historical work is crucial to the task. Racialized and foreign bodies are consistently disembodied in preaching because "they" are objects rather than subjects of discourse, and because often churches are not spaces where aspirations of Eucharistic sharing are instantiated. Recently my parish in Fullerton, California held a community forum about AB60, a new law enabling undocumented immigrants to apply for a driver license, so that they can drive legally without fear of deportation or an impounded car when pulled over for a routine traffic stop. To gather together in such a way as a community with invited guests from the DMV, Mexican Consulate, and the police chief, instantiates a radical resistance to the powers and principalities. The church becomes a space where the Eucharistic sharing on Sunday morning literally "gives flesh" to a resistance to the enclosure of bodies based on their legal status, or rather acknowledges that bodies at the edges of "legality" (undocumented yet "privileged" drivers) are in fact full community members who themselves lead our churches into gospel solidarity. Jesus's Parable of the Sower presents the rough ground as the place where the word is snatched away by the birds (Satan and the powers beholden to him). To work this rough ground is to forge spaces of

---

71. Nancey Murphy, "Traditions, Practices, and the Powers: A Radical-Reformation Epistemology," unpublished; utilizing James Wm. McClendon, Jr., *Ethics: Systematic Theology, Volume 1* (Nashville: Abingdon, 1986) 173–77.

72. J. Kameron Carter, *Race: A Theological Account* (New York: Oxford University Press, 2008); Willie James Jennings, *The Christian Imagination: Theology and the Origins of Race* (New Haven, CT: Yale University Press, 2010).

resistance and to live in hope that the principalities and powers too come under the reign of Christ. Nancey Murphy's embodied philosophy invites us to read Yoder through MacIntyre so as to embolden the people of God to resist the "smooth" narratives that keep us spinning our wheels in place. If we want to talk and walk the justice of God: "Back to the rough ground!"

12

"So Far As It Depends on You, Live Peaceably with All"[1]
On Pluralism, Particularity and Proselytizing

—Mark Thiessen Nation

Introduction: Steps in My Early Journey toward Plurality

"My mother is perhaps the wisest and most capable person I have ever met." I am fairly sure that was my unconscious assumption when I was a child. Thus, I took it for granted that the world shaped largely by my mother and my familiar surroundings, my extended family, and my friends offered a truthful understanding of reality. The attachments, affections, and convictions by which I lived my daily (convictional, moral) existence was mostly shared and reinforced by this world. That is to say, like most all of us, I assumed during my childhood that the world I knew was quite simply *the* world as it is.

Probably like most readers of this essay, this common sense understanding of what seemed to be simply reality did not remain undisturbed after I left home to enter college. But for me the initial disturbance occurred before I left home. For during my senior year of high school I became a Christian—which distinguished me convictionally (and thus also morally) from most everyone who had defined my world to this point, including my mother. No one in my family of origin, no one in my circle of friends was,

---

1. Rom 12:18, NRSV. I should say that I am conscious of the fact that I am addressing Christians in this essay. The formal dimensions of my argument would be relevant for others as well.

to my knowledge, a Christian. But of course these people, who now had a different "faith" from mine, were my family and friends that I loved. Thus I began at an early age to negotiate what it means to have loving, personal, caring relationships with people with whom one does not share the most central convictions and moral commitments.

This beginning prepared me for my college experiences, for by the time I arrived at Oakland City College, a Baptist school, it did not seem strange to me to encounter Christians with varying convictions. Nor did it seem odd that two of my best friends would be Muslims (one from Pakistan and one from Iran). And for that matter, during my last year at a state university, it seemed quite natural to have friends and acquaintances who were Hindus, Socialists, Libertarians, Vehement Ex-Christians, as well as a diverse array of Christians.

It would be a number of years, however, before I would begin to delve seriously into the intellectual and theological issues connected to this approach to life. By the time I did so I realized it was sociologist Peter Berger, certain postmodern writers, particular specialists in inter-faith relations and, most significantly, my Anabaptist perspective on the Christian faith which caused me to frame things the way I did.[2] And as I wrestled with the intellectual issues involved I also grew in my understanding of the scope of the diversity of religions (and other convictional communities).[3]

Plurality as a Sociological Reality

London, England is a cosmopolitan city, a microcosm of our contemporary world. On a typical day, so it is reported, over two hundred and fifty languages can be heard on the streets of central London. Living on the outskirts of London for more than five years before joining the faculty at Eastern Mennonite Seminary, I witnessed something of the reality of this marvelous diversity. Every trip on the underground train—through the sounds of many unfamiliar languages, the display of a glorious variety in dress and an interesting array of smells—reminded me of the multiplicity of cultures

---

2. I am very grateful for what I learned from Nancey Murphy regarding my particularist approach. Of her published works, most representative of what I learned from Nancey regarding the issues addressed in this essay are: Nancey Murphy, *Anglo-American Postmodernity: Philosophical Perspectives on Science, Religion, and Ethics* (Boulder, CO: Westview, 1997) and Nancey Murphy, *Beyond Liberalism and Fundamentalism* (Harrisburg, PA: Trinity, 1996).

3. One of my learnings, which took a number of years to fully grasp, was the realization that the community in which I grew up was in its own way a convictional community.

and religions that define contemporary London. Such diversity in one of the largest cities in the world is perhaps to be expected. More surprising is that there are approximately fifty languages spoken in the Harrisonburg, Virginia school system and that in the United States today there are more Buddhists than Episcopalians, more Wiccans than Mennonites.

This plurality is nothing new to Christianity. Christianity was born in the midst of a plurality of "religions," a greater diversity than most of us have ever experienced. In fact, plurality continued to be a part of the contextual reality for Christians for the first few hundred years of its existence. (And in various parts of the globe it has continued to be the context across the history of the church into the present.) However, by the end of the fourth century within Western Europe that reality began to give way to Christendom (and forcibly, to a more monolithic culture). The form of "Christendom" created in the United States differs in various ways from that in Western Europe. Nonetheless, to borrow from John Howard Yoder, we have had a neo-neo-Christendom here as well (which, it should also be said, has an increasingly waning influence).[4]

Because we in the Western world have for a long time lived with some form of Christendom, two things have happened. First, most of us—except perhaps for some of the very young among us, certain minorities, those from missionary families and those from other cultures—have grown up in a culturally and religiously monolithic world.[5] Second, and related, Christians in the United States have often been unconscious of the fact that a world of religious plurality was the context of our Christian origins. Our own monolithic worlds prevented us from being cognizant of what was true over the centuries, and remained true today: namely, that there was in fact, *then as well as now*, a plurality of cultures and religions in the world. Two things, however, have changed for us: our social worlds and our consciousness of this plurality.

Sociologist Peter Berger has for over thirty years been helping us see that pluralization is one of the defining features of our present world.[6]

---

4. On this, see John H. Yoder, "Christ the Hope of the World," in *The Original Revolution*, foreword Mark Thiessen Nation (Scottdale, PA: Herald, 1971; reprinted 2003) 144.

5. Most US Americans did, until fairly recently, grow up with some form of Christendom. Growing up in a non-Christian home, I was fairly unaware of Christianity. Nonetheless, I was in the choir in elementary school, and at Christmas time we sang various songs influenced by the Christian faith. Looking back on my experience, it is clear that my family was "not Christian," rather than, say, "not Muslim."

6. This is what his 1979 book *The Heretical Imperative* is all about. See Peter Berger, *The Heretical Imperative: Contemporary Possibilities of Religious Affirmation* (New York: Doubleday, 1979). He has affirmed this claim in many places since.

Various scholars have helped us name how this dramatic shift has happened. British historian Eric Hobsbawm refers to a "social revolution" that happened globally between 1945 and 1990. Though he means many things by this phrase, Hobsbawm says, "the most dramatic and far-reaching social change of the second half of the [twentieth] century, and the one which cuts us off forever from the world of the past, is the death of the peasantry. For since the neolithic era most human beings had lived off the land and its livestock or harvested the sea as fishers."[7] Mary Ann Glendon puts it this way, "As late as the 1970s, about two-thirds of the world's population still lived in villages where modes of life and work had changed little since agriculture was invented. By the year 2000, for the first time in human history, a majority of the earth's inhabitants [were] living in urban areas."[8] Rural communities defined by raising livestock or fishing tended to be stable across time, with little mobility, little interaction with "alien" cultures. Thus Hobsbawm names this "social revolution" provocatively by saying that, "For 80 percent of humanity the Middle Ages ended suddenly in the 1950s; or perhaps better still, they were *felt* to end in the 1960s."[9]

Urbanization, greater wealth in certain parts of the world, and significant immigration have all been partly responsible for dramatic changes in our social world and consciousness. But most significant in terms of pluralization is what social psychologist Kenneth Gergen calls the "technologies of social saturation." It is almost mind-numbing to reflect on the ways in which technologies of travel and communication have altered our world within the last seventy-five years, with the most dramatic shifts happening within the last few decades: automobiles, television, commercial airlines, videos, computers, the internet, cell phones, social networking, smartphones, tablets, twitter, etc. As Gergen puts it, "one detects amid the hurly-burly of contemporary life a new constellation of feelings or sensibilities, a new pattern of self-consciousness. This syndrome may be termed *multiphrenia*, generally referring to the splitting of the individual into a multiplicity of self-investment."[10] The way Peter Berger puts it is that "'the institutional pluralization that marks modernity affects not only human actions but also human consciousness: [we find ourselves] confronted not only by multiple

---

7. Eric Hobsbawm, *The Age of Extremes: A History of the World, 1914–1991* (New York: Pantheon Books, 1994) 289.

8. Mary Ann Glendon, "Villages and Virtues," *First Things* (October 1995) 39–42; quote on 39. (Writing in 1995, Glendon's original had: "will be living." I adapted her prediction to address 2015.)

9. Eric Hobsbawm, *Age of Extremes*, 288. Emphasis his.

10. Kenneth J. Gergen, *The Saturated Self* (New York: Basic Books, [1991] 2000) 73–74.

options of possible courses of action but also by multiple options of possible ways of thinking about the world.'"[11] This can, as Berger says, lead us to be "afflicted with a permanent identity crisis."[12]

To put it poignantly: My grandmother Nation died in her 50s in 1945. Devoid of virtually all of these technologies of social saturation, she lived with a persistent and monolithic understanding of reality throughout her life. I, in the year 2015, can easily experience more construals of reality in an hour than she experienced in a lifetime. We—many of us—are only beginning to learn to navigate such a world. As we do so, let us remember that in terms of an awareness of a plurality of convictions, we are moving closer, in some ways, to the experience of Paul in the first-century Roman Empire— and away from the experience of our grandparents or great-grandparents.

Three Responses to the World of Plurality

Of course one could organize the various responses to plurality in any number of ways. I will name three ways Christians have responded to the descriptively pluralistic world in which we live—a world where plurality is in our midst and very much forms our consciousness. These responses are sectarianism, pluralism and particularity/ism.

The first mode of response I would name is familiar to many who have grown up Mennonite: sectarianism.[13] This is the sociologically defensive response that attempts to build metaphorical walls to protect a community from the influences of those who are aliens—outsiders who are perceived to threaten our identities, including our particular Christian convictions.[14] Much of my wife's childhood was defined by this way of life. Growing up in southern Alberta, Canada, German was her first language. The children attended language school on Saturday. German continued for a number of

---

11. Quoted by Philip N. LaFountain, "Theology and Social Psychology: Pluralism and 'Evangel' in the Thought of Peter Berger and John Howard Yoder," *Theology Today* 69:1 (2012) 18–33, quote on 20. Also see the profound book, Thomas de Zengotita, *Mediated: How the Media Shapes Your World and the Way You Live in It* (New York: Bloomsbury, 2005).

12. Peter Berger, *The Homeless Mind*; quoted by Gergen, *Saturated Self*, 73.

13. For a discerning discussion of the sort of world I am alluding to here with reference to the Church of the Brethren, see Carl F. Bowman, *Brethren Society: The Cultural Transformation of a "Peculiar People"* (Baltimore: Johns Hopkins University Press, 1995). By mentioning the histories of the Mennonite and Brethren traditions, I don't mean either to stereotype them or ignore parallels with other groups. I name them simply because I am familiar with them.

14. This defensive mode of shaping existence, it needs to be said, has not been unique to Christians, nor has it been unique to religious groups.

years—in Canada—to be the worship language for these Mennonite Brethren. Along with this significant identity marker there were also moral strictures: no movies, music, jewelry, make-up, secular novels or inter-marrying (including other sorts of Mennonites)—with the threat of hell looming on the horizon if one's Mennonite Brethren identity was abandoned.[15]

The particulars would vary among different groups of Mennonites. But between the latter decades of the nineteenth century to the seventh decade of the twentieth, similar sociological barriers were erected by many who are now members of Mennonite Church USA. Peculiar forms of dress, language, and moral-doctrinal prohibitions were employed in often rigid ways in order to prevent what Peter Berger calls "cognitive contamination," and which in the case of Mennonites should also be referred to as the contamination of a way of life, since it wasn't simply about doctrinal convictions. Some have come to refer to this fear of contamination as "a will to purity."

A second mode of response is usually called pluralism. We should note that pluralism as a philosophical approach should be distinguished from plurality as a description of sociological reality. The most influential theorist of pluralism is philosopher John Hick.[16] Given the diversity of religions, pluralists ask, what is it that all the major world religions have in common? In short, this view attempts to reach beyond the particulars of all the major religions to name certain universally shared commonalities. Simply put, Hick says that this is a search for what is Ultimate in life, for the ultimate Reality—the Real itself, as he often puts it. It is the Real, which is beyond all the particular doctrinal claims of various religions, that finally matters. Correlatively, as all major religions recognize, it is important that people move from being self-centered to being Reality-centered (or God-centered). When people embrace this ultimate Reality, they also adopt a universal moral outlook which likewise leads them to embrace "unrestricted love and compassion."[17]

---

15. I don't want to understate the way in which, sometimes, a theological fundamentalism was interwoven with sociological sectarianism. In chapter one of his book, *Soul Survivor* (New York: Doubleday, 2001), Philip Yancey shows some parallels with how certain (non-Mennonite) fundamentalist churches have functioned.

16. Hick is influential among Christians. I don't know how influential he is beyond the Christian world. This present essay was originally given as a lecture in conversation with an Iranian Muslim who wrote his doctoral thesis on Hick. As such, my discussion of pluralism is directed at pluralist views influenced by or in alignment with Hick. I am aware there are other pluralist views, some of which would differ with Hick at certain points.

17. John Hick, "Is Christianity the Only True Religion, or One among Others," in *Can Only One Religion Be True? Paul Knitter and Harold Netland in Dialogue*, edited by Robert B. Stewart, (Minneapolis: Fortress, 2013) 105–15, quote on 110. His fullest

It is worth noting that in recent decades there seems to be a trend whereby a form of pluralism is becoming the dominant approach to issues of religion, truth, and living life in the United States. In their 2009 book, *Souls in Transition*, sociologists Christian Smith and Patricia Snell summarize their extensive research on the religious views and practices of young adults. In a summary statement, they say: "Most emerging adults are stuck at the place of thinking that nobody ultimately really knows what is true or right or good. It is all so relative and impossible to know in a pluralistic world with so many competing claims." Thus, these emerging adults affirm "individual autonomy, unbounded tolerance, freedom from authorities, the affirmation of pluralism, the centrality of human self-consciousness, the practical value of moral religion, epistemological skepticism, and an instinctive aversion to anything 'dogmatic' or committed to particulars."[18] It should be noted that Smith and Snell are saying that the convictions named here are replacing the nuanced, textured convictions of the specific religious communities to which these emerging adults had been or even presently are attached, at least in theory.

The third mode of response to our pluralistic reality is simply to admit that we—all of us—live with a particular set of convictions that form our ways of understanding the world and living within it. I will spend the rest of my time speaking about this approach, which I am calling "particularity," and briefly contrast it with the two other approaches.

Particularity (Neither "Parochialism without Tears" nor "Cosmopolitism without Content")

Put briefly, my claim regarding particularity is that we are *all*—every one of us—members of particular convictional communities. That is to say, there is no alternative to being *particular* people who live in *particular* places connected to *particular* communities, and thus we always have and embody *particular* convictions, whether we realize it or not.[19] Furthermore, every

---

philosophical defense of this view is: John Hick, *An Interpretation of Religion* (New Haven, CT: Yale University Press, 1989). For a critique of Hick, see Christopher Sinkinson, *The Universe of Faiths: A Critical Study of John Hick's Religious Pluralism* (Carlisle, Cumbria, UK: Paternoster, 2001).

18. Christian Smith and Patricia Snell, *Souls in Transition: The Religious and Spiritual Lives of Emerging Adults* (Oxford: Oxford University Press, 2009) 287, 288, emphasis mine.

19. On how this claim relates to theorists of pluralism such as John Hick and Paul Knitter who claim, in various ways, to be above particularity, see Gavin D'Costa, "The Impossibility of a Pluralist View of Religions," *Religious Studies* 32 (1996) 223–32; and

one of us desires to make converts for what we believe to be important, true, and will lead to human flourishing—assuming we care about others. On some occasions we actively promote our views (i.e., we proselytize). On other occasions we have discussions or dialogues. But in any event, we are not neutral about our central beliefs. But for some of us that *something*, that *truth* for which we proselytize, may not be our religion. (Or is it?) Before I proceed to elaborate on what particularism is, I need to offer some reflections on the use of the term "religion."

Religion is a word neither I nor the Christian Scriptures use very much, so if I am to use it in this context it is important that we have a definition or two in front of us. I believe the following two definitions are helpful. Robert Schmidt has said that religions are "systems of meaning embodied in a pattern of life, a community of faith, and a worldview that articulate a view of the sacred and of what ultimately matters."[20] Complementing this is another definition offered by Paul Griffiths, one that helps us to see that what we designate as our "religion" might not truly function as our religion—that is, as what ultimately matters to us. Griffiths suggests: "A religion ... [is] a form of life that seems to those who inhabit it to be comprehensive, incapable of abandonment, and of central importance."[21]

In real life there is no such thing as "religious" people. There are rather varieties of Buddhists, Jews, Muslims, Christians, Socialists, Capitalists, Libertarians, Republicans, Democrats, Civil Religionists of right or left, and so on. That is to say, there are people with particular convictions (who are usually connected to or members of convictional communities).

In this essay, I am mostly referring to "religions" and therefore interfaith relations for the sake of convenience. However, when the Christian faith is properly understood, we realize—as my list and descriptions above signal—that what we are dealing with is about much more than what we

---

Philip N. LaFountain, "Theology and Social Psychology," 18–33.

20. Quoted by Harold Netland, "Opening Remarks," in *Can Only One Religion Be True*, 19.

21. Paul J. Griffiths, *Problems of Religious Diversity* (Oxford, UK: Blackwell, 2001) 7. Since I originally delivered this lecture, I have come to see even more clearly that "religion" as we understand it in the United States is a modern invention, *and* that being aware of this is quite important. On this see William Cavanaugh, "The Invention of Religion," in *The Myth of Religious Violence* (Oxford, UK: Oxford University Press, 2009) 57–122; Tomoko Masuzawa, *The Invention of World Religions: Or, How European Universalism Was Preserved in the Language of Pluralism* (Chicago: University of Chicago Press, 2005); and Brent Nongbri, *Before Religion: A History of a Modern Concept* (New Haven, CT: Yale University Press, 2013). But even with this awareness, if one is to use the term religion at all, the two definitions I've employed move in the direction of naming what pre-Enlightenment Christians understood by their faith and faith communities.

normally place under the umbrella of "religion" (and thus, is pertinent to more than simply inter-faith relationships.) As Peter Leithart has provocatively put it, "The Church's competitors are nation-states and international political bodies like the United Nations. The Church's ethos and culture are not just a challenge to other 'religions,' but to the ethos of Americanism and the culture of globalization, insofar as such an ethos and culture exist."[22] Therefore, in the academic world I inhabit I worry much more about Christians effectively "converting" to a Civil Religion of the Left (what I call NPR- or Jon Stewart-Civil Religion) than from Christianity to, say, Buddhism.[23]

Croatian-born theologian Miroslav Volf has said: "It is not clear that all religions are essentially the same. Most of their adherents would disagree with the claim, and would feel that the one making it does not sufficiently respect them in their own specificity but is looking through them in search of an artificially constructed essence."[24] Put differently, it's not clear that what we have in common with others who are religious (even monotheistic) is more important (to us or them) than certain convictions that separate us.

Harvard professor Jon D. Levenson, a Jewish theologian, has helped us to see just how true this is in his recent book, *Inheriting Abraham*.[25] It is true, of course, that Judaism, Christianity, and Islam have Abraham in common. And discussing how this shared spiritual ancestor leads to common themes and points of identity is certainly worth exploring. However, Levenson argues that the particular ways in which Abraham is employed to constitute the identity of each of these living religions is really quite different. Similarly, it is also true that both Christianity and Islam hold Jesus in high esteem. Again, the connections this brings between these traditions are interesting to explore.[26] However, not only is Jesus of central importance

---

22. Peter Leithart, *Against Christianity* (Moscow, ID: Canon, 2003) 34. For an affirmation and critique of Leithart, see Mark Thiessen Nation, "Against Christianity and For Constantine: One Heresy or Two?," in *Constantine Revisited: Leithart, Yoder, and the Constantinian Debate*, edited by John D. Roth (Eugene, OR: Pickwick, 2013) 68–82.

23. So I am not misunderstood, I regularly listen to both NPR and Jon Stewart. However, I believe my convictions, morals, worldview, etc. should be formed by the Christian faith in a holistic way that substantially shapes by daily existence and not the worldview, etc. of these programs. (This requires careful work, deliberation and discernment.)

24. Miroslav Volf, "Be Particular," *The Christian Century* (January 25, 2003) 33. See also Miroslav Volf, "Living with the 'Other,'" *Journal of Ecumenical Studies* 39 (Winter/Spring 2002) 8–25.

25. Jon D. Levenson, *Inheriting Abraham: The Legacy of the Patriarch in Judaism, Christianity and Islam* (Princeton: Princeton University Press, 2012).

26. See, e.g., Robert F. Shedinger, *Was Jesus a Muslim?* (Minneapolis: Fortress, 2009).

to the Christian faith in a way he is not in Islam: some of the central claims of the Christian faith about Jesus regarding his divinity, crucifixion, and resurrection contradict in some basic ways the portrait of him in the Quran (and thus clash rather fundamentally with traditional Muslim beliefs about Jesus).

However, this is not to suggest that we should assume ahead of time that adherents of other religions or convictional communities are either totally different from *or* similar to us. Rather, it is to say that we ought to simply live out and articulate our particular faith, and as we so live and speak, we will note at what points there are overlaps, differences, and even contradictions between us and other particular convictional communities. In order to clarify what I mean and don't mean by affirming particularity, let me contrast it with sectarianism on the one hand and pluralism on the other. I turn first to sectarianism.

Clifford Geertz, a very influential anthropologist, helped us to see that the world today is far removed from the 1940s world of either my grandmother or sectarian Mennonites. Today, we live in a world of diversity—and importantly, with a consciousness of that diversity. With this in mind, Geertz writes that "we have come to such a point in the moral history of the world ... that we are obliged to think about such diversity rather differently than we had been used to thinking about it."[27] He continues by discussing how in the past it was common for cultural groups to employ various means to separate themselves from those other, alien peoples they saw as a threat to their identity. They lived in their own social spaces—distinguishable from those who were from other tribes, other people groups, other religions. But now, says Geertz, it is "getting to be the case that rather than being sorted into framed units, social spaces with definite edges to them, seriously disparate approaches to life are becoming scrambled together in ill-defined expanses, social spaces whose edges are unfixed, irregular, and difficult to locate." In this world, he says, "the question of how to deal with the puzzles of judgment to which such disparities give rise takes on a rather different aspect. Confronting landscapes and still lifes is one thing; panoramas and collages quite another."[28] He continues: "It is not necessary to choose, indeed it is necessary not to choose, between cosmopolitanism without content and parochialism without tears. Neither [is] of use for living in a collage."[29]

---

27. Clifford Geertz, "The Uses of Diversity," in *Available Light: Anthropological Reflections on Philosophical Topics* (Princeton: Princeton University Press, 2000) 85.

28. Ibid.

29. Ibid., 86–87.

Indeed, now that we live in something of a cultural collage, "parochialism without tears" can be recognized as the sectarianism of yesteryear. It should never have been defining of our Christian (and ecclesial) identity, for the church was always called to be missional. More specifically, we were meant to love our neighbors as ourselves. We were to care about the least among us. We were to welcome strangers. We were—and are—to weep when our neighbors weep and rejoice when they rejoice. We should want to share the Good News through word and deed. If we understand what it means to be followers of Jesus we will be relationally, lovingly connected to our neighbors, in ways that are appropriate to our identity in Christ, and to our enemies as well.

The alternative to "parochialism without tears" is not a "cosmopolitanism without content" (i.e., pluralism). Volf is particularly helpful on this point. In his extraordinary book, *Exclusion and Embrace*, Volf is aware that in our descriptively pluralistic world we need to attend quite deliberately to our identity, and to do this is to have boundaries for our existence—beliefs and moral practices that define us and differentiate us from those who don't share our central convictions and moral practices. "Without boundaries," Volf says, "we will be able to know only what we are fighting against but not what we are fighting for. Intelligent struggle against exclusion demands categories and normative criteria that enable us to distinguish between repressive identities and practices that should be subverted and nonrepressive ones that should be affirmed."[30] Without any boundaries, Volf argues, one is left with nonorder, "and nonorder is not the end of exclusion but the end of life."[31] "Vilify all boundaries, pronounce every discrete identity oppressive, put the tag 'exclusion' on every stable difference—and you will have aimless drifting instead of clear-sighted agency, haphazard activity instead of moral engagement and accountability and, in the long run, a torpor of death instead of a dance of freedom."[32]

Dietrich Bonhoeffer realized this. In the first half of the 1930s Bonhoeffer was a committed ecumenist. However, by 1937 he dropped out of the formal ecumenical movement in Europe. Why? Partly because he was very unhappy with the leaders in the ecumenical movement who refused to accept his claim that among the Protestants in Nazi Germany it was only the Confessing Church that continued to be Christian in any meaningful sense. Most of "German Christianity" was being centrally re-defined by an

---

30. Miroslav Volf, *Exclusion and Embrace: A Theological Exploration of Identity, Otherness, and Reconciliation* (Nashville: Abingdon, 1996) 63.

31. Ibid.

32. Ibid., 64–65.

amalgamation of historic German pagan traditions, the new "revelation" given in Adolf Hitler, and thinned-out elements from Christianity. As Bonhoeffer put it provocatively in a letter to his grandmother, "The issue is really Germanism or Christianity, and the sooner the conflict comes out in the open, the better. The greatest danger of all would be in trying to conceal this."[33] In other words, Bonhoeffer was aware that Christianity had a true identity, and that its boundaries needed to be defined.[34]

But just as this awareness did not lead Bonhoeffer to cut himself off from others within Germany, neither ought we cut ourselves off from others with whom we disagree (even in ways that are vitally important). Reiterating what I said above, Christians are called to engage in missional activities. We care for the least among us. We welcome strangers. We love our neighbors. And besides, we do not and should not attempt to live in hermetically sealed convictional communities. We just do interact with a variety of people, every day of our lives. As we do so, we realize that we acquire what Volf refers to as "catholic"/ ecumenical personalities. "A catholic personality," as he defines it, "is a personality enriched by otherness, a personality which is what it is only because multiple others have been reflected in it in a particular way. The distance from my own culture that results from being born by the Spirit creates a fissure in me through which others can come in."[35] However, he goes on to say that "any notion of catholic personality which was capable only of integrating, but not of discriminating, would be grotesque.... A truly catholic personality [in Christian terms] must be an *evangelical personality*—a personality brought to repentance and shaped by the Gospel and engaged in the transformation of the world."[36] In these senses we should want to create communities that are both catholic and evangelical.

Thus far, I have been comparing particularity with broadly sectarian responses to the presence of multiple convictional communities as a descriptive reality. What about the relationship between particularity and pluralism? I have become convinced by theologian Gavin D'Costa and philosopher Keith Yandell that in reality, there is no such thing as pluralism.

---

33. Quoted in Mark Thiessen Nation, Athony G. Siegrist and Daniel P. Umbel, *Bonhoeffer the Assassin?: Challenging the Myth, Recovering His Call to Peacemaking* (Grand Rapids: Baker, 2013) 42.

34. See Dietrich Bonhoeffer, "The Confessing Church and the Ecumenical Movement," in *Theological Education at Finkenwalde: 1935–1937*, Dietrich Bonhoeffer Works, Volume 14, translated by Douglas W. Stott, edited by H. Gaylon Barker and Mark S. Brocker (Minneapolis: Fortress, 2013) 393–412.

35. Volf, *Exclusion and Embrace*, 51.

36. Ibid., 52.

All so-called pluralists are really particularists. That is to say, it is simply not the case that they have risen above the world of particular convictions. As D'Costa says, "all pluralists are committed to holding some form of truth criteria and by virtue of this, anything that falls foul of such criteria is excluded from counting as truth (in doctrine and in practice)."[37] I would suggest that either D'Costa is right, or else that the vagueness of pluralism gives us no purchase on how to live our lives (in the real world) in a discerning way. That is to say, pluralism is either itself substantive and particularistic, or it does not help us to discern the difference between the convictions and moral practices of Bonhoeffer on the one hand, for instance, and typical German Christians in the 1930s and 1940s on the other.

As a Christian one of my central concerns with pluralism as an approach to religion is that I think those who espouse it uncritically accept Enlightenment-inspired definitions of religion. Referring to the ultimate as "the Real" and then joining this concept to unlimited love and compassion fits well with an understanding of religion as something basically private and only personal—and relevant to a thin understanding of what "religious activities" on a Sunday morning are for. However, this understanding of religion doesn't give us much of a purchase on daily life. Nor does it fit with the much more complex definitions of religion I gave earlier, for such affirmations of "the Real" are substantively thin, and thus unable to connect a community of faith in any rich way to moral and doctrinal convictions that are "comprehensive," "of central importance," and integrated into a way of life.

Fully embraced, pluralism suggests that this thin understanding of what is truly important in religion is *all* that religion is good for. Thus, some vaguely defined mystical practice connected to a general commitment to love and compassion are what we get from our religion, nothing more. Therefore, what truly shapes our daily existence—the convictions that are truly of central importance—is drawn from elsewhere than our stated religion. So, as Schmidt and Griffiths would say, it may be the case that something other than our formally designated religion is functioning as our actual religion. As Volf writes,

> The trouble is that an unknowable god is an idle god, exalted so high on her throne (and hidden so deep in the foundations of being) that she must have the tribal deities do all the work that every self-respecting god must do. Believing in a god behind

---

37. Gavin D'Costa, "The Impossibility of Relgious Pluralism," 225–26. See also Keith Yandell, "Has Normative Religious Pluralism a Rationale?" in *Can Only One Religion Be True*, 163–79.

all concrete manifestations amounts therefore to not believing in one: each culture ends up worshiping its own tribal deities, which is to say that each ends up, as Paul puts it, "enslaved to beings that are by nature not gods." (Gal 4:8)[38]

To put it differently, I think theologian Robert Webber is right to say that one of the central questions for Christians is: *who gets to narrate the world?*[39] The Christian faith gives us a way to narrate the world, which includes substantive theological and moral convictions. When I became a Christian I *knew* that John Wayne and the Westerns on television that I had grown up with could no longer serve as the narratives for defining my approach to violence. After I became a Christian I realized I would not become a soldier killing in the name of democracy—which certainly for many US Americans is a way of embodying compassion on a large scale for those who don't enjoy our way of life, our freedoms. No, my life was to be re-defined—re-narrated—by the gospel of Jesus Christ. This story was not just one more story among others, nor a manifestation of some more general truth, nor still a way to insulate me from difference, but a new and loving way to live with difference.

Conclusion: Reminders from a Late Medieval Muslim

Around the year 1438—almost a century before the Anabaptist movement began—a Western European knight asked a Turkish Muslim to convert to Christianity. The following is the remarkable response from this Muslim:

> I see that according to your Bible Christ has redeemed you with his death and chosen you for eternal life. But observing your actions I also see that not one of you truly loves Christ, nor do you desire to live by His word. In fact, you deny Him. You take away your neighbor's goods and wealth; you destroy your fellow man's dignity; you even claim his person for your own. Is this done according to your savior's word and command? Now you plan to come across the sea and wage war upon us, and gain eternal life by vanquishing us. But you deceive yourselves. It would be a far better deed were you to remain at home and do battle with the false Christians in your midst, showing them the way to righteousness![40]

---

38. Volf, *Exclusion and Embrace*, 44.

39. Robert E. Webber, *Who Gets to Narrate the World?* (Downers Grove, IL: IVP Books, 2008).

40. Quoted by C. Arnold Snyder, *The Life and Thought of Michael Sattler* (Scottdale,

This fascinating statement from this Muslim reminds us to be honest about the ways in which those who have carried the name "Christian" have often been unfaithful to Christ—especially in relation to those who have been profoundly different. It also reminds us that sometimes non-Christians may help us to re-capture what it means to be Christian.[41]

However, I am also reminded of Michael Sattler, one of the first leaders of the Anabaptists, who, a little less than a century later, took up the challenge contained in the last sentence uttered by the Muslim interlocutor. Sattler in fact did nonviolently "battle" with the false forms of Christianity he saw expressed in Switzerland and Austria. He evangelized—proselytized—for what he believed to be the true gospel (as all of us proselytize for what we believe to be true).

Michael Sattler and some of his contemporary Anabaptist descendants have strengthened my resolve similarly to do nonviolent battle against the Christianity that confuses the Christian narrative with the US American one. After six years of professional work as a peace and justice educator in more than 150 congregations throughout the Midwest, I am convinced that Volf is right: "At least when it comes to Christianity, *the cure against religiously induced or legitimized violence is not less religion, but, in a carefully qualified sense, more religion.* What I mean is this: Strip religious commitments of all cognitive and moral content and reduce faith to a cultural resource endowed with a diffuse aura of the sacred, and you are likely to get religiously inspired or legitimized violence." He continues: "Or—nurture and educate people in the tradition and, if you get militants, they will be militants for peace. . . . 'Thick' practice of the Christian faith will help reduce violence and shape a culture of peace."[42] He adds elsewhere that this must include a realization that "in order to *know truly* we need to want to exercise power rightly." And to do so is also to acknowledge that a "commitment to nonviolence must accompany commitment to truth; otherwise commitment to truth will [on occasion] generate violence."[43]

PA: Herald, 1984) 225, endnote 81.

41. I think it's also important to note a point from Philip Kenneson: "the impetus for change may come from any quarter, but change with integrity must be capable of being justified on terms 'internal' to the church." Philip Kenneson, *Beyond Sectarianism: Reimagining Church and World* (Harrisburg, PA: Trinity, 1999) 68–69.

42. Miroslav Volf, "More Religion, Less Violence," *Christian Century* 119:8 (April 10, 2002) 32. See also Mark Thiessen Nation, "The First Word Christians Have to Say about Violence is 'Church': On Bonhoeffer, Baptists, and Becoming a Peace Church," in *Faithfulness and Fortitude: In Conversation with the Theological Ethics of Stanley Hauerwas*, edited by Mark Thiessen Nation and Samuel Wells (Edinburgh: T. & T. Clark, 2000) 83–115.

43. Volf, *Exclusion and Embrace*, 249, 272.

In light of these affirmations, I hope that in the midst of our descriptively pluralistic culture Christians will not abandon the gospel of Jesus Christ for some other particular set of convictions (concealed under the banner of pluralism, or through an embracing of Civil Religion of the Right or Left, or through a private spirituality). I hope that we will not allow another story to narrate our lives, so that some other story forms our identities. Rather, I hope that Christians continue to allow the story of the God known in Jesus the Christ to offer a comprehensive framework for understanding life, a way of life in which this God is seen as centrally important for defining our lives as we navigate our present, pluralistic culture. And finally, I hope we can live and speak in ways consistent with this story so that others will indeed perceive it to be good news for the world.[44]

---

44. In thinking about this set of issues I would suggest, among other works, the following: Lesslie Newbigin, *The Gospel in a Pluralist Society* (Grand Rapids: Eerdmans, 1989); Bryan Stone, *Evangelism after Christendom: The Theology and Practice of Christian Witness* (Grand Rapids: Brazos, 2007); and Brad J. Kallenberg, *Live to Tell: Evangelism for a Postmodern Age* (Grand Rapids: Brazos, 2002).

13

Sexy Theology
Evolution and the Formation of a Theological Concept of Sexuality based on Kenosis

—James A. Van Slyke

In the past, sexual desire was defined in Freudian terms as a drive or instinct that needed to be satisfied. Current research in evolutionary psychology has modified this understanding of sexual instinct in terms of mate choice and preference. However, human sexuality is not just a product of individual preferences but also reflects the cultural and religious values embedded in social contexts. Theologically, a conceptualization of the value of human sexuality arises as a result of evolved aspects of human nature in dynamic relationship with different religious expressions that attempt to mirror the reality of a transcendent God. Nancey Murphy's work in the hierarchy of the sciences provides a helpful model for integrating a scientific understanding of the evolution of human sexuality with a kenotic view of both human and divine relationships. The primary divine expression of kenosis is in self-renunciation, which creates a unique moral perspective for human sexuality by focusing on the other rather than the self.

Sexual Desire and Evolutionary Psychology

Evolutionary psychology investigates various types of adaptations that occurred in human evolutionary history that play an important role in human psychology.[1] One of the primary areas of research in evolutionary psychology is the investigation of the evolutionary factors that contributed to the formation of human sexuality, including mating strategies, jealousy, and different forms of attraction. Evolutionary psychology works under the assumption that particular psychological adaptations must have evolved to solve the adaptive problems required for successful mating among our early human ancestors. Thus, human sexual desire is at least partially constituted by psychological propensities or preferences in mate selection that constrain human concepts of beauty and sexual attraction.

For example, the waist-to-hip ratio (WHR) specifies a male sexual preference for women with a particular body shape comprised of a ratio of the waist of a woman to her hip size.[2] Males showed a preference for a WHR between .67 and .80 over three different studies. The first study tracked the WHRs for Miss America winners and Playboy playmates over the past 30–60 years. Although there was some change in the ideal body weight for women, the WHR remained relatively the same. In the second and third studies, college-aged males and males from the general public (ages 25–85) rated women with lower WHRs as more attractive, healthier, and possessing greater reproductive potential. This adaptation was determined to be a result of discriminating between potential sexual partners based on their reproductive potential. Thus, males would be able to distinguish between females who were within their reproductive window and those who had not yet reached sexual maturity. To illustrate in a very simplistic way, if two males each have an equal chance of mating with several different females but one has a preference for women based on physical cues of sexual maturity, the male with that preference is much more likely to mate with a female who has a better chance at conception and will not waste as many resources on females who are not currently able to conceive.

In addition to being a physical signal for reproductive potential, WHR may also be a signal of better genetic quality; lower-body fat in women may have a positive effect on the supply of fatty acids that play an essential role in the neural development of offspring.[3] Children of women with lower WHR score higher on tests for cognitive ability when other factors are controlled.

---

1. Cf. David M. Buss, ed., *The Handbook of Evolutionary Psychology* (Hoboken, NJ: John Wiley & Sons, 2005).

2. Devendra Singh, "Adaptive Significance of Female Physical Attractiveness: Role of Waist-to-Hip Ratio," *Journal of Personality and Social Psychology* 65:2 (1993) 293–307.

3. William D. Lassek and Steven J. C. Gaulin, "Waist-Hip Ratio and Cognitive Ability: Is Gluteofemoral Fat a Privileged Store of Neurodevelopmental Resources?" *Evolution and Human Behavior* 29 (2008) 26–34.

Thus, the WHR may not just indicate sexual maturity but also health and good genes. Sexual selection theory in evolution assumes that many different forms of physical cues are proxies for the selection of good genes, which increases the possibility of survival and reproduction in subsequent generations of a species.[4] Besides WHR, several different psychological adaptations have contributed to male sexual psychology and what men indicate as attractive. Many of these have to do with indicators of youth such as clear and smooth skin, muscle tone, and energy level.[5]

Male preferences in mates should not be taken as an indication that men are the ones who are typically doing the choosing throughout evolutionary history. In fact, for most species females are the ones who do the choosing and males are the ones who are trying to grab the attention of the females.[6] However, female preferences are slightly different from males. Females favor some aspects of physical attractiveness similar to males such as facial symmetry. Both males and females favor facial symmetry in a potential long-term mate when compared to faces with less symmetry using computer-generated faces (although symmetry affected male preference to a greater degree).[7] Although women use physical attractiveness as a proxy for fitness, their overall preferences reflect different factors in the assessment of a potential mate.

Based on the history of human evolution, reproduction for females is much more costly. Females have relatively few eggs in comparison to the number of sperm typical of males, so females tend to be much more conservative in their choices for a potential mate. Once they are pregnant, they have to carry the child to term and care for the child once they are born. Thus, part of female mating psychology includes evolved preferences for men who are more likely to contribute to resources during pregnancy and help to raise their children. Women often prefer mates who have a higher perceived status based on their likelihood of success in a career, education and degrees, level of maturity, and ambition.[8] David Buss and Todd Shackelford suggest that women have an evolved adaptation that is able to raise or lower their standards for a potential mate based on their implicit assessment

---

4. Cf. Geoffrey, Miller, *The Mating Mind: How Sexual Choice Shaped the Evolution of Human Nature* (New York: Anchor Books, 2000).

5. Cf. David M. Buss, *The Evolution of Desire*, rev. ed. (New York: Basic Books, 2003).

6. Miller, *Mating Mind*, 88.

7. Randy Thornhill and Steven W. Gangestad, "Facial Attractiveness," *Trends in Cognitive Sciences* 3:12 (1999) 452–60.

8. Buss, *Evolution of Desire*, 25, 28–31.

of their own mate value.⁹ Standards for a potential mate were clustered into four basic categories: (1) fitness or good-gene indicators (i.e., physical attractiveness); (2) investment indicators (i.e., potential income) (3) good parenting; and (4) good partner indicators (i.e., being able to express love). Higher levels of the female's implicit assessment of their own mate value, assessed through correlation with levels of attractiveness assigned by observers, led to increased expectations in all four categories for potential mates.

Mating strategies typically fall along a continuum between long-term and short-term strategies, although males and females may engage in different types of strategies during their lifetimes depending on age and current life circumstances. Each strategy has different payoffs and drawbacks for both sexes. Historically, males would have been much more likely to engage in short-term strategies while females would have been more likely to engage in long-term strategies based on the relative differences of effort and cost involved in reproduction for each gender. However, this difference may not be conclusive, as with many different types of adaptations, changing environmental conditions often modify which type of strategy is used.

Female mate preferences actually change during their ovulatory cycle. During their high fertility phase, females demonstrate a preference for characteristics more associated with cues of good genes such as more masculine voices and faces, scents associated with males with symmetrical faces, and displays of dominance and competition.¹⁰ Elizabeth Pillsworth and Martie Haselton argue that females may have evolved two mating strategies: one for coupling with a primary partner and a second that involves a long-term partner while also seeking extra pair copulations (EPCs) with other males.¹¹ The possibility of EPCs primarily occurs during the high fertility phase of the female cycle, which would maximize the potential for seeking out good genes for new offspring even with the possibility of losing

---

9. David M. Buss, and Todd K. Shackelford, "Attractive Women Want It All: Good Genes, Economic Investment, Parenting Proclivities, and Emotional Commitment," *Evolutionary Psychology* 6:1 (2008) 134–46.

10. Steven W. Gangestad et al., "Women's Preferences for Male Behavioral Displays Change across the Menstrual Cycle," *Psychological Science* 15:3 (2004) 203–7; Steven W. Gangestad and Randy Thornhill, "Menstrual Cycle Variation in Women's Preferences for the Scent of Symmetrical Men," *Proceedings of the Royal Society B: Biological Sciences* 265 (1998) 927–33; Ian S. Penton-Voak and David I. Perrett, "Female Preference for Male Faces Changes Cyclically: Further Evidence," *Evolution and Human Behavior* 21 (2000) 39–48; David A. Puts, "Mating Context and Menstrual Phase Affect Women's Preferences for Male Voice Pitch," *Evolution and Human Behavior* 26:5 (2005) 388–97.

11. Elizabeth G. Pillsworth and Martie G. Haselton, "Women's Sexual Strategies: The Evolution of Long-Term Bonds and Extrapair Sex," *Annual Review of Sex Research* 17 (2006) 59–100.

the current partnership. It is important to understand that evolved mating strategies are not conscious strategies, but involve unconscious cognitive biases and attractions that affect eventual mating actions. Thus, the presence of a particular mating strategy may be in one's genetic interests, but may be detrimental based on psychological, familial, or social issues.

Females engaging in long-term strategies are primarily concerned with securing mates with a high level of parental investment to help with the many duties of raising children and securing resources to help provide for the family. Buss has found that females showed a preference for potential long-term mates that could offer resources to her and her offspring, had the ability to protect her children, showed promise as a good parent, and had similar goals and values for their family.[12] Males engage in long-term strategies for slightly different reasons. Pair bonding increases the fertility levels for both males and females over time during the mating partnership. Pair bonding also increases paternity certainty for males who do not have as reliable information as females do (genetic testing is relatively new for males, who typically had to rely on other means to assure paternity). Thus, jealousy for EPCs is higher among males, who are much more likely to make false positive accusations of female cuckoldry.[13]

Primate Sociality and Sexuality

Individual male and female sexual preferences obviously have an important effect on mate selection, but sexuality, especially in primates, is a very social process. In our closest primate relatives, sexuality is not just a means for procreation, but also serves an important role in social functioning of the group. For bonobo females, mutual clitoral stimulation or "GG-rubbing" is a part of female bonding and a regular part of social interactions.[14] Males often participate in similar acts, mutually stimulating the penis of their partner. Although this does not usually lead to ejaculation, it does seem to be a normal part of their social life; bonobos seem to include "genital handshakes" as a form of social communication.[15] Sexual intercourse may be used as a bargaining chip in social exchanges, such as offering sex for

---

12. Buss, *Evolution of Desire*, ch. 2.

13. David M. Buss et al., "Sex Differences in Jealousy: Evolution, Physiology, and Psychology," *Psychological Science* 3 (1992) 251–55; Paul W. Andrews et al., "Sex Differences in Detecting Sexual Infidelity," *Human Nature* 19:4 (2008) 347–73.

14. Frans de Waal, *Good Natured: The Origins of Right and Wrong in Humans and Other Animals* (Cambridge, MA: Harvard University Press, 1996) 104.

15. Ibid., 105.

food.[16] Sexuality is used as a way to ease social tensions in the group and is often the appetizer offered before a large meal; it can also be used to initiate sex, appeasement for anger, and as a sign of affection.

Reproduction between male and female chimpanzees involves many different social factors within the troop. In contrast, gorillas tend to have one dominant male who controls reproductive access to the females in a troop, while chimpanzee troops have several males in a particular group, though one maintains dominance. Although the dominant male has greater sexual access to the females, this does not necessary hinder the other males from gaining sexual access. If a female is willing to copulate with a lower-raking male, the male can find different ways to get around the defenses of the dominant male. Over time the alpha male can simply be worn out from having to monitor the advances of lower-raking males.[17] Males have been known to hide their erections from other higher-ranking males when they come close as male and female chimpanzees are preparing for sex.[18] Males will often groom the dominant male to try and soothe him to allow for copulation, and male grooming is often highest when sexual tension is high among the troop.

Sexual reproduction is greatly constrained by the social situations that exist in both human and nonhuman primate cultures. Humans are a highly cooperative species and any sexual preferences must have been exercised within a particular group. Sexual selection occurs mainly between individuals as both males and females use particular strategies to enhance their reproductive potential both in terms of their chances for mating and the quality of potential mates. However, these strategies must have been exercised in particular groups; the strategies could not have been isolated from corresponding issues such as coalitions, economy, and food. Thus, it seems highly probable that the group with social structures that help to effectively manage sexual selection among its members would have a slight advantage over groups lacking in such structures.

Group Selection, Religion, and Sexual Morality

Until recently, the primary component of evolutionary change was assumed to be at the level of individual differences, which were the result of

16. S. Kuroda, "Interactions over Food among Pigny Chimpanzees," in *The Pygmy Chimpanzee*, edited by R. Susman (New York: Plenum, 1984) 301–24.

17. Frans de Waal, *Our Inner Ape: A Leading Primatologist Explains Why We Are Who We Are* (New York: Riverhead Books, 2005) 122–23.

18. de Waal, *Good Natured*, 77.

differences in phenotypes that lead to relative fitness. Thus, the term "selfish gene" became a common phrase indicating the genetic factors that cause the formation of a particular phenotype, which enhances survival and reproduction in competition with other organisms.[19] However, in the history of the theory of evolution, groups were thought to be possible candidates as potential loci of evolutionary adaptation, but poor theoretical and empirical development lead many biologists to discredit this view, especially in the work of G. C. Williams.[20] Recently, there has been a revival of sorts in looking to groups and multiple levels of possible evolutionary change rather than focusing solely on the individual differences between and within species.

Group selection can be defined as a form of selection that occurs along a particular vector that includes multiple processes working at various levels of selection.[21] Thus, individual versus group selection is not a zero-sum game between two competing processes; both contribute, in varying degrees, to the evolution of some particular trait. The difficulty that arises in defining group selection is that any apparent trait that benefits the group is seemingly a deficit for the individual. For instance, in the case of a sentinel (an animal that warns a group of potential danger), it appears detrimental to the sentinel's own well-being to warn others, because it also singles out the warning caller as potential prey.[22]

One may guess that at the individual level foragers would have a higher level of fitness in comparison to the sentinels over time, who benefit from the calls without inheriting the same level of danger. However, P. A. Bednekoff has found that over time the absolute level of fitness for both sentinels and foragers is the same, but continues to refer to this behavior as "selfish" or "safe" for sentinels. As David Sloan Wilson points out, what is clearly an example of group-level selection becomes reinterpreted according to the constraints of individual-level selection, reflecting an apparent

---

19. Famously, cf. Richard Dawkins, *The Selfish Gene* (Oxford: Oxford University Press, 1976).

20. G. C. Williams, *Adaptation and Natural Selection: A Critique of Some Current Evolutionary Thought* (Princeton: Princeton University Press, 1966); David Sloan Wilson, "Human Groups as Adaptive Units: Toward a Permanent Consensus," in *The Innate Mind: Culture and Cognition*, edited by Peter Carruthers, Stephen Laurence and Stephen Stich (Oxford: Oxford University Press, 2007).

21. David Sloan Wilson, "Group-Level Evolutionary Processes," in *The Oxford Handbook of Evolutionary Psychology*, edited by Robin Dunbar and Louise Barrett (Oxford: Oxford University Press, 2007).

22. Wilson, "Human Groups," 85; P. A. Bednekoff, "Mutualism among Safe, Selfish Sentinels: A Dynamic Game," *American Naturalist* 150 (1997) 373–92.

bias in empirical interpretation.[23] To counter this form of bias, Wilson and Elliott Sober attempted a working definition of group selection. For group selection to occur there must be different groups in a population and those groups must vary in regard to the presence of a particular trait. The trait enables a difference in fitness in comparison to other groups in that the trait makes the group more likely to survive and reproduce.[24] Additionally, the trait that makes one group more fit than others must be able to override the potential differences in traits at work within the group.

It follows from the preceding analysis that the seeds for human sexual morality, promoted in some form or another by most religions, evolved in part as a consequence of both individual and group-level selection. This is not so say that sexuality or religion is *reducible* to these two forms of selection, but that many of the initial processes in the formation of these aspects of human nature required both forms of selection. In fact, it is probably the case that there was a highly complex interaction between several different factors in the evolution of sexual morality and religion, including cultural evolution.[25] The foundations for the emergence of sexual morality obviously included individual differences in sexual selection that occurred throughout the evolution of the human species. Cognitive adaptations such as WHR, facial symmetry, and perceived social status obviously inform aspects of human sexuality, but one of the most distinctive aspects of primate behavior is social and hierarchical relationships. Thus, human sexual preferences must have been exercised primarily in social groupings.

Therefore, at the group level, those social norms that benefit the group by managing individual sexual preferences and relationships would most likely lead to a higher level of fitness in comparison to groups that did not manage sexual preferences well. The early appearance of religion in human history makes it a very likely candidate for a special role in the formation of such social norms. And in fact, religion may have evolved as a consequence of the need to manage human relationships through social norms, of which religion has always played an important role. Many of the functions of the human brain and cognition evolved as a consequence of problems posed by complex social relationships.[26]

23. Wilson, "Group-level Evolutionary Processes," 86.

24. Elliott Sober and David Sloan Wilson, *Unto Others: The Evolution and Psychology of Unselfish Behavior* (Cambridge, MA: Harvard University Press, 1998) 26.

25. Cf. Robert Boyd and Peter J. Richerson, *The Origin and Evolution of Cultures* (Oxford: Oxford University Press, 2005).

26. Robin Dunbar, "The Social Brain Hypothesis," *Evolutionary Anthropology* 6 (1998) 178–90.

From an evolutionary perspective, morality emerged at the group level as a system of beliefs and practices that regulated behavior in early hunter-gather societies.[27] Religion can be defined as a set of sacred symbols that motivates different forms of behavior in terms of both regulation and encouragement of behaviors that benefit the group.[28] In terms of sexuality, then, religion has obviously played an important role in regulating the sexual behavior of humans living in groups. Religious doctrines often target marriage and sexuality as primary locations of behavioral regulation, and many competing interests—including mate preference, the possibility of mate poaching and retention, and certainty of paternity—have shaped human sexual desire.[29] However, religion is certainly not an exclusively positive influence on sexual behavior; there are several indications that suggest that religious leaders use their power and prestige as a way to gain sexual access to a wider variety of partners.[30] Religion and sexuality have a complex relationship that includes both positive and negative outcomes.

Recently, there has been renewed interest in investigating the relationship between sexual selection theory and religion.[31] Some researchers have found the highest positive correlation between a more restrictive sexual morality and higher rates of church attendance.[32] Thus, using the reproductive religiosity model, they argue that persons engaged in long-term mating strategies are much more likely to be involved in religious institutions because those types of organizations offer many different types of support for long-term partnerships. A different study found that persons increased their religious beliefs in the presence of same-sex persons perceived to be a competitor for potential mates.[33] Both males and females seemed to use religiosity as a way to advertise the potential for a long-term mate to compete with other same-sex rivals.

In addition to being related to mating strategies, religion has also demonstrated a positive effect for decreasing risky forms for sexual behavior in

---

27. Cf. David Sloan Wilson, *Darwin's Cathedral: Evolution, Religion, and the Nature of Society* (Chicago: University of Chicago Press, 2002) 25.

28. Ibid., 227.

29. David M. Buss, "Sex, Marriage, and Religion: What Adaptive Problems Do Religious Phenomena Solve?" *Psychological Inquiry* 13:3 (2002) 201–38.

30. Ibid., 202.

31. Cf. D. Jason Slone and James Van Slyke, eds. *The Attraction of Religion: A New Evolutionary Psychology of Religion* (New York: Bloomsbury Academic, 2015).

32. Jason Weeden, Adam B. Cohen, and Douglas T. Kenrick, "Religious Attendance as Reproductive Support," *Evolution and Human Behavior* 29 (2008) 327–34.

33. Jessica Yexin Li et al., "Mating Competitors Increase Religious Beliefs," *Journal of Experimental Social Psychology* 46:2 (2010) 428–31.

certain contexts. Higher levels of religiosity have been associated with lower levels of HIV infection in adolescents in the Wakiso district in Uganda and urban areas of Atlanta, Georgia.[34] Additionally, married couples that viewed their marriage as sacred or involving some type of transcendent value stay married longer and have higher levels of marital satisfaction.[35] Married individuals tend to be better off then unmarried individuals, which is actually most true for males. Married males are less likely to engage in violent crime, rape, robbery, substance abuse, and gambling.[36] Some have even argued that monogamous marriage may have been favored because of cultural evolution.[37] Social arrangements that encourage marriage decrease the detrimental effects of crimes and substance abuse, while encouraging positive social outcomes such as familial and economic investment. Thus, to the extent that certain religious morals and values may have aided in promoting monogamous marriages (and the corresponding positive social effects), religiosity may have played a unique role in cultural or group-level evolution as it contributed to competition among different groups and facilitated greater social cohesion and commitment to various moral values such as monogamous marriage.

Integrating Human Sexuality and Theology

Nancey Murphy and George Ellis provide a helpful framework for integrating insights from the science of human nature into a theology of sexuality.[38] In contemporary science, it has been widely accepted that the natural world

---

34. M. Kagimu et al., "Religiosity for HIV Prevention in Uganda: A Case Study among Christian Youth in Wakiso District," *African Health Sciences* 12 (2012) 1–9; Kirk W. Elifson, Hugh Klein, and Claire E. Sterk, "Religiosity and HIV Risk Behavior Involvement among 'at Risk' Women," *Journal of Religion and Health* 42 (2003) 47–66.

35. Annette Mahoney et al., "Religion in the Home in the 1980s and 1990s: A Meta-Analytic Review and Conceptual Analysis of Links between Religion, Marriage, and Parenting," *Journal of Family Psychology* 15 (2001) 559–96.

36. Martin Daly and Margo Wilson, "Killing the Competition: Female/Female and Male/Male Homicide," *Human Nature* 1 (1990) 81–107; G. J. Duncan, B. Wilkerson, and P. England, "Cleaning up Their Act: The Effects of Marriage and Cohabitation on Licit and Illicit Drug Use," *Demography* 43 (2006) 691–710; Robert Sampson, John Laub, and Christopher Wimer, "Does Marriage Reduce Crimes? A Counterfactual Approach to within-Individual Causal Effects," *Criminology* 44 (2006) 465–509.

37. Joseph Henrich, Richard Boyd, and Peter J. Richerson, "The Puzzle of Monogamous Marriage," *Philosophical Transactions of the Royal Society B: Biological Sciences* 367:1589 (2012) 657–69.

38. Nancey Murphy and George F. R. Ellis, *On the Moral Nature of the Universe: Theology, Cosmology, and Ethics* (Minneapolis: Fortress, 1996).

can be understood according to a hierarchy of different types of complex entities. Lower level entities include the smallest particles of matter such as quarks, electrons, and protons. Moving upwards on the hierarchy, one finds larger types of entities such as chemical compounds and cellular structures, followed by organisms such as different animals (including humans) and the environmental ecology specific to the planet earth. At the highest level would be the universe itself, with the billions upon billions of stars and planets contained therein.

Each level in this hierarchy has a specific science that studies entities and processes of its particular size and "level" (physics studies properties of the atom, human physiology studies the systems of the body, tectonics studies the earth's crust and changes in the earth's landscape over evolutionary time, etc.). Further, each science is dependent on sciences at different levels to provide various types of explanations about aspects of the phenomena that are being studied, in particular certain "boundary questions" in each discipline "that can only be answered by reference to entities or processes described at higher levels of the hierarchy."[39] For example, neuropsychology is dependent upon the science of neural functioning to help understand different brains systems and their role in traumatic brain injury. It follows that no one level of science is independent of the others. As is true in most domains of knowledge, each scientist is dependent on a large group of contributors and collaborators in the study of her small corner of the universe, and a long history of success and failure in trying to describe even the simplest of physical processes.

Following the work of Arthur Peacocke, Murphy and Ellis argue that the hierarchy of the sciences is incomplete without *some* type of theological (metaphysical, ontological) framework providing a description of ultimate reality. Technically, this description could be atheistic, drawing from different anti-theistic metaphysical systems, starting in the modern period and continuing through to contemporary forms of the "new atheism." The important point is that once questions are asked that require contributions from multiple levels in the hierarchy of science—such as (1) what is human nature? (2) what is morality? (3) how should governments be structured?— there are background assumptions contained in descriptions of ultimate reality that constrain and influence the types of conclusions drawn from these broadly based philosophical questions. Human sexuality is one of these important, yet ultimately contestable, questions. There are inherent difficulties in trying to establish a purely objective perspective on human sexuality. Murphy and Ellis's contribution to this discussion is their simple

---

39. Ibid., 16; cf. also ibid., 219–20.

acknowledgement of the background assumptions and theological commitments that constitute any attempt to articulate a narrative about the nature of morality.

Clearly, a concept of human sexuality impinges on multiple levels of the hierarchy of sciences. Evolutionary biology provides a general outline of the origins of human sexuality and its particular function as an adaptation in our species. Psychology studies the different manifestations of human sexuality in everyday thoughts, behaviors, and relationships. Theology provides an ethical and transcendent framework that relates human sexuality to goals or values beyond its function in evolutionary history or human psychology. However, this is a complex and highly difficult task because evaluations are made between competing claims about human sexuality at different levels. For example, some evidence suggests that male mating cognition and behavior naturally gravitates towards multiple partners, but this contradicts Christian theological commitments of fidelity in marriage. Thus, the theologian is left to weigh the theological moral guidelines regarding marriage against the relative merits of the scientific outlook and the types of behaviors possible for human beings based on their evolutionary heritage.

Theological Revelation and Human Sexuality

Theological conceptions of sexuality emerged from a diverse set of resources. Individual sexual preferences, as discussed by evolutionary psychology, play an important role in describing aspects of human sexuality that are both encouraged and cautioned by theological doctrines. The social character of early human life, also supported by primatological research, demonstrates that sexual preferences were mainly employed in a group context, which adds additional factors that are addressed by theological concerns about sexuality. These processes constitute the evolutionary factors that form the basis for theological concepts of sexuality, both historically and currently. Because sexuality played such an important role in early human behavior, it must have greatly affected the types of theological revelation that occurred in early primal religions. Keith Ward argues that theological revelation originated in primal traditions that do not have a written tradition, nor feel the need to have one.[40] Revelation about and from supernatural beings often revolved around natural concerns of the social group such as foraging for food, protection from enemies, and staying healthy. Revelations are

---

40. Keith Ward, *Religion and Revelation: A Theology of Revelation in the World's Religions* (Oxford: Oxford University Press, 1994) 58.

dependent upon different characteristics of the environmental context in which they are embedded.[41] For instance, the Inuit sea goddess Takanaluk expresses both the harshness and goodness of the sea and the people dependent upon it for their survival.[42] Early definitions of primitive religions focused on the way in which different aspects of the natural world take on a spiritual dimension. Edward Tylor originally came up with the term "animism" to describe the ways in which primitive religions animate trees, animals, and storms in terms of spiritual entities that control different aspects of their lives.[43] In this sense, the environmental and social context of early humans was conceived within a spiritual framework, not just a natural one. There was not a strong distinction between religious and practical values; they were essentially one and the same. Thus, theological concepts of sexuality emerged very naturally out of the social contexts where sexual preferences were employed, probably in both positive and negative ways. On the positive side, theological concepts developed that encouraged procreation, married life, and faithfulness to partners. On the negative side, some theological concepts developed that included extreme forms of punishment for adultery (almost always against women), forms of sexual repression, and using religion as a means of coercion for sex.

The issue remains to interpret what God may intend for a Christian theological concept of the value of human sexuality. Theological revelation is a form of persuasion in which God acts within the context and cognition of religious communities to generate values that more closely mirror the divine reality.[44] God does not insert propositional statements into the human mind, but works within a particular environmental and cultural context to attune humanity to a divine transcendent reality. Thus, human sexuality has emerged in different religious traditions in a variety of ways according to the ways in which sexuality has been informed by the divine. From the perspective of Christian theology, what can be discerned as the divine influence on the formation of sexual values within Christian communities? How can we articulate a theology of human sexuality?

---

41. Ibid., 67.

42. K. Rasmussen, *Intellectual Culture of the Iglulik Eskimos* (Copenhagen: Gyldendalske Boghandel, 1929).

43. Edward B. Tylor, *Primitive Culture* (London: John Murray, 1873).

44. Ward, *Religion and Revelation*, 24.

Toward a Theology of Sexuality

The work of Sigmund Freud strongly influenced the understanding of sexuality in Western Society. Freud not only brought human sexuality to the forefront of everyday behavior and thought (conscious or unconscious), but he also made sexuality a major component of human development throughout the lifespan.[45] Throughout development, the libido acts as a drive for pleasure that is focused on certain objects in different stages.[46] For example, during the oral stage pleasure is derived from the mouth, which is connected to the pleasure received during nursing, and is manifested in infants constantly putting things into their mouths. The Oedipus complex occurred during the latency stage in which the libido is directed toward the mother as a sexual object, which needs to eventually be repressed and directed towards other females that can facilitate a mature sexual relationship during the genital stage.

According to Freud, the human psyche consists of three parts, the id, ego, and super-ego.[47] The id is the impulsive, motivational aspect of the person that lives according to the pleasure principle. The ego tries to maintain balance between the id and the super-ego, while the super-ego acts as a moral constraint on the impulses of the id. This model views sexuality as a drive that must be satisfied and is always in direct conflict with the super-ego, which tries to repress this drive through moralizing and guilt. Freud's drive theory of sexuality views sexual desire as an impulse or need that builds up over time and then must be performed to bring the body back into homeostasis. The sexual drive creates tension in the person, which must be released for proper functioning.

This view of sexuality is in some ways unfortunate in that it seems to diminish the social and relational dimension of sexuality by *reducing* it to a drive; yet this view has had a significant influence on certain branches of Christianity that seem to reflect the work of the super ego trying to repress the expression of sexuality. Some conservative Christian views of sexuality often emphasize abstinence reflected in abstinence bands and father-daughter dances, while the secular view is supposed to emphasize promiscuity, which emphasizes having sex with several partners.[48] However, this di-

---

45. Cf. Sigmund Freud, *The Psychopathology of Everyday Life*, translated by Anthea Bell (New York: Penguin, [1901] 2002).

46. Sigmund Freud, *Three Essays on the Theory of Sexuality*, translated by James Strachey (New York: Basic, [1905] 1962).

47. Sigmund Freud, *The Ego and the Id*, translated by James Strachey (New York: W. W. Norton & Co., [1923] 1990).

48. Cf. Lisa Miller, "Sexual Revolution Part 2," *Newsweek*, Nov. 16, 2009.

chotomy is somewhat misleading for what average students are looking for in a sexual relationship. In studies conducted on seven college campuses, students reported that although they were not interested in complete abstinence, they were not necessarily promiscuous either and many wanted to be in a sexual relationship with someone who was both a partner and a friend.[49]

An emphasis on kenosis and relationality may provide a better theological context within which to explore concepts of human sexuality. This emphasis on relationality is a product of two cooperative features: evolutionary factors that dealt with social issues involving sexuality in groups and the relational properties of the divine nature as demonstrated in several recent areas of theological discourse. These areas include Christian theological models that emphasize a particular kind of relationality, such as kenotic versions of a self-emptying God, a metaphysical framework based on love, and the turn to relationality connected to developments in late modern philosophy.[50] Thus, a Christian theological interpretation of sexuality understands that the desire for sexual gratification cannot be divorced from the relationships in which sexuality occurs, primarily between partners but also in regard to larger social structures such as churches, families, and marriages. This is not the creation of a dichotomy between abstinence and promiscuity, but a realization that who we are sexually informs many aspects of our identity and cannot be defined simply as a biological drive that needs to be satisfied, but as a pleasurable experience that unites persons into a bond of intimacy and vulnerability.

Understanding sexual value through the categories of either abstinence or promiscuity is too rigid to be helpful in constructing a theological concept of sexuality, but emphasizing the relational dimension of sexuality affirms both the theological importance of marital relationships as well as the practical concerns of living in community. Defining sexuality as merely a drive that needs to be satisfied robs it of its relational significance and may lead to attitudes that foster satisfying that need at any cost. Placing the theological conception of sexuality in a relational context allows the behavior to be modified in terms of how it affects relationships both between partners and between partnerships themselves and their children, as well as the wider community. Human sexuality is a natural expression of intimacy

---

49. Donna Freitas, *Sex and the Soul: Juggling Sexuality, Spirituality, Romance, and Religion on America's College Campuses* (Oxford: Oxford University Press, 2008).

50. Cf. John Polkinghorne, ed. *The Work of Love: Creation as Kenosis* (Grand Rapids: Eerdmans, 2001); F. LeRon Shults, *Reforming the Doctrine of God* (Grand Rapids: Eerdmans, 2005); Thomas J. Oord, "A Metaphysics for the Love-and-Science Symbiosis," *Contemporary Philosophy* 25 (2005) 5–6.

and commitment in long-term relationships. This expression should be encouraged by theology as an important part of sexual desire. However, this is not the only sexual relation that should be kept in mind. As sexual expression increases, it is important to think about long-term consequences in terms of marriage, family life, and commitments. A theological definition of sexuality must include multiple aspects and consequences of sexuality in community including marriage, but also the affects of adultery and providing resources for children.

Kenosis is a unique theological resource in attempting to articulate a robustly theological understanding of human sexuality. Alasdair MacIntyre argues that ethical systems require some *telos* or goal in order to provide a standard for moral development and maturity over time.[51] Murphy and Ellis argue that kenosis is the primary *telos* or goal of their ethical system, referring to it as the "hard core" of their moral theory and defining it in terms of self-renunciation: "self-renunciation for the sake of the other is humankind's highest good."[52] This understanding of kenosis is drawn from Phil 2:5–11, where Jesus Christ, despite being in his very nature God, consciously chooses to let go his claims to authority and take on a servant's role. Christ's primary achievement is to not hold on to his own power, but to release it in order to become a servant for others in his earthly life, ultimately sacrificing his own life for others.

Kenosis is a helpful, yet difficult concept to put in tension with an evolutionary view of sexuality, let alone human nature in general. The most widely used analogy for the process of evolution is that of the "selfish gene," meaning that the genes that survived and reproduced over time were those that were "selfish" at the cost of other potential genetic alternatives.[53] Kenosis allows humanity to differentiate between genetic and personal or social interest. Our genetic interests do not have to solely define what is the good (or *telos*) for humanity; individuals and social groups can self-define *telos* according to their own individual goals and hopes for different social structures. Self-renunciation seems counterintuitive and perhaps even negative as a good to be sought for humanity, especially as a pathway for individual fulfillment.[54] Yet it is worth noting that similar concepts have been a part of many different types of religious traditions. For example, in developing a practice of nonviolent resistance, Gandhi's use of the concept *satyagraha*

---

51. Alasdair MacIntyre, *After Virtue: A Study in Moral Theory* (Notre Dame: University of Notre Dame Press, 1981).

52. Murphy and Ellis, *Moral Nature*, 118.

53. Cf. Dawkins, *Selfish Gene*.

54. Murphy and Ellis, *Moral Nature*, 121.

(an insistence on truth or holding onto truth) constitutes a notable parallel from the Hindu tradition.[55] John Hick's definition of the function of religion is also relevant here, as "a transformation of human existence from self-centeredness to reality centeredness."[56] For the Christian tradition, the idea of kenosis as a good for humanity is summed up in Luke 17:33 (NIV): "Whoever tries to keep their life will lose it, and whoever loses their life will preserve it." Kenosis is the perfect complement to sexual desire and mate preference because it directs attention to the other rather than the self in making decisions regarding sexual enjoyment and fulfillment, family, and social consequences. Males and females demonstrate a propensity toward both short-term and long-term strategies. News cycles continually provide examples of illicit sexual behaviors for all different kinds of persons from politicians and celebrities to pastors and schoolteachers. Thinking of the other rather than the self changes the dialogue regarding sexual behavior and hopefully provides the possibility of understanding the larger issues involved in the values a society associates with sex. There is still a unique tension here in that sexual repression, alienation, or suppression does not promote healthy sexuality either. Thus, rather than forming a moral absolute regarding human sexuality, it may be better to keep both self-interest and self-renunciation in tension when forming theological concepts regarding human sexuality. More discussion and careful introspection is needed regarding how Christian communities should engage contemporary sexual behavior, discussion which keeps kenosis at the forefront such that the theological conversation focuses not just on the individual, but also on the other, such that this becomes the central concern of human sexual relationships.

Conclusion

The relationship between human sexuality, evolution, and theology is complex. Evolution, at both the individual and group level, has played an important role in the formation of human sexual desire and religious concepts about sexuality. However, religion and sexuality are not necessarily reducible to evolutionary processes, nor does an evolutionary account rule out the possibility of developing a healthy theological understanding of sexuality. Rather, theological concepts of human sexuality emerged as a result of both evolutionary factors and the influence of kenotic conceptions of the divine. Relationality and kenosis, as expressed in several contemporary theological

---

55. Murphy and Ellis make a similar observation concerning *satyagraha*; ibid., 7.

56. John Hick, *An Interpretation of Religion* (New Haven: Yale University Press, 1989) 14; Cf. Murphy and Ellis, *Moral Nature*, 118.

accounts, provides a helpful theological framework for the formation of a contemporary ethic of human sexuality. Although religion and sexuality have had a tumultuous relationship throughout history, an emphasis on self-renunciation and concern for the other provides a fertile context for exploring these important issues for years to come.

14

Defacement and Disappearance
The Practice of Mourning with the Church of the Benevolent Self

—Craig Hovey

A messenger comes to the mourner's house.

"Come," says the messenger, "you are needed."

"I cannot come," says the mourner, "my spirit is broken."

"That is why you are needed," says the messenger.[1]

I.

Nancey Murphy helped many of us see how significant recent philosophical turns have been turns toward ethics. Christian practices both arise from and cultivate the virtues required for Christian living: this MacIntyrian insight helped pave the way for a resurgence of political theology as the study of Christian social existence in its own right as opposed to the attempt to make Christian beliefs "go public." Practices, in this way, are not only religious versions of political ones; they have their own integrity and their own theo-logic. In some cases, they can only be perceived to be "political" by downgrading rivals whose political character flows from the West's

---

1. Leon Wieseltier, *Kaddish* (New York: Knopf, 1998) 166.

preoccupation with certain notions—such as sovereignty—that too easily pass for or exhaust "politics."

Even before there were Anabaptists who embraced this non-sovereign-yet-still-political quality of certain practices, there were Church Fathers who understood that the Christian church sojourns in the world without making it its home. For Augustine, if Christian citizenship is in heaven (Phil 3:2), then people are called out of all nations and into a kind of exile within those same nations, only now as a gathered society of pilgrims whose way in the world is one of witness rather than rule.[2] The earlier *Epistle to Diognetus* celebrates how Christians "dwell in their own countries, but simply as sojourners. As citizens, they share in all things with others, and yet endure all things as if foreigners."[3] The *Shepherd of Hermas* challenges readers to recognize the absurdity of living in lavish homes since they "dwell in a strange land . . . for your city is far away from this one."[4] Tertullian claimed that Christians "acknowledge one all-embracing commonwealth—the world."[5] And Pontius the Deacon recognized that, while pagans consider banishment to be a severe punishment, it is different for a Christian like Cyprian since, for him, "the whole of this world is one home. Wherefore, though he were banished into a hidden and secret place, yet, associated with the affairs of his God, he cannot regard it as an exile. In addition, while honestly serving God, he is a stranger even in his own city."[6] The significance of exile and banishment, then, depends on the significance of one's national identity. When Origen argued that Christians should seek leadership positions in the church rather than in the state, his reason was that the church is itself a nation: "[W]e recognize in each state the existence of another national organization founded by the Word of God [i.e., the church]."[7]

In what follows, I draw on the non-sovereign quality of Christian political existence to investigate mourning as a distinctively political Christian practice. What is the nature of the remembrance that mourning enacts, especially in the face of injustices and indignities such as banishment and death? The memory of the unjust past can, and in many ways must, be sustained by repeated, ritual performances that both remember and protest, that simultaneously call the past to mind and declare a moral judgment over it. Mourning can be just such an act, I argue. Still, it may not be immediately

2. Augustine, *City of God*, XIX.
3. *Epistle to Diognetus*, ch. 5.
4. *Shepherd of Hermas*, Similitude 1.
5. Tertullian, *The Apology*, Chapter XXXVIII.
6. *The Life and Passion of Cyprian, Bishop and Martyr*, 11.
7. Origen, *Against Celsus*, Book VIII, Chapter LXXV.

obvious how mourning actually functions this way. What, if anything, does mourning try to do? What is required in order to say that it does so? Does the act of mourning in any way do justice to the dead? Can it condemn the injustice of a death unjustly caused?

My aim is to describe and illuminate these and related questions about mourning, disappearance, loss, and death primarily by way of two sources—Nathan Englander's novel, *The Ministry of Special Cases*, set in Argentina's "dirty war" of the 1970s, and several of Gillian Rose's discourses on death and mourning. Together, Englander and Rose expose the futility of human mourning, its passive politics, and its vulnerability to injustice. I argue that, while it is contested, mourning's political character can nevertheless be seen in how it enables resistance against the sovereign forms of injustice that conspire to render it amoral and apolitical. For this to happen, though, the church needs to reject the normativity of sovereignty and see itself as the sojourning, exiled, displaced, people of God.

The theology offered here in response is, to a considerable degree, a meditation on resurrection. Perhaps it is a paradox: resurrection both makes mourning possible as an activity of justice-seeking through just remembrance and also signals the transcendent end of mourning that displaces the hegemony against which, in Rose's terminology, "endless mourning" has thoroughly entrenched itself in the form of a postmodern ethic. Rose thought that the latter cannot escape a number of contradictions. Postmodernism's chief tragedy is the way that it consigns any mourning to the void of meaninglessness and certainly the realm of the unpolitical and the non-moral.

II.

In his novel *The Ministry of Special Cases*, Nathan Englander probes questions of death, disappearance, justice, and mourning. He shows how an injustice can be made all the more unjust when forces conspire to make mourning it impossible. The central character, Poznan Kaddish (whose last name comes from a traditional Jewish prayer of mourning), makes a pitiable living defacing gravestones under the cover of night. He is hired by prominent Jews of the city intent on disowning their disgraceful pasts by defacing all extant links with their prostitute mothers or their corrupt or unknown fathers. Their dishonorable ancestors were not permitted proper burial plots in the regular site. Instead, the graves reserved for this unconventional and marginal society known as The Benevolent Self were exiled to the other side of a wall from the others. But their gravestones only haunt the living who have now prospered and become respectable in the eyes of society, able to make use of Kaddish's services as he erases their ties to the past and to the dead. The past remains in the present at least at the site of the banished, interred bodies since the present is constituted in part by the activity of those who come to know who they are by their mourning.

This erasure—Kaddish's business—enacts an injustice beyond whatever brought about the deaths of those now being erased. Unable to pay for Kaddish's services, one client, a plastic surgeon, offers an exchange: Kaddish will deface a gravestone in the Benevolent Self parcel in exchange for plastic surgery—rhinoplasty—for Kaddish and his wife. There is nothing subtle in this. Even a shameful past is still an identity and, as it happens, supplies the most important, though most easily taken for granted, resource for engagement with the present. Defacing Jewish noses—the work of the plastic surgeon—is a respectable alteration of the living at the sacrifice of Jewish identity while Kaddish carries out his parallel work under a cloak of darkness. But they both achieve the same thing. Without Jewish identity, the disappearance of the Jewish youth, then, cannot be a holocaust and can issue in no determinative Jewish protest against it.[8] Without Jewish identity, it is "only" the disappearance of more Argentines and, even though there are certainly ways of naming the injustices Argentines suffer, the ability to cry out against the wrongs suffered by *this* people is greatly hindered and indeed constitutes an enlargement of *this* people's suffering to the extent that they are no longer sure what makes them a people in the first place.

Likewise, without a place to mourn, *even exiled beyond the wall*, it is no longer possible to name injustices. The names have been wiped from the gravestones. This irony runs very deep: Mourning preserves a link to what is mourned, leaving open the time of narration and re-narration that

---

8. A scandal of particularity is necessary to sustain this kind of claim that is otherwise very difficult to make against the strictures of universal modes of moral reasoning in modernity. Nevertheless, the particularity must surely go beyond tying Argentina's holocaust to other sufferings of Jews since all such suffering will finally find its narrative place in the story of the Exodus, including the possibility that the cry of protest against all of them will echo Israel's cry to God while in Egypt. Michael Wyschogrod makes this point explicit: "The fate of Israel is of central concern because Israel is the elect people of God through whom God's redemptive work is done in the world. However tragic human suffering is on the human plane, what happens to Israel is directly tied to its role as a nation to which God attaches his name and through which He will redeem man. He who strikes Israel, therefore, engages himself in battle with God and it is for this reason that the history of Israel is the fulcrum of human history. The suffering of others must, therefore, be seen in the light of Israel's suffering. The travail of man is not abandoned, precisely because Israel suffers and, thereby, God's presence is drawn into human history and redemption enters the horizon of human existence." Wyschogrod, "Faith and the Holocaust," *Judaism* 29:3 (Summer 1971) 293.

mourning enacts. It also commemorates the presence of what is now absent by marking a space with its exercise, a space reserved as a sign of disappearance. Such spaces witness to the fact that the absence is more than a lack of presence (of what might never have existed anyway), but is a loss that leaves a space by its absence—the space *is* the continued presence and is held open by mourning there. Beyond-the-wall is such a space even while its second-class status remains an inescapable aspect of the judgment that this mourning would enact. Without this space, mourning has no home—no place to return to in order to sustain the judgment against exclusion in which the mourner is identified as the mourner of these particular excluded people. The political risk is mitigated by continuing to exclude the excluded by ending mourning for them. And the mourners not only stop visiting the graves of their ancestors themselves: they positively ensure that no one else will be able to visit them. Their presence is therefore doubly disappeared: no work of mourning and no possibility of remembrance in the space that connotes the meaning of the mourning.

When Kaddish's own son falls victim to the junta's campaign of disappearance, Kaddish becomes caught between absence and mourning. He has strong suspicions that his son, Pato, has been killed although he lacks concrete evidence other than a vague report from the navigator of one of the military planes used to drop young people into the river. Even so, determined to do the right thing, Kaddish begins to mourn the death of his son while his wife refuses to give into despair, holding out hope for their son's return. Even though there is no body, Kaddish seeks a rabbi's advice on how to conduct a funeral.

> "I don't understand," the rabbi said, no judgment in it. "If there's no body, how do you know he's dead? How," the rabbi said, slow and careful, "how do you know your wife is wrong and you are right?"
>
> "How do I know?" Kaddish said. He hadn't expected such a question. "The navigator told me—the fisherman. I spoke to the man who did it, the one who throws the children from the planes."
>
> "A fisherman did this to your Pato?"
>
> "He might as well have," Kaddish said. "Of those he murdered, it's possible Pato may have been among them."
>
> "So there's no proof?" the rabbi said. His voice rose up in the asking. Again, it was without judgment. The rabbi was trying only to grasp.
>
> "This is the way in which it's Argentine," Kaddish said, now animated, eyes wide open wide. "It's neat and it's clean and,

> more than anything, it's well-mannered. The whole country turns away, as if they've caught the government with something in its teeth. It's become crass even to acknowledge the loss," Kaddish said. "You don't think it impolite, I hope, that my son has been made dead?"
>
> The rabbi began to mutter a *baruch shem kavod*. It wasn't a second *bracha*, it was instead the line mustered to undo the erroneous blessing. The rabbi dared not let a prayer over the death of a child stand when he thought the boy might live.[9]

I find Kaddish's character to be particularly compelling on account of his self-pity. In his grave-defacing world, he is surrounded by those whose identities are an embarrassment, whose very memories must be actively erased for the sake of the living. His response to his son's disappearance resembles the drive to "move on" that quickly sets in and aborts all modern mourning through the management of the so-called "grief process."[10] Yet because Kaddish himself freely visits his mother's grave among The Benevolent Self, he therefore reasons that only he is capable of truly mourning. Everyone else is in denial—*this* is, he says, the way in which it is Argentine. But the rabbi, like Kaddish's wife, Lillian, quickly analyzes Kaddish's flaw: it is only in the form of mourning that Kaddish can countenance the judgment that his dissent is.

> "She waits for him?" the rabbi said. "Lillian believes you're wrong?"
>
> "She doesn't wait. She searches and searches. Admirable behavior," Kaddish said, "if Pato were alive, if there were a boy to find."
>
> "Maybe," the rabbi said, "you're wrong in not waiting."
>
> "Me? I'm the same as always. Not right or wrong, only deficient," Kaddish said, "forever falling short. But this one thing, a father to a dead son without a son to weep over. This is an absence that's not right and not fair."
>
> "What am I to do?" the rabbi said. "I can't produce him."
>
> "I'm not a fool," Kaddish said. "I'm not asking for a miracle. Only advice. How without a body do I make a resting place for my son? You tell me not to leave my house during the first

---

9. Nathan Englander, *The Ministry of Special Cases* (New York: Knopf, 2007) 293–94.

10. I am indebted to Michael Hanby's observation that therapeutic techniques subject grief to managerial control that distorts our relationship to time while precisely mimicking the same distortion that capitalism enacts. See Michael Hanby, "Interceding: Giving Grief to Management," in *The Blackwell Companion to Christian Ethics*, edited by Stanley Hauerwas and Samuel Wells (Oxford, UK: Blackwell, 2004) esp. 243.

week of mourning, and I tell you, without a grave, the mourning never ends."

"Abandon the mourning," the rabbi said. "Go back to your wife. She's a sensible woman, Poznan. It sounds like she does the right thing."[11]

By the end of the conversation, the rabbi forbids Kaddish from mourning. But to Kaddish, the rabbi and Lillian appear to be all too Argentine, unwilling to declare the injustice of the military regime, reluctant to take a stand against the disappearing children—this is why they delay their mourning. A body is a kind of judgment. But the act of mourning the dead is also a kind of judgment.[12]

III.

Like life itself, mourning is not interminable. Hope runs out, as does patience, only to be replaced and overcome by resignation to the reality of loss. Kaddish's wife thinks her husband is wrong to give up hope and patience prematurely. But Kaddish is quick to figure out how to begin mourning since "without a grave, the mourning never ends." Gillian Rose described postmodernism as interminable mourning.[13] Without an end, mourning only mocks the perpetual march of existence that postmodern thought so much celebrates, for which history can have no final closure and therefore no judgment, but instead endlessly rehearses the pointlessness of nihilism—nothing has meaning since nothing ends.[14] Nietzsche understood that meaninglessness is a very real entailment of the eternal return of all things.

---

11. Englander, *Ministry of Special Cases*, 294.

12. Kaddish's self-pity is a great temptation. As one who has learned to mourn, he has also learned to judge. And yet it is all given away by his eagerness. In the book's opening scene, while defacing a grave, Kaddish and Pato stumble across a recently murdered body that has been dumped in the graveyard. Pato insists on investigating the matter and even on burying the body himself if it cannot be resolved. But Kaddish responds to Pato's interest in the body with exasperation. He is not moved by the injustice of a murdered body like his son is, suggesting a flaw in his understanding of what he was later to attribute to the work of mourning his very son. Put differently, we might imagine that mourning the Benevolent Self is a work of practical reasoning, a kind of training in the ability rightly to identify injustice and to know how and when to mourn it and how to protest against it.

13. Gillian Rose, *Mourning Becomes the Law* (Cambridge: Cambridge University Press, 1996) 11.

14. Robert W. Jenson, *Systematic Theology: The Triune God*, vol. 1 (New York: Oxford University Press, 1997) 327–28.

According to Rose, mourning attests to a transcendent ground of judgment or order. She likely has in mind thinkers like Foucault for whom "freedom" and "justice" are conceived of irrespective of metaphysics, and so quite straightforwardly will never constitute a proper ethic. Foucault, it will be appreciated, was happy to concede that his enterprise was never meant to prescribe an ethic since his genealogical efforts were only ever meant to be *descriptions*. In a helpful phase of Nicholas Adams and Charles Elliott, "ethics is ethnography."[15] Against such thinking, even as mourning designates and demonstrates the kind of emptiness it countenances as its object—namely, the loss of hope that the disappearance entails—it can still only do so because it remembers that justice only ever enabled, in the first place, the *presence* that has now disappeared.

Kaddish's wife would not equate disappearance with death; she refused to mourn. Disappearance without death still leaves the possibility of dying as much as it means the possibility of life—the fact that her son may still be alive also means he may still die. It is too soon to mourn. We will only mourn something lost when hope runs out that it may return.

Endless mourning is what Kaddish seems destined for. Thrust into mourning when there is no proper burial, there is nothing to mark dying with death. There is no *rest*. Ironically for Kaddish, in defacing the tombs, he undoes the proper burials of others. Now there is no way to commemorate these dead by visiting them or by involving them in the ritual acts of memory *in a particular place*. Kaddish is essentially a grave robber, unwinding the otherwise dignified deaths of undignified lives. He is in effect perpetuating for eternity the damnation of those whose lives were shameful to their children, those who now refuse to mourn for them—as deplorable, then, as the dominant, respectable Jewish community that insisted that the bodies be buried on the other side of the wall.

IV.

Let us recall now that for Christianity there is a polis that is the future and goal of human community; communion with God is not an earthly city. This eschatological city may be refracted (as for Augustine) into a secular political analogue. Yet the composition of the Christian community—its concept of heavenly citizenship—surpasses the inherently limiting secular politics. Communion across time, especially, preserves the dead within the church.

---

15. Nicholas Adams and Charles Elliott, "Ethnography is Dogmatics: Making Description Central to Systematic Theology," *Scottish Journal of Theology* 53 (2000) 339–64.

Christian burial attests to the presence of the dead with the living saints: the dead remain part of the church, often literally as they are enshrined in the architecture or in the floors. Christians remember the deaths of their fellows, if not as saints, then at least *in light of* the saints. What the dead saints are now doing is the inverse of mourning: celebrating their unmediated presence to God. Those disappeared from us—the dead in Christ—see God face to face.

Because the saints are present to God, Christian mourning may be an act of political resistance. Christians may take the time to honor those whose commitment to Christ has meant, in one way or another, that they must be buried outside of the city, removed from its honorific language and official sanctions for civic contribution and conformity to the overriding way of life of the polis. By continuing to mourn their dead, Christians are declaring that the way the world remembers is not an ultimate concern, nor can the world determine how the deaths of Christians will be remembered in the face of a people who so persist. Therefore, "persistence" describes how mourning is an active enterprise that does not simply pick up where patience leaves off. Rather, it is itself an act of patience. It still attests to transcendent order and justice and, just so, protests sin and mortality—objecting to it, awaiting resurrection. And where mourning takes a decidedly political form in the face of unjust memory or unjust disappearance, it does more than long for a lost presence. Rather, it positively objects to criminal death and disappearance as an act of protest *through* its determination to take the time to mourn and to recall the now lost presence as the very gift of existence that all existing things are and in which they share.

If mourning is an activity of representation and enactment of transcendent justice, it witnesses to a transcendence altogether at odds with the deferral of justice to the illimitable "beyond" in which present mourning is evacuated of all political significance and practiced function aimed at the good of social life in the polis. Rose reflects on the separation from the polis that Nicholas Poussin depicts as Phocion's fate in the painting "The ashes of Phocion collected by his widow" (1648; see below). Rose explains that this separation is not the primary injustice that Phocion's wife mourns. Instead, Phocion's wife's mourning is already a judgment against the city, a mournful cry that insists that *this* city has fallen into tyranny (Phocion had been a celebrated statesman but was executed by a tyrannical leader).

Nicholas Poussin, *The Ashes of Phocion Collected by His Widow* (1648)]

For Rose, it is crucial that Phocian's wife does not enact a mourning-judgment against the city as such, that the widow's weeping does not signal the despair over worldly (terrestrial) order. Here Rose disagrees with the interpretation Sister Wendy Beckett offered in her BBC documentary. According to Sister Wendy, burying Phocion's ashes outside of Athens is a wholesale condemnation of the politics of this world with its injustice in favor of the politics of heaven (symbolically, of Jerusalem) with its gracious acts of love. As Sister Wendy see it, *this* city (here Athens) is not condemned, but all cities are shown impossibly to execute the justice on which they stake their authority and therefore their existence. Therefore the mournful exclamation rises *over* the city walls since it cannot help now but originate from *beyond* them.[16]

Nevertheless, Rose argues that this cannot be. Such mourning is activated by an idolatrous knowledge that prevents mourning from being an activity, a work of the traumatized soul: this soul grasps at the certainty of what will arrive from the "beyond." It disqualifies all present knowledge and activity from being the work of justice on grounds that transcendent justice has no earthly and temporal representation. What is earthly and temporal are known quantities precisely in their known non-representation

---

16. In the Gospels, Lazarus, a resident of Bethany, was buried outside the city (cf. Matt 21:17). And later, the dead are raised in a way somehow connected with Christ's resurrection: "The tombs also were opened, and many bodies of the saints who had fallen asleep were raised, and coming out of the tombs after his resurrection they went *into the holy city* and appeared to many" (Matt 27:52–53, emphasis added). We might say that these bodies "of the saints" were judgments against the city that had condemned Jesus, symbolically (at least) emerging from outside.

and non-correspondence and hence empirical purity. All attempts at actual political justice are sheer tyranny. But even though tyrants may rule the city, "we understand that we, too, must constantly negotiate the *actuality* of being tyrannical."[17] Accepting a prior understanding of "tyranny" as a necessary description and therefore one half of a static binary relieves us of the need to negotiate the opposite existence—a just life even within an unjust city. The perpetuity of aberrant mourning only disguises this possibility.

Yet if mourning retains the possibility of just action in which Phocion and his wife may be declared just, despite present political corruption, it is by itself being simultaneously an act of judgment and a display of openness to learning what cannot be anticipated. One might come to learn that one has unknowingly been complicit in the city's abuse of power, as Rose says. But then mourning beyond the city walls is prevented from being a pious act of condemnation since the judgment enacted there is still the *city's own* judgment. For Rose, the stately buildings of Athens represent the justice of Athens under former regimes and at better times. The "outside" judgment grants safety to neither the city itself nor the prophet who denounces it: in the judgment, the city is *reminded* of its civic status and the prophet is reminded that the city produced him.

In Scripture, this situation is precisely seen in the way that neither prophet nor city could withstand Jeremiah's prophecy. Jeremiah 14:13–16, for example, illustrates that even though the city produced those prophets, their prophecy contained no justice. Instead, the prophets shared in the tyranny and corruption of the city and so symbolically stood firmly within its walls. They did not speak out against the failure of the courts to adjudicate cases with impartiality nor did they dare to expose the corruption of leaders. The traditional position of the prophet relative to the king—the holy fool who speaks, "you are dust" with indifference to the consequences—has been traded for false promises that speak of eternal kingdoms and unending sovereign reigns. Because there is no "outside," there is no mourning. There is only the indignity of unburied bodies on the streets of the city. And while Jerusalem will not witness the justice of anyone mourning for these prophets, the unburied dead nevertheless represent God's transcendent justice. There will be mourning in the form of the great dirges of Lamentations, a mourning only made possible for those who remember God's promises to the people and the wickedness of the city. Those who mourn know that the good life of the city is not at odds with good human life, life lived before God in faithfulness to God's righteous law. The political compromise of the false prophets had advanced on the short-lived promises of sovereign power

---

17. Rose, *Mourning Becomes the Law*, 122–23.

to grant civic dignity to the speakers of soothing words. In not receiving a fitting funeral, though, such promises can no longer be fulfilled. The reason is not primarily that the city has fallen, however, but that the promises were false. In other words, the fact that there is no one to mourn the false prophets only *derivatively* signals the city's failure to form and discharge righteous and virtuous citizens. This failure is itself the city's wickedness.

Still, those who lament the fallen city are vindicated in their refusal to mourn the false prophets. The reality of the true prophets who will stand over against the city is a witness to the city's insufficiency as a morally formative agent. Therefore, Jerusalem symbolizes neither a wholly transcendent political possibility that must always be frustrated in this world. Nor does it symbolize a political body with an exhaustive capacity to produce righteous citizens through its instantiation of law.

That notorious modern skepticism engendered toward its institutions, at its most politically enervating, funds a sublime reservation to those institutions' inability to achieve the goods they purport to serve. The "new ethics" that emerges from this conception of New Jerusalem as the only true city is, we might say, nothing more than the exasperated mirror image of the very discredited political forms with which it has become dissatisfied. Having failed to produce virtuous citizens, "Athens" (what Rose calls the symbolic first city) is not reformed by its sages—its prophets who, though they might denounce the city nevertheless refuse to escape it, cognizant that any choice between this political form and another cannot actually be a viable choice between one city and another (except in certain maladies of modern thought). Prophets do not denounce the city by preaching another law. Rather, they denounce by continuing to preach the law of the city despite the city's present lawlessness. In this sense, Athens and Jerusalem are not really so different.

My question to Rose is: Why must transcendent justice be symbolized by the city's buildings? It is, after all, one thing to say that the city's justice transcends this tyrannical period in the city's history. But why must we suppose that the return of that earlier justice will occur with the density that it previously had—splendid imperial buildings continuing to stand and declare the enduring nature of justice even after the unmourned deaths of today's corrupt rulers?

It seems to me that just as creaturely existence (preeminently as political existence) can never reassure us that exile might not actually be a permanent way of life, we cannot know with confidence that we will return to the old order. None of this would have surprised Pontius the Deacon given how he described Cyprian's banishment. In some ways, this is exactly Rose's point: the just acts of the women outside the city walls take just political existence into exile with themselves (with Phocion himself, whose ashes they bury) by committing themselves to the semi-permanent condition of internment in soil that lies beyond the city's configurations. Their mourning does not await "regime change" nor a more favorable political tide but (as it were) contents itself with the present injustice and even the possibility of never returning from exile. Then again, their mourning "contents itself" through a very act of discontent, which is to say, of determinate protest.

This dialectic between contentment and discontentment lies behind the connotation mourning intimates as a practice that aims at goods that exceed *mere* protest. As a positive act of judgment in affirmation of a good human life, it does not first have in view the proclamation of transcendent realities like justice, goodness, and truth. Instead, it finds these realities always already instantiated in the presence of lives the absence of which it is now determined to mark through its very exercise. So to return to my earlier question, does mourning require the buildings?

According to Rose, Sister Wendy's mistake was to presume that the city has now become *inherently* corrupt, that the powers, perhaps, form a timeless category of political life that is opposed to the purposes of God and are therefore beyond redemption—certainly beyond the possibility of discharging justice in this world. But I do not see why it is necessary to follow Rose in extolling the transcendence of the city's forms *as remaining with the city*. In my view, we need only correct Sister Wendy's insight by restoring to its judgment a contingent relation between the political and the state. Phocion's wife is simply acting politically and justly and we don't need the image of Athens in the background in order to see it. The relation between the political and the state is not *necessarily* divergent, on the one hand, where the state as-such is so corrupt that it cannot instantiate the political. But on the other hand, neither is the abandonment of justice necessarily temporary. What remains of the state (Athens, in this example) in no way ensures that the defiant actions of those who dwell in exile are just actions.

V.

Nathan Englander's *The Ministry of Special Cases* portrays Kaddish as a man for whom mourning is altogether tragic. Having made his living on account of graves as the persistent sites of unwilling mourning, his own all-too-willing mourning of his disappeared son can only be deemed pathetic for its lack of a proper site. This is the same homelessness that Rose imagines besets postmodern ethics without metaphysics. Nevertheless, Kaddish does live up to his name, albeit in a way that appears to be lost on the other characters. His readiness to mourn is appalling because he appears to be *foreclosing on justice prematurely*, to be looking heavenward too quickly while there is still work to do—a classic case of the failure of religion in the face of injustice when it counsels the faithful to "just pray." The failure of postmodern ethics actually to do anything at all is an exact corollary. In his book *Kaddish*—a moving reflection on mourning after the death of his father—Leon Wieseltier relates this objection to the Kaddish prayer for its seeming misguided focus: it is offensive for being servile and indifferent to human despondency. An old man objects,

> This prayer called the "Kaddish," it is the mourner's principal prayer, it is said during all the days of mourning, and according to our law it is enough, there is no need to say anything more. And what does it say? "Magnified and sanctified may His great Name be. . ." Only this. Nothing more. Not a word about the dead, not a hint about what has happened. Not even "I surrender to your holy will." Just a bunch of silly words: "Blessed and praised and glorified" and five or so more compliments of that kind. I'm sorry, but it reminds me of what Boris Mavrikovich wrote to Anna Mikhailovna from Italy: "Dear, Beloved, Honorable, Esteemed Anyatochka. . ." How can God stomach it? All these bowings and scrapings should make him nauseous![18]

The objection is that the prayer fails to do anything. At its worst, it does not even plead the case of the silenced dead against injustice before God. Instead of being a proper prayer of mourning, it seems to be a tedious series of praises for God's glory and greatness. Yet Wieseltier recounts that the Rabbi who composed the prayer, Rabbi Akiva, did in fact mean for it to have a purpose: he was damning the devil. The devil prods the mourner to ask for reasons, to stop worshiping God, to acknowledge that the contradiction between the dead's silence and God's justice must therefore lead to no-prayer. But Akiva reasons there may indeed be an absence of reasons, and that this is precisely a refutation of the devil and a "reason" for the prayer. "But who needs reasons? Satan, stay out of this. God and the Jew are partners."

Mourning is only possible because God has partners. Apart from this, mourning only furthers the injustice of wrongful death by seeming to do nothing about it, even conspiring in the silence that protects killers. This means that postmodernism conceived of as endless mourning perpetuates injustice at the point where it supposes that it stands most determinedly neutral on questions of justice. With Rose, we must conclude that "outside the wall" makes no judgment against the city since the wall cannot finally

---

18. Wieseltier, *Kaddish*, 164.

have any meaning at all. But the connection between justice and the state is not finally the most conclusive one, implying that the work of mourning may in fact be a revolt against the state's injustice, even though it is so on account of God's partnership with a people who will never rest easily with attempts to secure objections on more universal grounds, which is to say grounds that are readily deployable without such partnership (and, indeed, without God).

Christians too are God's partners. Gentile Christians have been brought within the crowded house of Israel through adoption. Their partnership with God is embodied and constituted through the reconciliation of the world to Christ in the person of Christ. Resurrection enacts a political judgment. In the same way that mourning can be a political act, resurrection is the *final* political act that throws back onto all mourning the condition of possibility, its reality actually enabling mourning to come to an end rather than ceaselessly resigning over and over again to the city's injustice. Nothing, it turns out, could be more universal. After all, the site of Christian mourning has been exploded to its widest possible extent: the entire universe. As Gregory Nazianzen said when recounting the interrogation of Basil the Great,

> Banishment is impossible for me, who am confined by no limit of place, counting my own neither the land where I now dwell, nor all of that into which I may be hurled; or, rather, counting it all God's, whose guest and dependent I am.[19]

In conclusion, it seems to me that there are two ways for a grave to cease being a mourning site. The first is through defacement—erasing the significance of the place, the ritualistically performed act of anti-mourning that converts loss into sheer absence, wiping all memory of existence, obliterating the place that marks the lost presence, refusing to be a mourning-presence at that site and ensuring also that the memory will fade from others by depriving them of the ability to remember. Thus the grave is transformed from memorial to meaningless stone and dirt, mimicking the decay of the body beneath.

The other way a grave ceases to be a mourning site is through resurrection. In resurrection, not only is the body no longer available to mark the site of mourning, but the loves that were severed by death are brought back together and are made available to each other once again. In Jerusalem today, Christian worshippers at Jesus's empty tomb are not mourners. The intention of the first Easter's visitors was to ensure a proper burial with

---

19. Gregory Nazianzen, *Oration XLIII*.49.

honorific spices and mourning. When they were interrupted with the good news of the gospel, the site was transformed into a site of miraculous presence rather than loss, presaging the end of all mourning at the end of the age when all loves will be present to their lovers in God.

> While they were going, behold, some of the guard went *into the city* and told the chief priests all that had taken place. And when they had assembled with the elders and taken counsel, they gave a sum of money to the soldiers and said, "Tell people, 'His disciples came by night and stole him away while we were asleep.' And if this comes to the governor's ears, we will satisfy him and keep you out of trouble." So they took the money and did as they were directed; and this story has been spread among the Jews to this day. (Matt 28:11–15, emphasis added)

"In the city," the empty tomb is falsely reported as being the work of grave robbers, the site of non-mourning enabled by defacement. In the Gospels, this is associated with the corruption of the city: soldiers who commit to spreading a false account through taking payoffs, chief priests who commit to lying to the Roman governor in order to keep the peace and protect the soldiers whose stories they believed to be true.

Like the Benevolent Self community, Christian existence, then, is originally and normatively beyond the polis wall. It may practice non-sovereign mourning—a mourning that nevertheless ends—recalling the dignity and honor of those whose banishments and deaths were orchestrated by others. No polis is needed in the background for its mourning to name injustice nor is a site needed for it to receive legitimation against the very structures that both build sites and kill.

Subject Index

anabaptist, anabaptism, 2, 5–6, 8, 9, 10, 29, 44, 46, 59, 61–63, 127, 138–45, 185–86, 189, 193–94, 196, 208–12, 214, 216–17, 219–20, 224, 228, 241, 262
Anthropic Principle, 24
anthropology, theological, 7, 8, 67–71, 180, 192–93
atheism, 2, 31–32

baptist, baptist vision, 8, 31, 34–35, 39
boundary questions, 7n19, 190, 253

church, 35, 78–82, 88, 90, 96, 109, 218–19, 262, 268–69
conversion, 83–101
cosmology, 14, 16, 129–32, 146–48, 186, 190–91
creatio ex nihilo, 16–18, 127–29, 182
creation, 16, 22, 128–29

divine action. *See* miracle.
dualism, 3, 8, 67–69, 86, 102–5, 109, 121, 126, 133, 140

embodied cognition, 71–74
epistemology, 5–6, 8, 27–30, 37, 45–59, 172–81, 187, 207–8, 221
evangelical, 29, 42n33, 44, 87–89, 96, 102
evolution, 1, 10, 14, 18, 19–20, 22, 128–29, 132, 151, 243–52
ethics, 7, 126, 159–69

extended cognition, 67, 74–77
extraterrestrial intelligent life, 19–20

foundationalism, 1, 27–29, 36–37, 46–50, 55, 58, 60, 174, 187
fundamentalist, fundamentalism, 8, 26–31, 38–41, 162–63

hard core, 15, 29–30, 51, 56, 58, 63, 201, 258
holism, 8, 30, 45, 50–54, 103–4, 174, 208

incarnation, 19–20
individualism, 48–49, 78–79, 87–88, 187, 192, 199
inerrancy, biblical, 27, 30, 35n25
inner self, 87, 90, 103, 114

kenosis, 3, 9, 10, 63–64, 186, 189, 192, 194–96, 198–202, 204–5, 243, 257–59

language, 28, 73, 81–82, 92, 105–7, 148
liberal, liberalism, 8, 29–31, 40, 48, 197–99

mathematics, 14, 149, 153–156
metaphysics, v, 7, 9, 172–82, 253
miracle, 1, 3, 9, 21–22, 27–28, 125–33
modernity, 29, 38, 187–188
mourning, 10, 262–76

narrative, 96–98
neurosciences, 14, 67, 69–70, 83, 90–95, 190
nonreductionism, 10, 21, 188, 190
nonreductive physicalism, 67, 69–70, 77, 84, 126n5, 180, 208
nothing, ii, vi, 12, 66, 124, 184
novel facts, 15, 30

ontology, 150, 152–58, 166, 253

peace, 6, 101, 209–10
philosophy of religion, 9, 171–72, 178–82
physics, 13, 149–51
pluralism, 10, 228–30, 231–33, 238–40
politics, 7, 10, 127, 133–35, 185–205, 261–62
possibility spaces, 9, 146–70
postmodern, postmodernism, 1, 2–3, 26–27, 43, 44–45, 60, 185–87, 205
power, powers, 6, 193–94, 215

practices, 5–6, 10, 60–61, 62, 97–98, 188–89, 193, 197–99, 218–20, 261–62
psychology, 67, 69, 243–47

quantum physics, 1, 16, 21–22, 148n7

radical democracy, 9, 186, 196–205
radical reformation. *See anabaptist.*
reductionism, 21, 175–76, 187–88, 192–93, 256
relativism, 47, 208

science and theology, 1, 13–15, 23–24, 53–54, 57, 186, 207–8
scripture, 31, 35, 212, 213–14
sex, sexuality, 10, 243–60

technology, 107–15
theodicy, 1, 24
tradition, 32–34, 36, 52, 63–64, 98–99, 188–89, 208, 210–13

virtue, 86, 98–100, 220–21

Author Index

Aquinas, Thomas, 17n13, 52n31, 127, 130, 140n39
Aristotle, v, 62, 97n29, 125n2, 133, 149
Augustine, 102–103, 212, 262, 268
Austin, J. L., 5, 39, 57, 188

Barbour, Ian, 13, 17, 21, 23–24
Begbie, Jeremy, 7, 115–21
Berger, Peter, 229–31
Berry, Wendell, 86
Bonhoeffer, Dietrich, 237–38
Burrell, David, 127n6, 140n39, 182n14

Cavell, Stanley, 4, 171
Clark, Andy, 7, 74–76
Clayton, Philip, 45n4, 53–54, 57
Coles, Romand, 7, 59–64, 186, 196–205

Descartes, 50, 56, 125, 174, 180

Feyerabend, Paul, 2, 15, 46–47, 51n28, 52

Geertz, Clifford, 236–37
Graham, Billy, 88–89

Hadot, Pierre, 4, 128n9, 171
Hauerwas, Stanley, 56n47, 62n72, 197n36, 198n41
Hick, John, 232, 259
Huebner, Chris, 55

James, William, 140–41

Kuhn, Thomas, 47n13, 51

Lakatos, Imre, 1, 2, 7–8, 13, 15–16, 24, 29–30, 47, 51–52, 58–59, 208
Lindbeck, George, 39

MacIntyre, Alasdair, v, 1, 2, 5–6, 7, 8, 9, 16, 31–34, 36–38, 45–46, 47, 52–53, 58–64, 97, 171, 188–89, 193, 207–26, 258, 261
McCabe, Herbert, 105–106
McClendon, James Wm., Jr., v, 2, 3n4, 8, 31, 34–38, 44n2, 56n49, 62, 127, 135n25, 141–45, 187–88, 196, 200n51, 204n68, 208
Mulhall, Stephen, 7, 103
Murphy, Nancey, 1–6, 14–16, 23–25, 26–28, 32–34, 43, 44–64, 68–69, 73n12, 77n20, 79n24, 82, 84, 100–3, 106n8, 107n11, 109, 121, 126–27, 136n28, 143n48, 146, 167n51, 180n12, 185–205, 207–8, 220n59, 228n2, 243, 252–54, 261

Nagel, Thomas, 158n27, 170
Newbigin, Lesslie, 89–90, 242n44
Newton, Isaac, 21, 131

Peacocke, Arthur, 17, 21, 24, 253
Pius XII, 17, 23
Plantinga, Alvin, 49
Plato, 9, 149

Polkinghorne, John, 17, 21, 257n50
Prigogine, Ilya, 7, 135–38, 140

Quine, W. V. O., 9, 48n17, 50–51, 171–82, 188

Shults, F. LeRon, 58, 257n50
Socrates, v, 4, 47

Teske, John, 97–98
Tillich, Paul, 31, 127n8
Toulmin, Stephen, 48n15, 133–35, 207

Volf, Miroslav, 235, 237–38, 241

Wittgenstein, Ludwig, 7, 10, 39, 46n7, 47, 48n17, 103n4, 110n15, 113n24, 114n28, 115–16, 120, 188, 207
Wolin, Sheldon, 186, 196–205

Yoder, John Howard, 7, 9, 55–56, 58, 60, 63–64, 203n65, 207–26, 229

www.ingramcontent.com/pod-product-compliance
Lightning Source LLC
Chambersburg PA
CBHW021655230426
43668CB00008B/635